# Take Back
# The Word

# Take Back The Word

## a queer reading of the Bible

**Robert E. Goss and Mona West, editors**

THE PILGRIM PRESS
Cleveland, Ohio

The Pilgrim Press, Cleveland, Ohio 44115

© 2000 by The Pilgrim Press

Printed in the United States of America on acid-free paper

05   04   02   03   01   00        5   4   3   2   1


**Library of Congress Cataloging-in-Publication Data**

Take back the Word : a queer reading of the Bible / Robert E. Goss and Mona West, editors
    p.   cm.
  Includes bibliographical references.
  ISBN 0-8298-1397-7 (pbk. : alk. paper)
    1. Homosexuality – Biblical teaching.  2. Bible – Reader-response criticism.    I. Goss, Robert E., 1948-   II. West, Mona, 1955-

BS680.H67  .T35  2000
220.6'086'64 – dc21                                                00-048293

# Contents

## Part 3
## TAKING BACK THE CHRISTIAN SCRIPTURES

# What Word Shall We Take Back?

Almost twenty years ago, I ended an article I had written about feminist interpretations of the Bible with the words, "to read the same Bible as enslaver and liberator, that is the paradoxical challenge of feminist biblical hermeneutics. It is, moreover, a challenge for every Christian living honestly in the modern world."[1] I remember being at that time quite optimistic about the ultimate success of such paradoxical readings of scripture in which the "textual harassment"[2] of female subordination and victimization in many biblical passages would be undercut, destabilized, or erased by the creative reading strategies of feminists. Now, after over thirty years of feminist work on the Bible, which has demonstrated the influential role of women in antiquity and the present, we are still faced with events like the recent call by the largest Protestant denomination in the U.S.A., the Southern Baptists, for wives to be obedient to their husbands and for churches to stop ordaining women. In light of the increasingly powerful backlash against women, which has unfortunately even crept into some recent queer theory,[3] I find myself much less optimistic about the ultimate success of creative strategies of reading for disarming the Bible's potential for "clobbering," as many essays in this present volume term it, marginalized or oppressed groups. As lesbians, gay men, bisexuals, transgendered and seeking people, do we really want to "take back the word"? And if we do, what "word" is it we want to "take back"?

As I see it now, there are two main problems involved in opposing the Bible's long history of "textual harassment": the text itself and its authorized readers. The books of the Bible were produced mostly by marginalized groups within the ancient cultures of the Mediterranean basin over a span of slightly more than one thousand years. Not only did these groups participate in cultures that were deeply patriarchal and nationalistic; they for the most part were located socially on the marginalized fringes of those cultures, colonized by the dominant powers of the period from Assyria to Babylon to Persia to Greece and finally to Rome. That these groups developed hopes for themselves as a specially chosen people, as set apart from the rest of the world, which was generally regarded as composed of warring, idol-worshiping imperial overlords, or that they worried seriously about their survival as a people, physically, culturally, and religiously, all makes perfect sense in the ancient Mediterranean contexts of "us" versus "them" in which they experienced their particular walk with God. For them to reject disdainfully the supposed sexual, religious, and social practices of outsiders or foreign colonizers was as much a political statement bolstering group survival as it was a religious belief. Indeed, this very categorization of separate realms of politics, religion and social practices would seem unusual to the biblical writers or their cultures for whom religion most frequently paralleled state boundaries. Consequently, that many of the biblical stories and metaphors confirm God's people as separate from others, often entailing the active exclusion of those who are different, in order to prove their own nomination as the chosen few whom God blesses, should come as no surprise at all given the political contexts in which these texts, their authors, and first audiences were located. Clearly, cultural exclusivity, fear of difference, insistence on unity, and a rigidly ordained social order were understood as the necessary tools of survival in such a marginalized, colonized context. However, these same traits could be transformed into tools of oppression when Christians ceased being the colonized and became instead the colonizers, those with the power to control and dominate the lives of others.

All of the biblical books bear the stamp of their contexts of production, contexts that are for the most part massively different from those of any of the Bible's contemporary Western readers. Nor does it matter that some contemporary Christians, especially those connected with more evangelical or fundamentalist positions, often refuse to consider the significance of these formative contexts on the Bible, for that refusal does not make them go away or lose their crucial formative power. In fact, one might argue that to ignore the degree to which every page of the Bible reflects the presence of its ancient context of production actually results in increasing the influence of that context on the final interpretation of the text. Those ancient hero stories and social mores, created in the particular situations of resistance or acquiescence to imperialism and marginality, become "naturalized" or universalized in contemporary evangelical readings by remaining unremarked.

Most, though not all, of the essays in this volume evince a deep ambivalence about the Bible either explicitly or implicitly, an ambivalence that I believe every thoughtful, serious Christian should have as well. For many Christians, to be reared in the church means to be raised with the stories and heroes of the Bible woven into the fabric of every memory of community from childhood onward, and this Bible-immersion is especially true for those of us reared in the more conservative or evangelical branches of Christianity. Because of such nostalgia or perhaps because of profound personal experiences of inspiration or even continuing tenets of belief or all three combined, many Christians sustain and are sustained by a kind of love affair with the Bible—or at least parts of it. However, whether we are in love with the Bible or not, it is simply morally unacceptable to ignore the profound damage done to millions of people over hundreds of generations in the name of the Bible. Queer people are only the most recent victims of biblical "textual harassment." Jews have long been subject to rejection, torture, and death on the basis of the witness of New Testament texts; Native Americans, Africans, Latin Americans, and Pacific Islanders had their lands and cultures ripped away by Christian European colonizers in the name of taking the "Word of God" to the heathens of the world; African Americans were kept in slavery by pious Christians who believed that the Bible's view that "slaves should obey their masters" justified the abomination of owning another human being; and generations of women have been abused, burned at the stake, subordinated, blocked from education or leadership by men quoting biblical passages as the reason for their religiously legitimated acts of oppression and victimization. And these are just a few highlights of a list that could be greatly lengthened in numbers and specificity. It is inconceivable to me that any morally conscious person who has taken even a few moments to review the history of Christianity's use of the Bible could fail to feel extreme discomfort in the seemingly easy complicity of the Bible with regimes of violence and death.

Of course, the Bible itself does not kill people; groups of readers of the Bible do that in its name. Since every interpretation of a text in the Bible is a combination of the stories themselves and the interests, commitments, and beliefs of the person or group reading the stories, the power of those reading the Bible and how they decide to apply what they have read can make the difference in whether or not anyone gets killed and in who gets killed. In the history of the Bible's use by the Christians, such killing has come in many forms, from the grosser forms of burning at the stake, stoning, torturing to death, gassing in ovens, slaughtering by the sword, gun, or bomb to the more subtle but still quite effective forms of ostracism, derision, defamation of character, cursing, casting out of the community, etc. The power and influence of the authorized readers of the Bible raises the second problem I see in the project of taking the Bible back for queer communities. No matter how creatively and even joyously queer readers of the Bible reclaim some of its texts by destabilizing them, playing with them, laughing at them, allegorizing them, tricking them—all wonderfully inventive strategies employed by the essayists in this volume—as long as there are groups of Bible readers who fear, hate, or want to make invisible lesbians, gays, bisexuals, transgendered or sexually seeking people, a barrage of killing interpretations will continue to be aimed at queer communities in public and church debates.

In the case of queers, as in the case of so many other, earlier groups harassed by biblical interpretations, the fact that all texts, including the biblical texts, are generally ambiguous and indeterminate, thus requiring readers to refine and complete their meanings, is something of a two-edged sword. Since reading is always and inevitably a process in which the commitments, views, and cultural and social location of each reader profoundly influences the way those ambiguities and indeterminacies are decided, readers of texts literally become the co-creators of their meanings. Indeed, one of the enduring techniques of liberative readings, whether used by queer readers, feminists, womanists, or any others, is to reveal the textual gaps that interpreters have consciously or sometimes unconsciously filled in from their own beliefs to arrive at their particular interpretations. Such "bias" is not the provenance of one group or another but the necessary accompaniment of *all* textual interpretation: to read is inevitably to interpret. To make the judgment that a certain interpretation of the Bible is unbiased is actually only to admit that its particular bias agrees with one's own. The conservative Christians who use certain Bible passages to "clobber" lesbians and gay men are deciding to clarify the ambiguities and gaps in those passages in ways that fit their pre-conceived notions concerning the sinfulness of homoeroticism or the normality of heterosexism. To point out the importance of these preconceived notions to the resulting interpretation of the text, as a few of these essays do, is a freeing and crucial strategy for liberation. It undercuts the inevitability of these harassing interpretations and is a vital contribution to stopping the violence. Nevertheless, the same sword can also cut the other way, demonstrating how affirmative readings of scripture by queers develop analogies, fill in gaps, and clarify ambiguities in ways that fit their own assumptions about the morality and normality of different sexualities. While such readings may be a wonderful inspiration and a wonderful relief to queer audiences, and that benefit in itself is sufficient reason to publish a book such as this one, in the ongoing battle over the Bible those with different starting assumptions will likely conclude that these readings, too, are only one more set of "biased" interpretations.

That all readings are "biased," reflecting the commitments and social and cultural locations of each reader or group of readers, should relativize all claims to having the final and definitive "truth" about the Bible, but in the history of Christianity's use of the Bible it has not. It has not because that claim has had less to do with the Bible than with who was proclaiming its "truth." The powerful, institutional voices of the Christian church in all of its many divisions have generally had the ability to proclaim their particular version of the Bible's "truth" as absolute, inspired, commonsensical, or the only objective reading possible. In terms of the dynamics of reading, such claims have always been and still are ludicrous, but since these groups have generally controlled not only the publication of biblical interpretations but also the education of those who read the Bible—from scholars to pastors to congregants—their particular reading biases have been spread to large groups of Bible readers. Reading, after all, is a learned activity, not an innate one. Everyone learns to read in the ways their particular culture and educational systems deem appropriate. Reading the Bible as a special form of reading is taught by conscious effort and unconscious modeling in every church and Christian community. Through Bible study materials, Sunday School materials, sermons, liturgy, and just general discussion, Christians learn their own denomination's or church's distinctive practices of Bible reading. Institutional leaders within the church can thus have their "biased" readings confirmed by their followers in part because they have themselves trained those followers to read the Bible in that way. Perhaps the most revolutionary contribution of this present volume is in its presentation of new and resistant practices of reading the Bible that challenge some of the prevailing "authorized" patterns of reading that allow the Bible to "clobber" oppressed people. By learning new ways to read the Bible, contemporary Christians may begin to see the sandy foundation under the house of "truth" constructed by some of the present institutionally authorized readers.

The Word is powerful and powerfully dangerous. The text itself and the biases of those who read it have made the Bible something of a loose cannon in history, with the potential to destroy as much as to console and inspire. If lesbians, gay men, bisexuals, transgendered and seeking people are to take back this word for themselves, they must take it back in a new way, a way that attempts to obviate its potential for harm while engaging its message of liberation and love. For me that new way entails first and foremost the firm rejection of any normative authority or doctrinal priority given to readings of the Bible. I do not reject the Bible's pivotal role in the beginnings of Christianity or its later development, but I do reject any theological position that claims the authority of the Bible as the primary guide for Christian life in the world today or in the world of the future.[4] The Bible will always be a book I—and many other lesbians, gay men, bisexuals, transgendered and seeking people—love and value, but for our sake and for the sake of the next group still waiting in the wings for their chance at dignity, respect, and community, I want to learn to value the Bible, not as the only and ultimate arbiter of God's plan for humanity, but as one source among many that God has provided to fund our future possibilities of participating in the new thing God is always doing in the world.

MARY ANN TOLBERT

George H. Atkinson Professor of Biblical Studies,
Executive Director, Center for Lesbian and Gay Studies
in Religion and Ministry, Pacific School of Religion

## Notes

1. Mary Ann Tolbert, "Defining the Problem: The Bible and Feminist Hermeneutics," *Semeia* 28 (1983): 126.

2. This phrase is drawn from the early work of Mary Jacobus, "Is There a Woman in This Text?" *New Literary History* 14 (1982): 119.

3. See the recent discussion of the very problematic "fight" between some queer theorists and some feminists in Judith Butler, "Against Proper Objects" in *Feminism Meets Queer Theory*, ed. Elisabeth Weed and Naomi Schor (Bloomington and Indianapolis: Indiana University Press, 1997), 1–30.

4. For a fuller discussion of my position on biblical authority, please see my article "A New Teaching with Authority: A Re-evaluation of the Authority of the Bible," in *Teaching the Bible: The Discourses and Politics of Biblical Pedagogy*, ed. Fernando Segovia and Mary Ann Tolbert (Maryknoll, N.Y.: Orbis Books, 1998), 168–89.

# Contributors

Rabbi Rebecca T. Alpert, Ph.D., is the codirector of the Women Studies program and assistant professor of religion and women's studies at Temple University. She is a rabbi and the former dean of students at the Reconstructionist Rabbinical College. She has taught and published extensively in the areas of women in religion, medical ethics, contemporary Judaism, and gay and lesbian studies. She is the coauthor of *Exploring Judaism: A Reconstructionist Approach* (Reconstructionist Press, 1985) and author of *Like Bread on the Seder Plate: Jewish Lesbians and the Transformation of Tradition* (Columbia University Press, 1997).

Sharon A. Bezner, Ph.D., is member of the clergy within the Universal Fellowship of Metropolitan Community Churches (UFMCC). She is coordinator of Christian Programming at the Cathedral of Hope, a twenty-five-hundred-member inclusive church composed primarily of gay, lesbian, and transgendered people, where she serves as the director of wellness.

Rev. Thomas Bohache has been a member of the clergy in the UFMCC since 1988, having pastored congregations in California, Virginia, and Delaware. He has served on the faculty of Samaritan Institute for Religious Studies for over ten years. Bohache has undergraduate degrees in classical languages and theology and a master of arts degree in religious studies.

Rev. Celena M. Duncan has served in pastoral ministry with UFMCC for fifteen years, as associate pastor and then as pastor of Good Shepherd Parish (UFMCC) in Chicago, and currently is senior pastor of the Metropolitan Community Church of Johnson County in Overland Park, Kansas.

Robert E. Goss, Th.D., is chair of the Department of Religious Studies at Webster University and has served as managing editor of the *Journal of Religion and Education*. An activist and former Jesuit priest, he is the author of *Jesus ACTED UP: A Gay and Lesbian Manifesto* (HarperSanFrancisco, 1993) and coeditor of *A Rainbow of Religious Studies* (Monument Press, 1996) and *Our Families, Our Values: Snapshots of Queer Kinship* (Harrington Park Press, 1997). In addition, he has transferred his clergy credentials to the UFMCC, where he serves as clergy on staff in St. Louis. Goss has served as cochair of the Gay Men's Issues in Religion Group of the American Academy of Religion.

REV. THOMAS HANKS, PH.D., currently living in Latin America, is executive director of Other Sheep (Ministerios Multiculturales con Minorías Sexuales), an ecumenical organization committed to reaching out to sexual minorities in developing nations. He has taught in Costa Rica and Argentina. Hanks is author of *God So Loved the World* (Orbis Books, 1983) and Old Testament editor of the *New Illustrated Dictionary of the Bible in Spanish* (Caribe, 1968). He is the father of two children.

CHRISTOPHER KING, D.PHIL., has completed his doctoral thesis for the University of Oxford on the subject of Origen of Alexandria's *Commentary on the Song of Songs*. He is an ordained priest within the Episcopal Church.

VICTORIA S. KOLAKOWSKI is a lesbian transsexual attorney, political and religious activist, and minister-in-training. She holds a master of divinity degree from Pacific School of Religion and is a candidate for ordination in the UFMCC, serving at the Metropolitan Community Church of San Jose. She is the author of "Towards a Christian Ethical Response to Transsexual Persons" in *Theology and Sexuality* (1997, the first published article on religion by a transgendered person in a mainstream academic journal). She is also author of "The Concubine and the Eunuch: Queering Up the Breeder's Bible" in *Our Families, Our Values: Snapshots of Queer Kinship* (Harrington Park Press, 1997).

REV. JAMES MARTIN has served in pastoral ministry with the UFMCC for twelve years, as pastor of the Metropolitan Community Church of Charleston, South Carolina, as associate pastor of the Metropolitan Community Church of Greater St. Louis, Missouri, and currently as pastor of the Metropolitan Community Church of the Palm Beaches, in West Palm Beach, Florida.

REV. JIM MITULSKI is a gay man living with HIV and has been the pastor of the Metropolitan Community Church of San Francisco since 1986. He has a B.A. in religion from Columbia University and an M.Div. from the Pacific School of Religion and was a Merrill Fellow at Harvard Divinity School. He is currently enrolled in the doctorate in ministry program at San Francisco Theological Seminary.

DR. VIRGINIA RAMEY MOLLENKOTT is professor emeritus of English language and literature at William Paterson University, Wayne, New Jersey. She is the author of eleven books, including *The Divine Feminine* (Crossroad, 1983), *Sensuous Spirituality: Out from Fundamentalism* (Crossroad, 1992), and (with

Letha Dawson Scanzoni) *Is the Homosexual My Neighbor? A Positive Christian Response* (Harper & Row, 1978).

IRENE MONROE is a Ford Foundation Fellow and doctoral candidate at Harvard Divinity School. She is author of "Louis Farrakhan's Ministry of Misogyny and Homophobia," which appears in the anthology *The Farrakhan Factor* (Grove Press, 1998).

BENJAMIN PERKINS is a Unitarian-Universalist and a graduate of Harvard Divinity School. He organized the 1999 translesbigay Seminarians Conference, Claiming Our Faith: Celebrating the Spiritual in Our Lives.

REV. MICHAEL S. PIAZZA is senior pastor of the Cathedral of Hope, the largest lesbian and gay congregation in the world. He is a graduate of the Candler School of Theology, the author of four books, including *Holy Homosexuals* (Sources of Hope, 1997) and *Rainbow Family Values* (Sources of Hope, 1995), and the proud father of two beautiful girls named Marie and Jordan.

RABBI DAWN ROBINSON ROSE, PH.D., is the director of the Center for Jewish Ethics at the Reconstructionist Rabbinical College. She graduated summa cum laude and Phi Beta Kappa from the University of California at Berkeley in the field of feminist literary criticism, where she also received her M.A. She received a second M.A. in a rabbinic program and a Ph.D. in Jewish philosophy at Jewish Theological Seminary. At Reconstructionist Rabbinical College, Rose teaches classes in ethics, feminist theology, and hermeneutics. She is also a visiting assistant professor at Jewish Theological Seminary, where she teaches feminist theology. She is a rabbinic leader of Durham Community Synagogue in Durham, New Hampshire, where she is making a home with her lover, Maria Brettschneider. Author of articles, she is working on a manuscript entitled *Approaches to Jewish Feminist Theology* and with her partner is coediting a volume on multicultural reciprocity in Jewish feminism entitled *Meeting at the Well*.

KEN STONE, PH.D., is assistant professor of Hebrew Bible at Chicago Theological Seminary. He is the author of *Sex, Honor, and Power in the Deuteronomistic History* (Sheffield Academic Press, 1996) as well as several articles that deal with gender, sexuality, and biblical interpretation.

ELIZABETH STUART, D.PHIL., is professor of Christian theology at King Alfred's University College, Winchester. She is executive editor of the academic journal *Theology and Sexuality* and author of a number of books on queer theology and theology and sexuality, including *Just Good Friends: Towards a Lesbian and Gay Theology of Relationships* (Mowbray, 1995), *People of*

*Passion: What the Churches Teach about Sex* (with Adrian Thatcher, Mowbray, 1997), and *Religion Is a Queer Thing* (Cassell, 1997).

REV. JUSTIN TANIS is currently the director of clergy development for the UFMCC. Prior to joining the denominational staff, he served at the Metropolitan Community Church of Boston, Ke Anuenue O Ke Aloha MCC Hawaii, and the Metropolitan Community Church of San Francisco. He received a B.A. from Mount Holyoke College and an M.Div. from Harvard Divinity School.

REV. IRENE TRAVIS is an African American pastor on staff at the Cathedral of Hope in Dallas. She is coordinator of Family Ministries, which is responsible for the children's center programs, single men fellowship, Lavender League, the Silver Sisters, Parents for Parents, and much more. Irene taught as an elementary school teacher for thirty years, and she retired to take up a second career in full-time ministry as a pastor in the UFMCC.

REV. MONA WEST received a Ph.D. in Old Testament studies from Southern Baptist Theological Seminary in 1987. She taught biblical studies at Austin College in Sherman, Texas, and at Anderson College in Anderson, South Carolina, and she was academic dean at Samaritan Institute of Religious Studies. Her most recent publications include "Ruth," "Song of Songs," and "Lamentations" in the *Mercer Commentary on the Bible* (Mercer, 1995), "The Book of Ruth: An Example of Procreative Strategies for Queers" in *Our Families, Our Values: Snapshots of Queer Kinship* (Harrington Park Press, 1997) and "Reading the Bible as Queer Americans." She is Pastor of Spiritual Life at the Cathedral of Hope, the largest gay and lesbian church in the world.

# Take Back
# The Word

# Introduction

When queer people think about their relationship with the Bible,[1] the phrase "Word of God" is probably the last thing that comes to mind. Queers find themselves in the company of women and African Americans who struggle with embracing the Bible as the Word of God when it has been used to justify our oppression. Historically, the relationship queers have had with the Bible has been defensive—warding off fundamentalist attackers wielding the Bible as a club condemning homosexuality. A handful of scriptures (Gen. 19:1–28; Lev. 18:22; 20:13; Rom. 1:26–28; 1 Cor. 6:9; 1 Tim. 1:10) is often called the "clobber passages" by the queer community because they are used to promote homophobia and violence against us. In borrowing Phyllis Trible's term, Bob Goss has identified them as our "texts of terror."[2]

Early queer biblical interpretation took on a defensive stance toward the attack of these texts. The defense included historical criticism and linguistics, which set these passages in their historical and cultural contexts and demonstrated that there is much ambiguity concerning the translation and interpretation of such words as *mishkav zakur* (the lyings of a male) in Leviticus, *para physin* (against nature) in Romans 1:26–27, and *arsenokoitai* (lying with males) in 1 Corinthians 6:9.

Nancy Wilson, in her book *Our Tribe: Queer Folks, God, Jesus, and the Bible*, calls for a queer strategy of reading the Bible that is more positive. Certainly there is more to the message of the Bible for queers than just silencing the texts of terror. Wilson's offensive stance toward scripture includes identifying texts that affirm same-sex love and the goodness of human sexuality (Jonathan and David, Naomi and Ruth, the Song of Songs). The bulk of Wilson's work, however, focuses on reconstructing queer identities of some of the characters in the biblical text. Wilson calls this queer biblical hermeneutic "outing the Bible." She claims,

> What if we just assumed that lesbians, gay men, and bisexuals were always in the Bible? What if we just accepted the fact that our counterparts followed Moses and Miriam in the Exodus, wandered in the wilderness, and walked with Jesus by the sea of Galilee? We were there! Even when we were silent or closeted about our sexuality or never expressed it (which is doubtful!), we were there. It is time boldly to "liberate" some biblical gay, lesbian, and bisexual characters from an-

cient closets. It may seem unfair to "out" these defenseless biblical characters, but I'm tired of being fair. Centuries of silence in biblical commentaries and reference books have not been fair. A passionate search for biblical truth about sexuality must be undertaken. It is time for seamless, wild speculation about the Bible and about human as well as "homo" sexuality.[3]

She goes on to reconstruct the queer identity of eunuchs not only as sexual minorities in the ancient world but also as persons who can be characterized as "messengers" and "go-betweens," persons often engaged in subversive roles and palace intrigue. These characteristics parallel the ways in which queers have been identified throughout our history as "berdache," "two-spirited ones," and "shamans." Wilson then outs the eunuchs in the Joseph story and the story of Esther, as well as Nehemiah, as characters in the Bible who exhibit some of these traits and therefore function as queer ancestors of faith.

This anthology attempts to provide examples of a queer biblical hermeneutic that engages the entire Bible and its message, not just selected texts and characters. It is a strategy that outs the queer community by articulating the community's lived experience in and beyond the closet as well as its particular concerns when encountering and appropriating the biblical text. It is a strategy that attempts to take back the Bible as the Word of God for our community, instead of a club. It is a strategy that takes into account the multifaceted nature of our community as gay men, lesbians, transsexuals, and bisexuals from different ethnicities, socioeconomic standings, and religious communities. Queer biblical scholarship, which intentionally employs this method, is just beginning to appear. *Take Back the Word* gathers some of this scholarship to provide a context for these voices to be heard.

With the rise of postmodernism we have seen a shift in biblical hermeneutics that considers the role of the reader in assigning meaning to the biblical text. Not only have we come to realize that readers make meaning of texts, but readers also bring particular "selves" to the text, which is shaped by a variety of factors such as race, ethnicity, gender, class, religious affiliation, socioeconomic standing, education, and, we would add, sexual orientation. This focus on the reader has produced many new voices in the discipline of biblical criticism. These new voices have pointed out, among other things, that there is no completely objective reading of the text. The scientific and objective stance of historical-critical methods of modernity has been nothing more than a reading from a privileged location described as European American, male, and heterosexual.

These new voices have also produced a biblical hermeneutic that considers the particular social location of flesh-and-blood readers. Readers are members of specific communities, and their history with that community shapes the way they approach the biblical text. According to James Earl Massey, reading the Bible from a particular social location can be characterized in the following way:

1. Groups such as African Americans and women (and queers) read and interpret the Bible as members of a particular social community.

2. Another term for social location is "community situation approach." The community's life experiences and the relation of scripture to the community's needs determine the ways in which the community appropriates texts of the Bible.

3. Most of the communities who employ this method have a social history of oppression and marginalization and are wary of "mainstream" biblical interpretation. Many of these groups have had the Bible used against them by the dominant culture to justify their oppression and marginalization.

4. Each group with this particular social history has found a point of reference from which to read, reclaim, and reappropriate the meaning of scripture for the community in liberating and affirming ways.[4]

The "point of reference" from which marginalized and oppressed communities read the Bible is one of the distinguishing characteristics of social location. This point of reference functions for each group as a means by which "to define and affirm themselves in the midst of a problematic social environment whose skewed perspectives and sub-Christian values steadily and systematically worked against them."[5] The point of reference for an African American reading of the Bible is the theme of deliverance and freedom.[6]

What is the point of reference for a queer reading of the Bible that allows us to "define and affirm ourselves" in the midst of a social environment that uses the Bible to justify violence and hate toward us? How does a queer person of faith who grew up hearing that the Scripture condemns her sexuality and that she is an abomination to God open and begin reading the Bible? Many queer people are afraid of the Scriptures. The whole Bible is a text of terror because of the ways in which our abuse has been justified by the misinterpretation of a few obscure passages. We believe the point of reference for a queer reading of scripture is the notion that the Bible is our friend. When we approach the Bible as a friendly text, as a text that "does no harm," the terror of the Scriptures is transformed into the life-giving Word of God.

Approaching the Bible as our friend is easier said than done, however. The contributors in this volume read the Bible from a queer social location, and in their reading they cross boundaries in order to take back the Word from fundamentalist, exclusionary readings that demonize our community or justify a rhetoric of hate that leads to violence against us. The contributors throughout the volume are resistant readers who struggle against heterocentric privilege that erases us from the text. As queer readers, we want to befriend the Scriptures to find our voices and allow subversive memories and diversities to emerge. The Hebrew and Christian Scriptures are not the privileged possession of heterosexuals but belong to all Jews and Christians of faith.

The essays in this anthology represent a limited cross section of trained readers. It is obvious from the contributions that we are only beginning to read biblical texts from a wide variety of queer social locations with diverse reading strategies. The authors have foregrounded themselves as flesh-and-blood readers, variously situated as they transgress heterosexist boundaries and even the sexual orthodoxies of "gay" and "lesbian."

The first section of the anthology presents a cross section of strategies for reading the Hebrew and Christian Scriptures from a queer social location. From her fundamentalist upbringing, Virginia Mollenkott had learned to read the Scriptures from a perspective of "low and outside" because she had been trained to read them from a white heterosexual male point of view. Like the biblical Rebekah, Mollenkott learned to read as a trickster to recover our voices within the biblical traditions. She notes that as we recover our voices, we are required to use our voices to bring the good news to the poor, release the captives, and free the oppressed. In a way similar to the trickster strategy, Elizabeth Stuart reads the Scriptures with laughter. Too often, queers have allowed themselves to be wounded by particular passages by mainline and fundamentalist churches. Laughing at those texts is a strategy that subverts their efforts of destructiveness and distances us from the pain of being a target. Stuart notes how "camp" becomes a means for queer reading that empowers us to work for liberation.

Irene Travis, a retired schoolteacher, mother, and member of the UFMCC clergy, writes as a cross between a modern Jeremiah and Isaiah. Passionately she challenges patriarchy and the churches for their failure to include lesbians and gays. Her womanist perspective invites people to reflect on oppressive Christianity and reenvision a Christian practice from the perspective of God as mother. Justin Tanis, a transgay male, reads the story of Jesus turning the Canaanite woman away. The woman was convinced that Jesus was capable of more than he seemed to believe he was able. Like the mother of a female-to-male transsexual, the Canaanite woman had to fight for the wholeness and well-being of her child. For Tanis, this is a story of advocacy, transformation, and healing; it looks forward to changes within the Christian churches to welcome transfolks.

Ken Stone begins the process of "taking back the Hebrew Scriptures" by reading the foundational texts in Genesis. Stone reads the Genesis creation accounts that have been argued by conservative critics as the basis for the heterosexual contract. They are accounts filled with inherent contradiction, which Stone exploits to open interpretive space for alternative queer readings.

Mona West continues the process with her essay on Exodus. West explores how the Hebrew Exodus functions as a coming-out story for queers, articulating an event of liberation and transformation. The Exodus tradition reminds queers that the silence of the closet does equal death and that the dominant culture will try to cut queers off from their past by rendering them invisible. It is the retelling of our stories of coming out that shape the journey of queer lives from enslavement to freedom. Irene Monroe provides a provocative reading of Exodus from the social location of an embodied African American lesbian. African American males have interpreted the text from the "endangered black male" social location, thus excluding African American women and translesbigays. Monroe's reading challenges African American heteropatriarchy with inclusiveness.

Whereas gays and lesbians have threatened the boundaries of heterosexuality, they have also set up their own orthodoxies or their own insider boundaries. Celena Duncan reminds us of bisexuals who transgress the sexual identity categories of straight and gay in her reading of the book of Ruth. She embraces a "both/and" rather than an "either/or" notion of identity. Victoria Kolakowski violates the orthodoxies of gender, criticizing Nancy Wilson's appropriation of "eunuch" for gays/lesbians and the exclusion of transsexuals. Her reading of the death of Jezebel at the hands of her eunuchs reaches into the soul of the queer community with her provocative analysis.

Michael Piazza, the charismatic senior pastor at the Dallas Cathedral of Hope, writes about Nehemiah. Like Nehemiah, Piazza has facilitated the building of a "mega" community of faith, whose members have been exiled from their churches for their sexual orientation and discovered a place where they can practice their faith. He speaks a vision of a queer Christian church imprinted with the values of servant leadership.

When queers "take back the Word," we see within the Scriptures visions of hope and dreams of liberation. Reading from a queer location means also to read from a location of hope and with faith. Irene Travis shares a psalm written in the midst of a diagnosis of breast cancer. It expresses her faith as a "blessed" child of God. Transgressing boundaries is a rebellious act that breaks conceptual categories, and when applied to textual readings, our queer contributors provide a creative rebellion driven by the diversity of our imaginations and commitments. Christopher King provides a queer reading of the Song of Songs, which celebrates the gift of human life and sexuality apart from its procreative value and conformity to social conventions. By loosening the reading of the Song from exclusive heterosexuality, he envisions queer love identifying with the passionate that prefers the outsider enhanced by sexual differences. His reading opens the text to the sexual outsider and the social outlaw.

Dawn Rose looks at the texts of some of the prophets. She calls these texts pornographic and demonstrates how traditional readings of these texts have been used to justify violence and abuse toward women. As a lesbian feminist rabbi, she concludes that her God is not an abusing God and is to be found in the midst of empowered actions of women to intervene and break cycles of violence.

Jim Mitulski writes from the perspective of faith living with HIV. As a modern-day Ezekiel, who has witnessed the tragedy of the AIDS pandemic in the heart of San Francisco's Castro district, he looks to God for memories of hope and resurrection. Sharon Bezner queers the book of Jonah with some interesting twists and turns. Jonah is sent to a modern-day Nineveh to preach a message of hope. Bezner likens Jonah's hatred of the Ninevites to that of the Christian Coalition toward queers. She challenges queer people of faith to proclaim God's love and justice to the religious right.

Many of the essays express a restlessness about justice, indicating that translesbigay people of faith have discovered the biblical word of God as the source of our spiritual power and a source for empowering liberating action. Rebecca Alpert reads Micah 6:8, exploring what it means "to walk humbly with God" as a Jewish lesbian: how to live with and present oneself in the world, how to establish social relationships, and how to make the world a better place.

In "Taking Back the Christian Scriptures," Tom Hanks, impacted by evangelical teaching in his youth, empathizes with Matthew/Levi who writes a gospel. Like Matthew the tax collector, he felt a deep call beyond legalism to follow Jesus to the marginalized, sexual minorities, and sex workers. Hanks founded Other Sheep to bring the good news of hope and acceptance to sexual minorities and sex workers in Latin America and Africa.

Ben Perkins, a student leader at Harvard Divinity School, reads the Lazarus narrative as a coming-out story in which gay men have had to exit the tombs that bind and destroy their spirit for a life of God's sacramental grace. Perkins writes, "We are called to leave a mode of existence that encourages dishonesty and deception for a life that celebrates authenticity and vulnerability. In answering this call to come out, we are also resurrected."

Many translesbigays have witnessed the sufferings and death of loved ones through tragic illness. Bob Goss identifies the beloved disciple in John's Gospel as Lazarus. He uses the symbolics of the relationship of Jesus and the beloved disciple to reflect upon his relationship with his lover Frank, Frank's diagnosis of HIV, and Franks's suffering and death. How many gay men have died in the presence of their mothers and lovers just as Jesus died on the cross before his mother and the beloved disciple? Goss traces the transformation of his grief into resurrection solace and a discovery of the continued presence of his lover.

For centuries men attracted to the same sex have intuited an erotic relationship between Jesus and the beloved disciple. Jim Martin reads the Emmaus account with an erotic undertone. It reminds us of Michelangelo's risen Christ, in which the risen Jesus represents an icon of male beauty for the artist's homoerotic devotion. Such a homoerotic resonance has played a significant role in the spiritualities of countless Christian men erotically attracted to Jesus the Christ.

Tom Bohache concludes the volume by reading Paul's letter to the Galatians, a letter that struggles with issues of promise and inclusion within the early Jesus movement. He reads Paul's letter as a manifesto for the inclusion of queer Christians in which queers do not have to circumcise the "foreskins of our sexual orientation" to be acceptable to God. His vision expresses a hope that closed faith communities will one day face courageously the question of queer inclusion just as early Christianity faced the question of Gentile inclusion.

Most of all, the contributors in this volume "take back the Word" for queer faith communities that need to hear scripture as the life-giving Word of God. We want to proclaim with the psalmist, "Your word is a lamp to my feet and a light to my path" (Ps. 119:105).

## Notes

1. We use the word "Bible" in this anthology to refer to both the Tanak of the Jewish faith and the Old and New Testaments of the Christian faith. For us "Bible" is a designation for scripture and is a term Jews and Christians use to refer to scripture.

2. Robert E. Goss, *Jesus ACTED UP: A Gay and Lesbian Manifesto* (San Francisco: HarperSanFrancisco, 1993), 90–94. Goss borrows the phrase from Phyllis Trible, who applied it to unredeemable texts in the Hebrew Bible that promoted violence against women.

3. Nancy L. Wilson, *Our Tribe: Queer Folks, God, Jesus, and the Bible* (San Francisco: HarperSanFrancisco, 1995), 112.

4. James Earl Massey, "Reading the Bible from Particular Social Locations," in *The New Interpreter's Bible*, ed. Leander Keck et al. (Nashville: Abingdon Press, 1994), 1:150–52.

5. Ibid., 151–52.

6. James Earl Massey, "Reading the Bible as African Americans," in *The New Interpreter's Bible*, ed. Leander Keck et al. (Nashville: Abingdon Press, 1994), 1:160.

*Part 1*

# QUEER STRATEGIES
# FOR READING

*1*

# Reading the Bible
# from Low and Outside

## Lesbitransgay People as God's Tricksters

### VIRGINIA RAMEY MOLLENKOTT

*Many queers grew up in fundamentalist and evangelical churches, receiving nega-*
*tive messages about their sexuality. From her fundamentalist upbringing, Virginia*
*Mollenkott had learned to read the Scriptures from a perspective of "low and out-*
*side" because she had been trained to read them from a white heterosexual male*
*point of view. Like the biblical Rebekah, a woman in a culture that valued her*
*only within a rigid gender model, Mollenkott learned to read the text as a trickster*
*to recover queer voices within the biblical traditions. Tricksters are agents of cul-*
*tural change; they incorporate a spirit of disorder and threaten hardened cultural*
*boundaries. They bring a type of social vision that provides alternatives to the*
*way things are. Mollenkott honors biblical tricksters whose subversive strategies*
*recover oppressed voices and subvert an unjust system. Finally, Mollenkott points*
*out that we are required to use our trickster voices as queers to bring the good*
*news to the poor, release the captives, and free the oppressed.*

As a lesbian Christian born in 1932 and growing up in the '40s and '50s, I
have had to learn to read the Hebrew and Christian Scriptures from low and
outside. From low because my status as female was secondary and silenced
in the church of my youth, where girls and women wore hats to signify our
submission to male authority and where even in Bible studies we were not
permitted so much as to ask a question. From outside because my lesbianism
(fully recognized by age eleven) took away from me even the humblest
of insider status in a community that never mentioned that kind of sin.

---

Parts of this essay were originally published in Virginia Ramey Mollenkott, "Practicing Privacy and
Timing: An Ethic for Lying When Necessary," *The Witness* 79 (April 1996): 10–14.

Someone did read Romans 1 to me when I was thirteen, telling me that if I continued to love women I would prove I was "without God in my mind" and "worthy of death." Being a compliant type and passionately devoted to God, I did try to kill myself, as so many queer teenagers do. But worse than that attempt were the years of living death in marriage to a man who was convinced that I was divinely created to clean up after him.

I had to learn to read the Scriptures from low and outside because I had been trained to identify with the white heterosexual male point of view when reading the Bible. What an amazing and life-transforming shift occurred when I learned to see myself, not as Abraham, but as Sarah or Hagar or one of the lesser concubines, not as one of Jesus' disciples, but as the determined Greek woman who cried for Jesus to heal her daughter but at first was told to go away (Matt. 15:21–28). When battered women from conservative denominations learn the "core insight" that "God . . . sides with those who are out of power" and when they realize that women are "included in the biblical category of the poor, the oppressed, and the outcast," they are empowered to leave the batterer.[1] That process worked in my life: as I divested myself of the male-identified androcentric and heterocentric mindset and became woman-identified and queer-identified, I realized that the God of scripture lifts up the lowly and brings the outsider into the community. (Think of Ruth, a woman who became "better than seven sons," a poverty-stricken Moabite widow who became part of King David's ancestral line, partly because she seduced Boaz on the threshing floor.) Not only that, but I realized that God repeatedly uses "those with less clout . . . to challenge those with more, in order to equalize or reverse the flow of energies that constitute power, be it cosmological, national, or personal."[2]

Eventually, I learned on my own pulses what Hebrew Bible professor Carole R. Fontaine describes as typical not only of the Bible but of the divine entities of the ancient Near East from Sumer to Egypt: "Those who find themselves disadvantaged, on the 'outside,' in the margins as it were, make use of trickery and other forms of manipulative behavior (like gossip, misinformation, nagging, playing possum, distractions and deceptions) because they do not have what sociologists refer to as 'assigned power.' Assigned power is just that: assigned (usually by the elite in favor of the elite), but masquerading as divinely ordained, cosmically correct and unquestionably true—in short, an unassailable 'given.'"[3]

It seems to me vital that queer people learn to empower ourselves by reading the Bible from low and outside instead of identifying our agenda as we read with that of the heterosexual normative group. Some of us, of course, have more power than others, and to the degree that we have power, we must use it responsibly. But it is equally important to recognize those aspects of our experience that are systemic and oppressive and beyond our individual ability to change and then to find ways to undercut and subvert those inequitable systems.

One trickster who did exactly that is the Reverend Dr. Jeanne Audrey Powers. A year before she retired from lifelong ministry in the United Methodist Church, Powers came out as a lesbian.[4] She made clear that she had been working for gay and lesbian liberation all her life, although the church forced her to remain closeted by its statement that homosexuality is incompatible with Christian faith. Powers described to me her pain when recently "out" lesbian women or gay men would express joy at having "regained their integrity." She felt (and I agreed) that she had always been a person of integrity but had been forced to practice subversion in an occupied territory that was the locus of her ministry and had thus silenced the fullest range of her voice as the price of that ministry. I know that her experience is typical of many who serve not only in United Methodism but in many other denominations of Christianity and Judaism or in public schools, for that matter. For their sake, and for the sake of clear thinking in general, I want to reclaim the Bible's words about God's tricksterism and God's use of tricksters and to suggest that queer people who work for justice from within the closet may validly be honored as the trickster servants of God. "When the power-brokers simply will not listen, when the center forgets the margin—well, then, a trick may be in order."[5]

My thesis is that it is time for queer people and all other oppressed people openly to espouse an ethical system that honors necessary subversion and ceases to shame those who practice it. Most Christian and Jewish congregations are still operating under heteropatriarchal assumptions that silence, marginalize, or distort queer experience. In occupied territory, subversion is necessary for two reasons: to survive and to move society toward justice.

This is not a popular thesis. When I discussed it at the annual Gay, Lesbian, and Christian event at Kirkridge Study and Retreat Center (Bangor, Pennsylvania), it caused pain and dissension, especially among the men. But I think that queer folk and our feminist and womanist allies must lead the way in acknowledging a more subtle and nuanced ethical stance than the reigning Eurocentric absolutes that work well only for the people with the power to make and circumvent the rules. I think we can develop greater sensitivity to the contexts that govern ethical decision making without encouraging flagrant and self-serving dishonesty.

In fact, more sensitive ethical nuancing should lead to greater honesty. During my heterosexually married and closeted years, I once heard an American Baptist minister preach a powerful sermon about the importance of absolute truthfulness because God hates and punishes liars. Afterwards, I asked the preacher whether he was aware of various lies that according to scripture had received God's blessing: for instance, the Egyptian midwives' lying to the pharaoh (Exod. 1:18–22) or the tricky deviousness of Miriam and her mother in hiding their relationship to Moses, the baby in the bulrushes (Exod. 2:1–10). Following the pharaoh's order to throw all boy babies into the river, they did that but first put him into a basket that would float![6] With obvious discomfort, the preacher admitted that, yes, he was aware of those lies and of the blessing of God upon the liars, but he insisted that his job was to teach people to be truthful. I pressed on: "So by leaving the Bible's ethical complexities out of your sermon, you were lying by omission, but that was okay because you did so in the service of truth?" He nodded miserably. At the time, I could think of nothing to do but to shrug and walk away, ruefully reflecting on my own "living a lie" concerning my sexual orientation. I am completing that conversation here and now, in this article.

Womanist theologians have always been frank about doing whatever is necessary in order to survive. For instance, in her book *Black Womanist Ethics*, Katie G. Cannon pointed out that in this "white-oriented, male-structured society," black women "do not appeal to fixed rules or absolute principles of what is right or wrong and good or bad, but instead they embrace values related to the causal conditions of their cultural circumstances."[7] Similarly, womanist Bible scholar Renita J. Weems states: "A challenge for marginalized readers in general, and African American women in particular, has been to use whatever means necessary to recover the voice of the oppressed within biblical texts."[8] That voice would include the perspective of the Bible's many tricksters, those whose presence turns the worldly status quo upside down and inside out or even such strange moments as Abraham's fooling potentates into thinking his wife was his sister because at the time that charade seemed necessary for survival or the Great Trickster's sending the King of kings to be born in a lowly stable. Fontaine comments, "The trickster exists to redistribute power: From the snake who beguiles to the Lamb who Redeems, readers of the Bible watch the interplay of potencies move from the 'Haves' to the 'Have-Nots.'"[9]

Within the contemporary lesbitransgay Christian community, the widespread assumption is that all community members should—must—proclaim their identity openly. I question this ethic that "everybody must come out" because it neglects the diversity of our contexts. In this regard, Judith Butler asks some important questions: "For whom is outness a historically available and affordable option? Is there an unmarked class character to the demand for universal outness? Who is represented by which use of the term and who is excluded? For whom does [universal outness] present an impossible conflict between racial, ethnic, or religious affiliation and sexual politics? What kinds of policies are enabled by what kinds of usages, and which are backgrounded or erased from view?"[10] I do not question that it would be best (for both individuals and society) for everyone to come out if they can afford to. But within the queer community, there is such a huge variety of race and class differences that it is oppressive for some of us to put pressure on others of us.

I was not surprised that at Kirkridge opposition to my thesis about honoring necessary subversion came from certain well-heeled white gay males, not from lesbian women or queers of color or of poverty. An affluent white gay male has encountered oppression in only one area of his experience and hence can hope in most cases to achieve the standards of the Kantian categorical imperative ("always act in such a way that your actions could be willed as universal laws"). But queers who are poor and/or nonwhite and/or women have experienced several interconnected oppressions. Hence they can more readily sense the need for subversion or tricksterism as survival and justice-making tactics.

But desperation is an outstanding teacher. When Hitler had achieved power in Germany, theologian Dietrich Bonhoeffer was forced to face complex moral questions, and his integrity assured that he could not oversimplify human reality. As Robin Lovin has pointed out, Bonhoeffer wrestled with such questions as "What are the limits of loyalty to one's people and one's nation when the government is corrupt? Can we use lies and violence and not become brutalized and deceptive ourselves?" By such struggles, Bonhoeffer shows us that "morality is ... what we must risk in extraordinary times to restore the possibility of what is ordinary and normal and sustaining. Times do not come neatly labeled as 'ordinary' or 'extraordinary.' Indeed, every time is a mixture of both."[11]

And although Lovin did not say so, for queers who are committed to economic, racial, and sexual justice, the turn of the millennium is a rather extraordinary time. Unrestrained capitalism is exploiting poor people all over the world, ruining local economies by building factories to take advantage of cheap labor and moving on when that labor begins to organize. Racial, gender-motivated, and orientation-motivated hate crimes are frequent. Elected public officials feel free to label queerness as sin. Lesbitransgay young people—especially transgendered youth—suffer outrageous assaults in a society that accords to children no rights to speak of.[12] We queers need to trust our inner knowing, held in tension with more conventional values, in order to find the balance suggested by Bonhoeffer's *Ethics* and his life: that lying is sometimes necessary, "that the real world is always more complex than our simple answers, and that the moral certainty that we can truly admire requires us to pay attention to everything that is there."[13]

During my Protestant fundamentalist childhood, I was taught that it was a Christian's responsibility to avoid even the appearance of evil (1 Thess. 5:22 KJV). It was years before it dawned on me that in Jesus' story of the good Samaritan, the two priests who refused their help to a man fallen among thieves were doing exactly that—abstaining from all appearance of evil. Had they assisted the bleeding man, they would have gotten dirt and blood on their stainless garments—and, God forbid, someone might think that they themselves had been involved in the mugging!

It is time, I think, for religious congregations to become less simplistic and more mature in their ethical stance, showing less concern for stainless absolutes and righteous images and more concern for supporting people in the often painful and messy realities of their lives. Queer people can lead the way in this as in so many other areas, by honoring God's tricksters among us and the Great Trickster within us.

John Milton, the great Puritan poet and theologian who risked and nearly lost his life for what he believed, had something vital to say about living with integrity: "I cannot praise a fugitive or cloistered virtue, unexercised and unbreathed, that never sallies out and sees her adversary, but slinks out of the race where that immortal garland is to be run for, not without dust and heat."[14] Milton's point is that no justice-oriented life can be lived without mistakes, occasional co-option, controversy, and making people angry. Queer people need to know that, I think, and to teach it to their "straight" contemporaries of faith. Some of us face the distressing claustrophobia of working for justice from within various closets. The important thing is that we do indeed work for justice and drain away none of our energy by judgmentalism, or even by celebrations of openness that may unconsciously assault the integrity or courage of our closeted and less privileged sisters and brothers.

Consider the story of Rebekah and her son Jacob. God told Rebekah that she was pregnant with twins who were struggling in her womb and would continue to struggle after birth, with the elder to serve the younger (Gen. 25:21–23). Because of her inner knowledge, Rebekah is the only one who can see to it that the divinely ordained switch of inheritance and power actually will take place. To that end Rebekah instructs Jacob in an elaborate scheme to trick his old father into giving him the blessing, inheritance, and power of the firstborn son (Gen. 27:1–33).

Gwenyth Mapes, who had the courage to open a Planned Parenthood clinic in Montana after the former clinic had been burned to the ground, had this to say about Rebekah and her son:

> Jacob becomes the archetypal trickster, a role that is lauded in many cultures because it is so versatile and ultimately necessary in the survival of the species. But what we forget is that Rebekah trained Jacob in this, thus forging the very nature of survival in him and in their descendants. What we also forget is that this trickster trait is the very

quality for which women and minorities are lambasted throughout history: deception, subterfuge, lying, cheating, etc. These qualities are necessary qualities of any person or group who is denied social power and has to achieve it in ways other than the system allows. So we laud Jacob in this story, but lambaste the Rebekahs of the world, unless we reinterpret the story and realize the important role Rebekah played and why she had to resort to lying and deception in order to achieve God's plan for her sons. No one else could do that for God, since only she knew the plan. And she could achieve God's plan in no other way but trickery, because society offered her no other power.[15]

Lesbitransgay people should have no trouble recognizing themselves in the figure of Rebekah (a woman in a culture that does not value women except in certain rigidly prescribed roles) or in the figure of Jacob (the relatively powerless second son). In a heteropatriarchal culture like our own, queer people are distinctly "other" and distinctly secondary, forced to compete uphill on a slanted playing field. I offer Rebekah's and Jacob's gaining of power through subterfuge as a paradigm for all the queer people who are forced to disguise all or part of their reality as the price of fulfilling their vocation, their divine calling in life.

I am aware of the dangers of espousing a complex ethic that includes the integrity of subverting unjust systems. I know all too well that the human ego can deceive us about our real motives, so that we can wrong ourselves and others while simultaneously assuring ourselves that what we are doing is necessary and good—indeed, that we were divinely guided to do it. And I am keenly aware that many queer religious leaders insist that there must be no secrets in our lives. But I would argue that there is a difference between emotional dishonesty to ourselves and our trusted friends and the preservation of privacy in occupied territory. So I am arguing for a realistically complex "underground" or "resistance" code of ethics, which is this: I will do what is necessary to preserve the loving values I believe in, and at the same time, I will try to survive in order to work yet another day. Such a code honors the integrity on both sides of the closet door.

Returning to the trickster motif: what else can we call a God who allows the previously quoted statement about abstaining from all appearance of evil to become part of canonical scripture yet chooses to honor by naming in the genealogy of Jesus five women—Tamar, Rahab, Ruth, Bathsheba, and Mary—all of whom are associated with moral irregularities and none of whom succeeded in avoiding the appearance of evil (see Matt. 1:1–16)?[16] Not to mention the many evils associated with the men named in Matthew's genealogy! Surely juxtaposing these biblical facts with the advice to avoid even the appearance of evil should be enough to prove that the biblical ethic is paradoxical and anything but simplistic! The same Bible that tells us to "be subject to the governing authorities" (Rom. 13:1) tells us that "we must obey God rather than any human authority" (Acts 5:29). Paradoxically, both are true, although in different contexts.

As a matter of fact, the Christian Scriptures tend toward what could properly be called a relativistic or situation ethic. Consider 1 Corinthians 6:12, where Paul says, "'All things are lawful for me,' but not all things are beneficial. 'All things are lawful for me,' but I will not be dominated by anything." How else could we know what is beneficial for us, or when we might be getting addicted to something, except by assessing our behavior in specific situations and contexts? Furthermore, in 1 Corinthians 10:23–24 Paul said something similar but more community oriented: "'All things are lawful,' but not all things are beneficial. 'All things are lawful,' but not all things build up. Do not seek your own advantage, but that of the other." Then Paul goes on to discuss eating meat that had been sacrificed to idols, a hot ethical controversy in the early church. He counsels not eating such meat in the presence of a person whose conscience would be distressed. But he has no objection to eating sacrificial meat when people will not know about it (speaking of tricksterism!). Paul suggests that it is okay to eat anything in moderation with gratitude, but that for the sake of immature consciences, sometimes it is necessary to eat our sacrificial meat "in the closet," so to speak.

The whole direction of the Hebrew and Christian Scriptures moves toward a contextual or situational ethic, including but not stopping with the many references to tricksterism. Jesus told us that the whole law and the prophets hang on just two commandments, to love God and to love our neighbor as we love ourselves (Matt. 22:36–40). Since "the law and the prophets" was a phrase used to describe the Hebrew Scriptures, which was of course the only Bible of Jesus' time, he was telling us that love of self, God, and neighbor is to be the norm against which we interpret everything we see, think, do, or read—including the other commandments. So it is left to us to decide within each context what is the way to be loving to our God, our neighbor, and ourselves. Sometimes we might wish that a voice from heaven would tell us exactly what to do. But if we quiet ourselves, ask for guidance, and listen without preconceptions, a loving and perhaps unexpected course of action will make itself known to us in the dark still center of our being.

During her previously mentioned coming-out sermon, Jeanne Audrey Powers pointed out that the Christian church was intended to "overcome [the] powers and principalities of this world" (cf. Eph. 6:10–12). Therefore, she said, "the whole Christian church is vocationally called to be subversive." Instead, the Christian church chose to model itself after heteropatriarchal Greek and Roman models, subverting the best interests of humankind by silencing the voices of half of the human family.[17] In the process the church adopted an ethical system that works well only for the elite who created it and excludes by definition all of us who are lesbian, gay, bisexual, or transgendered. Our challenge, then, is to use whatever means is necessary to recover our voices within the biblical text, within religious institutions, and within society as a whole and as we regain them, to use those voices to bring good news to the poor, release to the captives, sight to the blind, and freedom to the oppressed.[18]

## Notes

1. Susan Brooks Thistlethwaite, "Every Two Minutes: Battered Women and Feminist Interpretation," in *Feminist Interpretation of the Bible*, ed. Letty M. Russell (Philadelphia: Westminster Press, 1985), 100, 102.

2. Carole R. Fontaine,"Tricksters in the Bible," *The Witness* 81 (July/August 1998): 8.

3. Ibid., 10.

4. In a sermon preached at the convocation of Reconciling Congregations, July 15, 1995, at Augsburg College in Minneapolis, Minnesota.

5. Fontaine, "Tricksters in the Bible," 10.

6. See Virginia Ramey Mollenkott, *Sensuous Spirituality: Out from Fundamentalism* (New York: Crossroad, 1992), 41–50.

7. Katie G. Cannon, *Black Womanist Ethics* (Atlanta: Scholars Press, 1988), 75.

8. Renita J. Weems, "Reading Her Way through the Struggle: African American Women and the Bible," in *Stony the Road We Trod: African American Biblical Interpretation*, ed. Cain Hope Felder (Minneapolis: Fortress Press, 1991), 57–77 (Weems's italics).

9. Fontaine, "Tricksters in the Bible," 10.

10. Judith Butler, *Bodies That Matter* (New York: Routledge, 1993), 227.

11. Robin W. Lovin, "Bonhoeffer's Ethics: A Complex Obedience," *Christian Century* (April 26, 1995): 446–47.

12. See Gianna E. Israel and Donald E. Tarver II, M.D., *Transgender Care* (Philadelphia: Temple University Press, 1997).

13. Lovin, "Bonhoeffer's Ethics," 447. Cf. "What Is Meant by 'Telling the Truth'?" in Dietrich Bonhoeffer, *Ethics* (New York: Macmillan, 1965), 363–72. In this unfinished essay, Bonhoeffer states, "It is only the cynic who claims to 'speak the truth' at all times and in all places to all men in the same way....Every utterance or word lives and has its home in a particular environment" (365–67). And in a letter dated December 1943 Bonhoeffer wrote, "Truthfulness does not mean the disclosure of everything that exists but includes respect for secrecy, confidence, and concealment," and he quotes Nietzsche's comment that "every profound mind has need of a mask" (*Ethics*, 372).

14. John Milton, *Areopagitica*, in *John Milton: Complete Poems and Major Prose*, ed. Merrit Y. Hughes (New York: Odyssey, 1957), 728.

15. Gwenyth Mapes, "Feminist Theology: Hearing Old Stories into New Speech" (paper presented at the National Women's Studies Association Conference, Washington, D.C., July 1993).

16. On Tamar's sexual tricksterism, see Genesis 38:6–26; on Rahab's political trickster-ism and sexual questionability, and her heroism in faith, see Joshua 2:1–24; Hebrews 11:31; and James 2:25; on Ruth's tricking Boaz, see Ruth 3:1–9 ("uncovering his feet" is a eu-phemism for exposing genitals); on Bathsheba's passive role in King David's cruel trick vis-à-vis Uriah, see 2 Samuel 11:1–27; on Mary's status as an unwed youthful mother, see Matthew 1:18–20.

17. The latter concept comes from a nineteenth-century womanist foresister named Anna Julia Cooper, quoted by Elisabeth Schüssler Fiorenza in *Sharing Her Word: Feminist Biblical Interpretation in Context* (Boston: Beacon Press, 1998), 25.

18. This is the primary agenda of God's anointed messengers as described in Isaiah 61:1 and Luke 4:17–21.

## 2

# Camping around the Canon

## Humor as a Hermeneutical Tool
## in Queer Readings of Biblical Texts

### ELIZABETH STUART

*The Hebrew and Christian Scriptures are often used as texts of terror by conservative religious denominations. Too often, queers have allowed themselves to be wounded by particular passages by mainline and fundamentalist churches. Laughing at those texts is a strategy that subverts their efforts of destructiveness and distances us from the pain of being a target. Elizabeth Stuart traces the history of laughter within Christianity and how dangerous it was to the established social order. Laughter can burlesque sacred authority and question it. In a brief essay on the history of laughter, Stuart locates "camp," the tactics of queer parody. Camp includes humor as well as a subversive critique. Stuart notes how "camp" becomes a means for queer reading that empowers us to work for liberation, and she suggests a naturally queer strategy of reclaiming laughter in responding to scriptures that are used to harm. For Stuart, to read the text as a queer is to learn to laugh at the reading. Camping around the canon of scriptures has the potential of restoring the Word to the queer community.*

Why do human beings laugh? This question has exercised the minds of scientists, philosophers, and sociologists for centuries. Ingvild Gilhus collapses these reflections into three major theories: (1) the superiority theory, which links laughter to power over another; (2) the incongruity theory, which attributes the laughter to the bringing together of two opposite meanings in such a way as to produce an unexpected meaning; and (3) the relief theory, which claims that laughter is a means of relief from the psychological pressure of keeping certain things taboo, a form of safety valve which in allowing pressure to be occasionally released keeps the taboos and order of a society in place.[1] All of these theories assume that laughter is a universal, disembodied phenomenon, but it is not: laughter takes on different meaning in different cultures. As far as we can tell, only human beings laugh. Laughter is induced either by some kind of interaction between the body and the mind or by some agitation of the body itself. In either case it is a bodily reaction.

The early Christian attitude to laughter was forged in a matrix of different attitudes to laughter. From Judaism the early Christians inherited a scriptural tradition which in many respects was suspicious of laughter. The wisdom tradition, in particular, associated laughter with the rejection of wisdom (Sir. 21:14f.; 27:12f.). In many ancient Greek cultures laughter was associated with the erotic and with fertility cults. Homer and Hesiod taught that the gods laughed but their laughter was cruel, directed at the stupidity of mortals. Their laughter emphasized their transcendence, their detachment from human standards of ethical behavior. Both Plato and Aristotle warned that laughter threatened the moderation and dignity that was crucial for an ethical life. Plato maintained that laughter was unethical because it usually arises from an aggressive pleasure in the unconscious folly of another.[2] Aristotle recognized the usefulness of laughter in debate and as a means of relaxing. The issue for Aristotle was what kind of laughter was appropriate for a free man—certainly not the uncontrolled, vulgar hilarity of the buffoon. He came to the conclusion that irony was superior to buffoonery and humorlessness because it was an understated, modest, and moderate form of humor.[3]

The Gnostics, who caused various crises of identity within the Christian community in its infancy, took great pleasure in ridiculing and mocking their opponents, and so laughter became in their philosophy a symbol of gnosis. The association of laughter with fertility cults, doubt, folly, the unethical, and the illiberal as well as with Gnosticism did nothing to endear it to the early Christian theologians. Many of the early theologians concluded that immoderate laughter left the body out of control and open to sin. Early monastic rules are full of warnings of the dangers of laughter and punishments for those who succumb to it. Weeping, on the other hand, was approved of because it was considered to be an appropriate reaction to sin and the redemptive suffering and death of Jesus. While great ascetics like Anthony were admired for never having laughed, others like Arsenios and Abba John were admired for their crying.[4] John Chrysostom famously claimed that Jesus never laughed but he did weep and declared that those who mourn are blessed.[5] Those who mourn demonstrate their closeness to God and consequent awareness of their own sin, the sin of the world, and the suffering of Christ; those who laugh demonstrate their alienation from God. Yet, some laughter was considered a sign of holiness: the laughter of ascetics at the tricks demons tried unsuccessfully to play upon them and the laughter of spiritual joy, which demonstrated the extent to which the person's body had already been transfigured into a near resurrection state of joy.[6]

Despite many theologians' suspicions of laughter the church could not stop it altogether. Qoheleth reminded them that there was "a time to weep, and a time to laugh" (Eccles. 3:4), and the focus on joy in the New Testament (particularly the Gospel of Luke) and the promise of laughter in the coming reign of God (Luke 6:22) prevented a complete marginalization of laughter. The medieval period, with its increased emphasis upon embodiment in the sacraments and the lives and relics of the saints, also saw controlled expressions of laughter in a sacred context. The earthy comedy of the English mystery plays written to be performed during the Feast of Corpus Christi is well known. Much of the humor in those plays is focused on the body and the failure of various people to grasp the nature of the incarnation. The Feast of Fools, widely celebrated throughout the West on January 1 during the medieval period but particularly associated with France, was a feast of outrageous buffoonery in which the lower clergy ridiculed the higher clergy, dressed as animals and women, ran around the churches, brayed like donkeys, and mocked the liturgy.[7] There are several ways of interpreting the feast. It could be understood simply as a controlled explosion of the tension that accumulated in a highly structured church with an ambiguous attitude to the body and women. By barely tolerating this annual eruption, the hierarchy actually managed to keep order the rest of the year. But the feast's positioning in the wake of the Feast of the Incarnation suggests that there may have been other forces behind the laughter. The story of the nativity reminds all who celebrate it of the raising of the lowly and the casting down of the mighty, of the messy reality of God become human within female flesh to inaugurate a reign that overturns all human values. The Feast of Fools could be interpreted as an explosion of incarnational energy. Laughter as an integral part of that explosion, exposed the extent to which the church failed to realize in its own organization and beliefs the reality of the incarnation.[8]

An outpouring of resurrection spirit in the form of laughter took place in the German-speaking medieval world at Easter. The *risus paschalis* (Easter laughter) had preachers reducing their congregations to fits of laughter through bawdy humor.[9] This laughter must have expressed many things: relief at the vindication of Christ, joy at the defeat of death, and delight in the transfiguration of the body. A modern poet has described the resurrection as "a laugh freed forever and forever."[10] The anarchic nature of the resurrection can only be truly celebrated with an anarchic response, and this is what Easter laughter was all about.

Laughter was an important tool in the discourse of Renaissance thinkers, particularly Erasmus, who characterized human life as the mad laughing at the mad; the worldly fool laughs at the Christian, who cuts a foolish figure by the standards of the world but who laughs at the worldly fool, for the Christian sees things from God's perspective and can see that the world of the fool is vanity.[11] Following Aristotle, many Renaissance writers drew a distinction between appropriate and inappropriate laughter (the latter being lewd, vulgar, and vengeful), choosing to interpret Paul's condemnation of levity (*eutrapelia*) in Ephesians 5:4 as condemnation of this type of jest, a reading that was disputed by others.

The postmodern world with its emphasis on embodied knowing and suspicion of the hegemony of rationality has found a central place for laughter. Psychologists and medics tell us that laughter is good for us, and philosophers too have redeemed laughter. Perhaps the most famous modern treatise on laughter is in the form of a historical detective novel, Umberto Eco's *Name of the Rose*. An English friar, William of Baskerville, investigates a series of murders in an Italian Benedictine monastery where the manuscript is hidden of Aristotle's lost reflections upon laughter as an instrument for uncovering truth: "through witty riddles and unexpected metaphors, though it tells us things differently from the way they are, as if it were lying, it actually obliges us to examine them more closely, and it makes us say: Ah, this is just how things are, and I didn't know."[12] Jorge, the blind librarian who does all he can to keep the manuscript hidden, aligns himself with John Chrysostom—to him laughter is an expression and force of doubt, the enemy of truth. Laughter threatens the religious, moral, and social order because it is base, associated with the belly rather than the brain, the plebeian rather than the master. But the very experience of trying to solve the murders has convinced William that human beings are misguided in their attempts to establish a clearly defined and stable divine order in the world. The "signs" that he had believed to be divine were created by the librarian. And so he remarks to his pupil Adso, "Perhaps the mission of those who love mankind is to make people laugh at the truth, *to make truth laugh*, because the only truth lies in learning to free ourselves from the insane passion for truth."[13]

For William laughter is the embodied recognition of the ultimate omnipotence and freedom of the divine that makes a mockery of all human attempts to order the world in God's name. For many postmodern theologians this is the body's grace, its resistance to totalitarian truths, its "wild wisdom" resisting the "will-to-truth" which seeks to establish immutable truths,

> only through the suppression or oppression of the sensual, that is those markings of culture subject to the limitations and vicissitudes of finite existence which engage the senses of sight, sound, touch, smell and

taste. Thus, the site for new thinking or reconstruction is just those "sensual remainders" or "sensate markings of culture" that survive the clash between forces of the "will-to-truth" and their opposition.[14]

The theologian examines these neither to establish some universal truth from reflection upon them nor to apply some universal truth to them in the process of interpretation but in order to understand what forces are at work in them and to draw attention to the possibilities for a loving and transforming encounter with "the other" within them. In this type of body-based theology the divine, like the self and the text, is not a stable Being either inside or outside the world but a wild being, untamed, an eternal recurrence of difference that opens possibilities for wild love.

This postmodern understanding of laughter recognizes and attempts to avoid the pitfalls of some other forms of body theology that identify the divine with an unconstructed, innocent natural body, which has to be discovered and uncovered. Such an approach can lead to a complete identification between the divine and human bodily experience as interpreted by one group or another. In other words there is an annihilation of difference, and with difference the very bodily desire that most body theologians want to claim is the royal road to the divine. Desire, most postmodern philosophers agree, is born of difference. The need to emphasize this difference is obvious when we consider the bodily reaction of laughter. Not all laughter is subversive; it can be a weapon of conformity, as queer people are only too aware. Jokes about queers are one of the most effective strategies for keeping people in the closet. And humor directed against various groups within the queer community by other queers is an effective strategy of division. Comedy can be cleverly manipulated to dull people to the pain of injustice; it can be used to divert our attention away from the truly subversive. Laughter can be used to ridicule the victims of social systems; it can be used to stir up hate; laughter can be an expression of scorn.

The early church fathers were certainly right to recognize that laughter can be both a sign of divine grace and a sign of alienation from the divine. Sometimes the refusal to laugh, to assume a closed bodily position, is an incarnation of divine grace, but knowing when to refuse to laugh or recognizing when the laughter being produced is not of God and to be resisted can only be grasped out of a desire for the divine that is itself rooted in a recognition of the difference between the divine and human. However, the postmodern alternative to an overoptimistic identification between the divine and bodily reactions such as laughter is equally problematic because its tendency is to render God so other that the very existence of God becomes a matter of insignificance. The body may rebel occasionally against human constructions of the divine through laughter and other forms of bodily epistemology, but the divine is rendered so wild that ultimately one cannot speak of it at all. At the end of *The Name of the Rose* both William and his pupil are reduced to stuttering silence about God, a silence devoid of joy or energy. In such a silence ethics easily become a matter of competition and might makes right.

An awareness of the fallibility of bodily reaction can lead to a rejection of any kind of useful and certainly theological body-based epistemology. This explains why camp may frequently appear to reinforce the status quo and dominant order: it is dependent on it to subvert it. Queer Christians are often accused of merely buttressing oppressive systems by remaining within the churches, as if a person related to religion as a subject to an object. Parody recognizes the complexities of the relationship of queer to dominant structures and nevertheless creates a praxis for resistance and transformation. Parodic thought is not alien to the Christian tradition; indeed it is central to it. It is the means by which Christians relate the nature of God to their own relationships, as in the current trend to speak about human sexuality as an echo of the life of the Trinity. As Gerard Loughlin notes, however, by referring to such discourse as metaphor or, more usually, analogy, there is a tendency to forget that each parody carries cultural and historical content with the result that the difference between parody and the "Other" is overlooked.[15] Philip Core has defined camp (using Jean Cocteau's definition of himself) as "the lie that tells the truth";[16] this is also an appropriate definition of parody and is reminiscent of Eco's Aristotle and his definition of laughter.

Despite various studies that have drawn attention to the presence of the comic in the Hebrew and Christian Scriptures,[17] laughter, let alone camp laughter, has not been appropriated as a tool by the biblical scholars guild! Yet, as the foregoing discussion has shown, it deserves a place in every Christian's hermeneutical toolbox. Queer Christians have been socialized into relating to the Bible tragically, and it is only in very recent years that any attempt has been made to relate to the Scriptures other than through and on the terms of "original" readings. As a community we are learning to read all the texts of our lives as comedic stories (in Dante's sense of a story of ascent). If queer Christians are going to deal creatively and vitally with the intertextuality of their lives, then my contention is that they must learn to camp around the canon and learn to relate to the Scriptures comically, for it is a comic story. Laughter is something that needs to be restored to the heart of all Christian discourse. Queer Christians are therefore fortunate that camp humor is at the heart of their culture. Of all the critical methodologies developed within the academy to read the biblical text, reader-response criticism has the clearest potential to incorporate camp within it.

## Queer-Response Criticism

Historically based forms of biblical criticism have attempted to read the text by focusing on the horizon behind it, the world that gave rise to it. But a growing awareness of the influence of the response of readers on the problems that a historical-critical approach set out to solve plus the influence of poststructuralism helped to shift the focus onto the horizon in front of the text, the reader and her world. Reader-response criticism is an extremely diverse movement and in a constant state of evolution. What unites most reader-response critics is the conviction that meaning is generated, not by the text, but by the reader and reading process. They differ on some key issues such as the nature of the reader (is he an academically skilled or "ordinary" reader?), the nature of the reading experience (is it primarily an individual or socially constructed experience?), and the balance of power between the reader and the text (which dominates the experience the reader or the text?).

The Bible and Culture Collective has drawn attention to the fact that within biblical studies the mildest form of reader-response criticism has tended to be adopted, which leaves largely intact the notion of a stable text and circumscribes meaning.[18] This type of reader-response criticism has been influenced by the early work of Wolfgang Iser,[19] who developed the notion of the "implied reader" who is both the creation of the text but also the reader, "a realization of the potentialities *in* the text but produced *by* a real reader."[20] The reader reads through a dialectical journey of expectation and recollection and reevaluation within the text. Iser emphasized the transformation of the reader through the process of reading the text, an emphasis that has been extremely appealing to biblical critics as is his contention that reading strategies developed in the academy and among professional guilds provide the circumscribing framework for the reading process and the maps that help the reader negotiate the fissures within the text. So the readings of nonexperts and scholars who for various reasons exist on the margins of the academy are discounted.

Yet, as the Bible and Culture Collective has noted, postmodern and poststructuralist literary theory has shattered the notion of the stable text and the understanding of the relationship between text and reader as subject and object.[21] This collapse should pose few problems for those who stand within the Christian tradition for whom the relationship between text and reader is infinitely more complex than the scholarly guild is often willing to acknowledge. Christians are baptized into the biblical story; it "consumes" our reality and molds our experience. The church both constitutes and is constituted by the Scriptures, and in the attempt to body forth the story anew in every age and circumstance the church continues the narration of the story and becomes part of its development.[22] The collapse of the radical distinction between text and reader is therefore implicit in the Christian understanding of the dispensation of grace. Not only have many biblical scholars been reluctant to acknowledge this reality; they have also chosen to ignore the other great insight that postmodernism has afforded us, namely, that both texts and their readers are created by the interpretive conventions of the interpretive community to which they belong. This in turn has led to the failure to interrogate the sociopolitical nature of various reading strategies and the voices that these strategies exclude or marginalize, with the result that readings simply reinforce the worldview of the group with no space created for transformation.

Biblical reader-response critics have thus generally failed to appreciate that meaning is generated in and by the act of reading, which is always contextual. Queer readers, on the other hand, should have no difficulty integrating postmodern insights into their reader-response criticism, for the very concept of "queer" is a product of postmodern discourse. The whole notion of "queer" challenges the understanding of the concept of the stable self and replaces it with an understanding of the self as unstable and constituted by "performance" and improvisation within and in resistance to dominant discourses. Queer readers of biblical texts are already self-consciously constituted in such a way as to engage in the "truest" form of reader-response criticism, a reading that also reflects the theological relationship between readers and the biblical text.

What does it mean to read biblical texts as a queer reader? It means to read texts in an interpretive community and tradition that has not only, to use Judith Fetterley's phrase, "immasculated women," that is, assumed that the reader is male and taught women to read as males, in other words, assumed the universality of male experience,[23] but also de-queered readers, teaching us to read as people who accept the universality of heterosexual experience. To read as a queer is therefore to join the swelling ranks of resisting readers who read against the grain of the reading traditions we have inherited, not only resisting the de-queering but also all other racist, sexist, and classist strategies. This is part of the process of parody, to retell with significant differences—if you will, a drag reading of scripture—a performance designed to subvert dominant readings and understandings. To read as a queer is also to learn to laugh at a reading of a text, whether yours or another's, to learn to accept one's body as a site of epistemology, to subject that reaction to analysis, and to determine the nature of the laughter—is it porous to heaven or hell?

Certain groups of queer Christians will find this easier to do than others. As British black theologian Robert Beckford has pointed out, particularly within black churches there is a tradition of "call and response" to scripture:

If the Scripture reading moves us then we say "Amen." If the text really registered, then we say "Hallelujah." Hermeneutically speaking, these responses are oral affirmations which recompose the meaning of the text to fit with the needs of our contemporary situation. This "meeting of two horizons"—that of text and that of the lives of Black people in church—produces a rereading: new meanings arise as we affirm a passage, theme or concept.[24]

Beckford identifies this "call and response" as a clear form of reader-response criticism. What stops the oppressive reading of biblical texts in these communities is the fact that the reading was communal: "The responses of verbal affirmation or complete silence were a clue to those 'interpreting' that their thoughts were acceptable or errant."[25] Obviously, as Beckford points out such rereadings are inevitably limited by a group's theology, and this is an important point. The dialogical relationship between theology and reading is often denied or ignored by those who stand in the historical-critical tradition of reading who regard themselves as the front-runners in the race of theology, handing on the baton of their discoveries to theologians for them to work with. Nevertheless Beckford is convinced that reader-response criticism in a communal context is a vital experience for groups of marginalized people because it brings the Bible to bear on their existence in a liberating fashion; it is a form of praxis.

Although many evangelically based queer Christian groups already practice this kind of reader-response criticism, it is a way of reacting to scripture largely alien to other types of Christianity, and laughing at a reading is alien to most Christian cultures. Perhaps laughter reading is something we will have to learn to do on our own first, just as many of us "practice" coming out to our friends, parents, lovers, and children in the privacy of our rooms for weeks, months, years, before daring to do so in public. Perhaps a few of us will begin to dare to laugh in public, as preachers, proclaimers, and receivers. Perhaps there will be a Stonewall-type moment of laughter when queer Christians sitting in a cathedral hearing the intonement of Romans 1:26-7 one more time or one of the stories of the biblical eunuchs or Jesus' words about marriage in heaven in Matthew 22 told "straight" will begin to laugh, quietly at first but building to a crescendo that will sweep the queer world and disturb, disorder, and transform the straight church and its relationship with the biblical text. But learning to laugh at texts—to read them with camp humor communally and critically—must become an integral part of queer reading strategies if the Word is to be taken back.

I will conclude with an analysis of a text I have come to find very funny. I am conscious of the fact that humor like the grace that it so often incarnates is very fragile; it slips through one's fingers and analysis can kill it.

Nevertheless, an example is called for. The passage in question is Ephesians 5:21–33. The reading tradition in which I was nourished taught me to read this text as a magnificent theology of marriage, which took that sexual state and that state alone into the mystery of the triune God. Later as a feminist and a lesbian I learned to react to this text tragically as a heteropatriarchal and colonial manifesto for the ordering of male/female relationships. My bodily reactions to hearing it read (often at weddings) were to wince or churn with anger but never to laugh. It was an analysis of this passage by my friend Gerard Loughlin in a paper on Balthasar and the Trinity that changed my reaction to this passage from tragic to comic. Loughlin argued that the heteropatriarchal readings of this text are

> undermined and washed away in the deeper waters of the Christian symbolic, for insofar as women are members of the body, they too are called to be Christ to others; so that they too must also act as "groom"; and "husband"; to the "bride" and "wife" of the other, whether it be an actual man or woman. For it cannot be said that within the community only men are called to love as Christ does. . . . Being in Christ does not mean that one ceases to be Jew or Greek, slave or free, male or female; but it does mean that such social-symbolic orderings no longer have true solidity—a final oppression—but are liquefied and made to flow, so that they can in fact become a sign and means of freedom to us—though this some of us may hardly dare believe.[26]

Loughlin's reading of the text had transformed it into a queer text. The very incongruity of this reading with the "original" reading is enough to stimulate laughter. I find it funny that this passage should be read so often and so solemnly at weddings, the great ceremony of heteropatriarchy. I find it ironic that it should be among the texts of terror used against queer people. And I find it delightful that this should be part of the Pauline corpus, which most queer people relate to tragically. But this reading in which I find the grace of liberation and affirmation also challenges my narrowly feminist knee-jerk reactions to transgendered persons, for in this passage Christ himself is represented as transgendered—a male with a very female body, and the church is represented as a female body with a "male head." I now read this text with the transforming grace of laughter, and my parodic retelling of it stands firmly within the camp tradition.

Camping around the canon (and I use "around" here in its broadest sense to include a subversive taking seriously of texts the church tried to dismiss as frivolous and excluded from the canon) as a reading strategy has the potential to restore the Word to the queer community as a whole (and not just to biblical specialists with it) in a manner that will resonate with queers beyond that community and perhaps do something to alter the dominant image (at least in Britain) of both the Bible and the religions of the Book as texts of unmitigated terror for sane queer people. The Christian story teaches us that we are part of a divine comedy; our queer-response criticism teaches that it is a camp comedy at that.

## Notes

1. Ingvild Sælid Gilhus, *Laughing Gods, Weeping Virgins: Laughter in the History of Religion* (London and New York: Routledge, 1997), 5.

2. Plato *Republic* 2–3.

3. Aristotle *Nicomachaen Ethics* 4.4; *Rhetoric* 18.7.

4. Gilhus, *Laughing Gods, Weeping Virgins*, 64.

5. John Chrysostom *Homilies on the Gospel of Matthew* 6.5–6.

6. Gilhus, *Laughing Gods, Weeping Virgins*, 69.

7. E. K. Chambers, *The Mediaeval Stage*, vol. 1 (London: Oxford University Press, 1954).

8. Gilhus, *Laughing Gods, Weeping Virgins*, 78–88.

9. Karl-Josef Kuschel, *Laughter: A Theological Reflection* (London: SCM Press, 1994), 83–87.

10. Patrick Kavanagh, "Lough Derg," cited in Daniel W. Hardy and David F. Ford, *Jubilate* (London: Darton, Longman and Todd, 1984), 73.

11. M. A. Screech, *Laughter at the Foot of the Cross* (London: Allen Lane, 1997).

12. Umberto Eco, *The Name of the Rose* (San Diego: Harcourt, Bracc, Jovanovich, 1983), 472.

13. Ibid., 491.

14. Diane L. Prosser MacDonald, *Transgressive Corporeality: The Body, Poststructuralism, and the Theological Imagination* (Albany: SUNY Press, 1995), 118–19.

15. Gerard Loughlin, "Sexing the Trinity: Balthasar, Parody, and the Suprasexual" (paper presented at the annual conference of the Catholic Theological Association of Great Britain, 1997).

16. Philip Core, *Camp: The Lie That Tells the Truth* (London: Plexus, 1984).

17. See, e.g., J. Cheryl Exum, ed., *Tragedy and Comedy in the Bible*, Semeia 32 (Decatur, Ga.: Scholars Press, 1995); and Dan O. Via Jr., *Kerygma and Comedy in the New Testament: A Structuralism Approach to Hermeneutics* (Philadelphia: Fortress Press, 1975).

18. The Bible and Culture Collective, *The Postmodern Bible* (New Haven: Yale University Press, 1995), 20–69.

19. Among Iser's works are *The Implied Reader: Patterns of Communication in Prose Fiction from Bunyan to Beckett* (Baltimore: Johns Hopkins University Press, 1974); *The Act of Reading: A Theory of Aesthetic Response* (Baltimore: Johns Hopkins University Press, 1978); *Prospecting: From Reader Response to Literary Anthropology* (Baltimore: Johns Hopkins University Press, 1989); and *The Fictive and the Imaginary: Charting Literary Anthropology* (Baltimore: Johns Hopkins University Press, 1993).

20. The Bible and Culture Collective, *The Postmodern Bible*, 31.

21. Ibid., 51–57.

22. Gerard Loughlin, *Telling God's Story: Bible, Church, and Narrative Theology* (Cambridge: Cambridge University Press, 1996).

23. Judith Fetterley, *The Resisting Reader: A Feminist Approach to American Fiction* (Bloomington: Indiana University Press, 1978).

24. Robert Beckford, *Jesus Is Dread: Black Theology and Black Culture in Britain* (London: Darton, Longman and Todd, 1998), 167.

25. Ibid., 168.

26. Gerard Loughlin, "Baptismal Fluid" (unpublished paper, 1997), 9–10.

**3**

# Love Your Mother

## A Lesbian Womanist Reading of Scripture

### IRENE S. TRAVIS

*A womanist is a black feminist who frequently uses methods of survival involving boldness and courageousness, an appreciation of women's culture, and a commitment to survival and health. It is an idea involving such qualities as being relational, mutual, and family centered. Alice Walker's definition embodies a vision of freedom in which all women and men are respected and treated equally.[1]*

*What follows is a womanist vision expressed in fragments and lines of biblical texts, challenging assumptions of those who read the text from a white male perspective. It is a vision of wholeness, connection through love, community building, and the survival of an entire people of faith.*

> Ask now, and see,
>> can a man bear a child?
> Why then do I see every man
>> with his hands on his loins like a woman in labor?
>>>>> (Jer. 30:6)

Obviously, not every woman wants to be a mother. Nor does every man wish to become a father. Throughout history, however, there has apparently existed this incredibly strong biological, psychological, and sociological urge to propagate the species. Up until this century, women who wanted to parent alone, or with other females, had very few options. Lesbians of former generations usually settled on becoming surrogate mothers like Hagar raising someone else's children, or women attracted to women chose to settle into traditional families, forming subversive bonds among themselves. During slavery, African American women attempted to maintain relationships with their children and among themselves. With as few physical contacts as possible, lesbians were able to achieve their motherhood goals while "doing their duty" toward their husbands. Most managed to stay married, often forming enormously strong emotional attachments to special female friends.

Husbands functioned as protectors, providers, and social stabilizers. The traditional-looking family was held in high esteem in each community and supported male control of women.

> Thus says the Lord God, Ah, you shepherds of Israel who have been feeding yourselves! Should not shepherds feed the sheep? You eat the fat, you clothe yourselves with the wool; you slaughter the fatlings; but you do not feed the sheep. (Ezek. 34:2–3)

In this new era of budding gay and lesbian liberation, many mainline churches continue to preach a seemingly tidy "open but not accepting" solution to their homosexual members. All these problem congregants have to do is review the ancient texts, engage in a bit of behavior modification, and act as though they are really heterosexual, and they will be saved. All is forgiven, the perfect opposite-gender mate is found, marriage ensues, children arrive, and everybody lives happily ever after. It is all so decent and in good order. The clergy folks are satisfied with their roles as mentors, guides, and counselors. They collect their paychecks and retreat to the comforts of their own traditional families. Thinking that everybody is happy, they never look back to see the heap of dead bodies littering their doorways. Soul murderers! They enslave gay and lesbian people, destroying their spirit. These same churches once excluded black men and women from full participation. Now they exclude gays and lesbians.

What is the caring heterosexual clergyperson to do? Not try to help someone change her or his homosexual orientation? Unthinkable! And so these clergy folks perpetuate the myth of sexuality change and continue to recruit members of the gay and lesbian community to join their hetero-ranks! Through individual spiritual counseling and therapy, weekend seminars and retreats, leaders of the ex-gay movement brainwash the innocents until the gays themselves are convinced that a change has occurred. Then they unleash these repentant new converts upon unsuspecting heterosexual partners-to-be.

Merciful God, how the straight husbands and wives suffer along with their mates. They wonder why their wonderful spouses find it so difficult to respond to their sexual invitations and advances. They cannot fathom why so many escape and evasion maneuvers take place in their bedrooms. How is it that back rubs and hugs have come to replace more distinctly sexual activities? Why are there so many late nights at the office or frequent business trips, so many school clothes to iron and lunches to pack? How come there are so many bad backs and headaches? Straight spouses question their own desirability. Their self-esteem is damaged. Invariably little flirtations outside of the home begin as a way of testing their attractiveness to the opposite sex. They may wonder if anyone at all finds them desirable. Affairs may develop. Suspicion and jealousy enter the equation. Avoidance and/or lying become a way of life. Straight or gay, the truth is not in us. We cannot face our marital situations or ourselves.

But the church is self-satisfied. Church leaders are saddened and even shocked when, years later, many of these mixed couples decide to divorce or to accept outside relationships as a part of their renegotiated covenants with one another. Some couples are able to remain together, gradually falling into semicelibate relationships. Sex is no longer that important. The parenting urge remains mostly intact, both on the part of the straight spouse and the gay partner.

The biblical injunction "Thou shall not lie with a man, as thou liest with a woman" (Lev. 18:22) only works for lesbians! Obviously the Holiness Code in the book of Leviticus was not intended for a female audience. Either women's relationships with women did not matter or remained unnoticed. The only seeming reference to lesbianism is in the book of Romans. It tells of women giving up the natural use of their bodies and turning lustfully to other women. It speaks of women exchanging their attractions to men for women, a truly subversive act that Paul understands as a result of idolatry. Much has been written recently on just what that might mean, so we won't dwell on it here.[2] Suffice it to say the majority of mature lesbians do not abandon God, reject their "natural attraction" to men, and rush out in a frenzy to use and abuse other females. If they were naturally attracted to men, they would not be lesbians in the first place! By definition, lesbians are innately bonded to other women, both physically and emotionally. Being with males has proven to be a poor substitute. The vast majority of lesbians have excellent nonsexual relationships with men. They just don't want to marry them. It is patently unfair to all parties concerned to foist the seemingly heterosexual lifestyle upon those born gay.

So what are today's women to do if they are attracted to other women yet long to become parents? Nowadays they adopt, they use alternative insemination methods, they provide foster care, and they coparent with males. Some still marry, have children, and divorce. A few remain trapped, eschewing change.

What did women attracted to women do in ancient times? They definitely had little choice and were compelled to marry men. Often these marriages were arranged, making input from the bride unnecessary. Many of these arranged marriages were the result of economic and power deals among men. Women were just so much property, like children or cattle. But women have always been resourceful and have created clever ways to remain together. In those times, having offspring was not only expected but required. Techniques varied little, and rules were developed regarding problems of conception. Barren women were a disgrace. Enslaved women and barren women found God in their struggles for life and wholeness despite what patriarchs believed. They found the stories of Hagar, Rachel, Ruth, Esther, and other women inspiring hope in the midst of their struggles. They founded diverse communities, crossing age, race, and religion; they created womanist ways of mutually relating to each other and testifying to the image of God in their relationships of mutuality.

> Do not press me to leave you
>      or to turn back from following you!
> Where you go, I will go;
>      where you lodge, I will lodge:
> your people shall be my people,
>      and your God my God. (Ruth 1:16)

So, it appears that most lesbians of previous ages married, reproduced, and found comfort in one another's very close company. What about the plight of widows and single lesbians? Widows certainly found strength in their children and in one another, and single women created bonds with other women. Were all of the sisters actually biological siblings? Were Mary and Martha sisters? These bonds between women were primary, nurturing, and sustaining. Audre Lourde writes, "We cannot settle for the pretenses of connection, or for the parodies of self-love. We cannot continue to evade each other on the deepest levels because we fear each other's angers, nor continue to believe that respect means never looking directly nor with openness into another Black woman's eyes."[3] Women have often called each other "sister," and lesbians have found that ploy useful throughout the centuries. It also leads women to ponder the extraordinary bond between Ruth and Naomi that crosses boundaries of age, ethnicity, and religion. Female friendships have formed across cultural, racial, intergenerational, and religious boundaries.

What if more portions of the Bible had been written from the unique points of view of women? In the case of the particular time-honored female couple of Ruth and Naomi we query, where does duty and honor end and romantic love begin, if at all? What was Ruth thinking? It is a story of the love between women, celebrating faithfulness, passionate care, commitment, devotion, and loyalty. Ruth was willing to leave her homeland for the love of another woman. We now know that many women such as Ruth and Naomi exist, and have existed throughout the history of the world, as emotionally intimate lesbians and that genital expression is not necessarily the defining quality of lesbianism. (Some men find that hard to comprehend.) And, of course, lesbianism does not exclude motherhood. The biological urge and the psychosocial desire to perpetuate the human race continue to remain strong. Women are discovering more and more resources for obtaining sperm. Naomi instructed Ruth how to become impregnated by her kinsman Boaz. Once Ruth had given birth to a son, the women of the village gathered, saying, "A son has been born to Naomi" (Ruth 4:17).

I look at my own life and remember that I rejected my postadolescent lesbianism soon after college graduation. Preferring instead the safety and security of the traditional route, I married a good-looking young man. We had much in common: same race, same age, and same religion. This was, after all, the early sixties, and I had no role models for establishing a lesbian-headed Christian family. The only gay couple I knew were so deeply into butch-femme role playing, with one mannish woman working outside of the home and the high-heeled "wife" being the homemaker, that I decided I must be straight after all. I talked to no one about these feelings. Whom could I consult? My Presbyterian pastor? I think that he was not prepared to help me.

Now, almost forty years later, I find that I am the divorced mother of two grown and married children. I am in a lovely committed relationship with another woman. At times, I see myself as both Naomi and Ruth. Having retired from thirty years in the classroom, I am now in the fifth year of pursuing a second career as a UFMCC (Universal Fellowship of Metropolitan Community Churches) clergyperson at the Cathedral of Hope. Today's generation of homosexuals can find a variety of denominations and/or congregations that are open and affirming. They sometimes have to be willing to leave behind their former denominations and do a little church shopping, but welcoming congregations do exist. These churches will embrace and support them, their long-term partners, and their children. The only way that ever happened in the past was under the unacknowledged "don't ask, don't tell" policy. Nothing and no one was out in the open. This was another way that the soul was murdered . . . choked to death by the lack of fresh air in the closet . . . a miserable way to live and a terrible way to die. It's funny how something can be both miserable and comfortable at the same time. Misinformation, discrimination, and internalized homophobia will do that for you.

Thus says the LORD,

> A voice is heard in Ramah,
> lamentation and bitter weeping.
> Rachel is weeping for her children;
> she refuses to be comforted for her children,
> because they are no more. (Jer. 31:15)

How many of today's progressive churches actually support and affirm the notion of their gay and lesbian members creating intentional families without traditional marriage? Many are struggling with this issue because it is no longer theory—it is a reality. The voiced concern has always been, "What about the children?" They claim not to care what the grown-ups do privately, but they are certain that the children will suffer. Let's face the truth. They know and we know that the only way any children ever suffer in situations like these is if they are isolated, ignored, pitied, ridiculed, or vilified by the adults in their environment.

Children willingly accept all kinds of other children and a multitude of diverse family structures until they begin to pick up the attitudes of the adults around them. Girls and boys who are disabled, are of mixed racial backgrounds, or are born "out of wedlock" have gone through this, as have the children of gays and lesbians. More and more, one sees children in wheelchairs or with obvious mental or emotional challenges out in pub-lic. Why should these youngsters not go shopping or to sports events just like anyone else? We see many more children of "mixed blood," too. Some official documents have even dropped the use of "other" when requiring in-formation about the informant's race. They now use such terms as biracial. Children born of unmarried parents are no longer labeled and shunned. It's too bad that Hollywood stars were the agents of liberation instead of the church. God looks to other communities when the church is not prepared to be a community of liberation. Eventually the offspring of gay and lesbian parents will be accepted by society as well. In view of what has happened to other formerly despised children, why don't we fast-track them? We could easily bring them into the mainstream if we had the will.

During one of the last appearances of the resurrected Jesus, Peter in-quired about his relationship with the beloved disciple. Jesus curtly replied, "What is that to you?" (John 21:22). God has allowed humans to create this wonderful garden of children, of all different races, colors, abilities, parentage, and so on. If you, dear reader, have no appreciation for the wonderful diversity of our world's population, just go on about your busi-ness and leave this incredibly vital link to the future outside of your realm of experience. If God has chosen to allow the children of gays and lesbians to grow and thrive, what is that to you? Are we not all made in God's image, an image that is both male and female in all its diverse colors and sexual variations?

> For a long time I have held my peace,
>     I have kept still and restrained myself;
>   now I will cry out like a woman in labor,
>     I will gasp and pant. (Isa. 42:14)

God, as female, as Mother, is incredibly creative and nurturing. Mother God has fashioned animals, flowers, landscapes, and seascapes of such beauty and variety that one catches one's breath at the sights, sounds, and smells of it all. Why would the infinitely talented Supreme Being stop at creating only one type of human? She didn't. She has birthed this overwhelming potpourri of peoples. Like any mother she does not have one preferred child. She, who will not be limited by our tiny minds, never imagined into being one better race, one superior gender, one allowed sexual orientation. Healthy mothers love and accept all of their children. Will Mother God do any less?

What are we lacking? Is it safety, security, acceptance, compassion, empathy, or unconditional love? Humans who have experienced all of these things are not loath to share them with others. Those who have pitiable backgrounds in these realms find it very difficult to accept others, people unlike themselves. Inbred cultures, bereft of experience with "outsiders," ignorant of current psychological thought, and knowing little of biblical scholarship, tenaciously hold on to "old think." Their thought patterns and ideas remain unchanged. What they learned and believed at twelve years old remains true for them at fifty! How can we say that we love God yet despise those whom God has created in her own image?

What will it cost the world to encourage and protect, maybe even cherish, the children of homosexual marriages until such marriages are legally sanctioned and socially accepted? Since heterosexual couples continue to produce gay and lesbian offspring, right along with their heterosexual children, it cannot be the home environment that makes one homosexual. Neither will it be the homosexual household that either encourages or discourages its children to become one way or the other. In time, statistics will undoubtedly demonstrate that in either type of household 90 percent of the children will turn out to be straight and 10 percent will not. We would quickly discover that truth if gay people were not afraid to be honest. One would think that all churches would promote honesty as a virtue, but they obviously do not. Really, who cares if one child has gay parents and one has straight? Can their children not be best friends? Is it that folks like the religious right are still confusing homosexuality with pedophilia? Are we not more enlightened about this painful subject?

I read the biblical texts from an African American and lesbian perspective. I hold certain truths from my reading:

Child abuse is an abomination.

Homosexual acts for the purposes of degradation and humiliation or for asserting power over the weak and the vulnerable are an abomination.

Homosexual orientation is not an abomination.

Everyone knows that there are many more heterosexual pedophiles, yet the notion persists that gays in general are harmful to minors. Why is that? Your Mother knows better. Her gay and lesbian offspring know better. And her straight progeny now know better. Let's drop the pretenses of the past. If we are going boldly into the twenty-first century, don't we have an awful lot of old garbage that needs to be jettisoned?

What, in the long run, is really required of us? Nothing more than our Creator required centuries ago. Love God, show mercy and justice toward others, love yourself, and care for your neighbors. Human mothers have often chided their young ones, "What are you two doing in there? If you can't get along, you'll have to take a time-out. Why don't you treat each other the way you want to be treated?" It is the desire of every mother's heart that her children live in peace and harmony and learn to love one another. Can we do anything less for our God who has mothered us, nurtured and sustained us? We have loved our earthly mothers because they first loved and spiritually suckled us. Our mothers may have been biological or adoptive. Our mothers may have been the feminine nature of each male, gay or straight, who took on the mothering role for us.

Reasonable children obey their parents out of respect. They are obedient because it is from their parents that they receive instruction. The parent is the one who provides the basic necessities of life, who gives aid and comfort, and who ideally gives them unconditional love. If God does this for us, can we not respond as obedient children? Love all of God's human creatures including those of a variety of races, religious beliefs, ages, abilities, and sexual orientations. This is the desire of God's heart. Love your Mother.

## Notes

1. Alice Walker, *In Search of Our Mothers' Garden* (New York: Harcourt Brace Jovanovich, 1984), xi.

2. Bernadette J. Brooten, *Love between Women: Early Christian Responses to Female Homoeroticism* (Chicago: University of Chicago Press, 1996).

3. Audre Lourde, "Eye to Eye: Black Women, Hatred, and Anger," in *Sister Outsider: Essays and Speeches* (Trumansburg, N.Y.: Crossing Press, 1984), 153.

**4**

# Eating the Crumbs
# That Fall from the Table

## Trusting the Abundance of God

### JUSTIN TANIS

*Rigid gender constructions have been used to oppress women and queers alike. Gender bending has had a long history in many cultures, but institutional Christian responses have been tragically violent or inept. Justin Tanis, a transgendered male, explores the story of Jesus and the Canaanite woman from a female-to-male perspective. Jesus did not deal with his biases until challenged by the Canaanite woman. He learned from her challenges and was subsequently transformed to a position of acceptance. The ecclesial inclusion of transgendered persons presents a challenge for Christian churches. Can they learn as their founder learned to become more inclusive and accepting?*

And Jesus went away from there and withdrew to the district of Tyre and Sidon. And a Canaanite woman from that region came out and cried, "Have mercy on me, Sovereign, Heir of David, my daughter is severely possessed by a demon." But Jesus did not answer her a word. And the disciples came and begged Jesus, saying, "Send her away, for she is crying after us." Jesus answered, "I was sent only to the lost sheep of the house of Israel." But she came and knelt before Jesus, saying, "Sovereign, help me." And Jesus answered, "It is not fair to take the children's bread and throw it to the dogs." She said, "Yes, Sovereign, yet even the dogs eat the crumbs that fall from their owners' table." Then Jesus answered her, "O woman, great is your faith! Be it done for you as you desire." And her daughter was healed instantly. (Matt. 15:21–28)

The image of Jesus turning away a woman who is seeking healing for her sick child is not the image of Jesus that I was taught in Sunday school. It is troubling, disturbing, and challenging. Yet, I also find hope in this story because it contains a powerful message of inclusion, of determination, and of Jesus' own growth in his vision of ministry and hospitality. It is a familiar tale to those of us on the margins of "acceptability" who have experienced rejection from those in power, from those who, we were told, were our guardians and advocates, and from those who have the power to touch our lives. Those within the church have resorted, as Jesus did initially, to epithets rather than compassion, all in the name of Christ.

Jesus' first reaction, however, was not his last word. Jesus himself is transformed during this interaction. For me, as a transsexual man, this story is a powerful one with its dual message of human determination and God's abundance. It connects me both with those who have talked back to power and with a dynamic and growing God. Most of all, it speaks powerfully that God's goodness is for everyone, regardless of the status or position in society.

I began looking at this story when I was asked to preach at a conference on hospitality and welcome in the church. It was the first time I was asked to speak to a church group after coming out publicly as a transgendered person. The combination of the conference theme and my own journey as a transsexual seemed simultaneously appropriate and ironic. I have experienced both affirmation and condemnation from the church. I chose this scripture passage from Matthew precisely because it brings the irony of the situation into full view. It was my hope to provide those who heard the sermon with perhaps a little more knowledge of the experience of the transfolks in their midst and to show that Jesus' journey from rejection to affirmation was possible for us as a community of believers. This interaction between Jesus and the unnamed Canaanite woman seeking healing for her daughter speaks of God's call for us as people of faith to be advocates, to be transformed, and to be whole.

Throughout my own struggles with gender, I never felt any sense of fear or condemnation about what God might think about my gender. I knew very defiantly that God had created me as I was, whatever I discovered and may discover that to be. Over and over again as I have faced each step of this journey, I have had a profound sense of God's presence and comfort with me.

My journey of transforming my physical body has been simultaneously a journey of transforming my spiritual self. I have discovered previously untapped reserves of joy within me. I have a far deeper personal experience of God and a much firmer sense of God's calling in my life. The more congruent I felt in terms of gender, the more free I felt to express myself to God.

It never occurred to me that God would not accept me, but I was very afraid that God's representatives within the church might reject me. The church has only recently begun to look at its own issues of gender and continues to struggle with issues like inclusive language with reference to God, despite the Bible's use of both male and female names for God. The Southern Baptists' recent affirmation of the call for women to submit to their husbands tells me that the body of Christ has a long way to go in examining gender. If the church is still struggling with the role of women and men, it is even less prepared to deal with those who break free of the categories of gender itself.

I have encountered several people who, when their pastor discovered somehow that the person was transgendered, were instructed, shamed, and harassed to return to the gender of their birth. The pastors in these instances claimed that gender transformation was against the will of God. And yet, God, as part of a diverse and awesome creation, created these people. When will the church celebrate the goodness of the varieties of life and expression that God created, rather than try to force nature to conform to our categories of gender and sexual orientation?

To be authentic followers of Jesus, we must be willing to step outside the bounds of our comfort and into the realm of God's creation. We must be willing to follow Christ into the places that make us uncomfortable, places that we never imagined going. Jesus himself broke the bounds of gender in his own life and ministry, speaking to and including women and men around him. As a Christian, I look to Jesus and his encounter with someone quite different from himself for a model of how I am to live in this world of differences.

## The Encounter

This story details Jesus' one and only recorded trip outside the borders of Palestine. Some scholars say he went to Canaan to visit the large Jewish population there. Others say it was because of the political trouble he faced at home. Whatever his reasons for going, he arrived and encountered a local Gentile woman. There were strong ethnic tensions and deep-seated hostilities between the Jews and Gentiles in that region.

This woman approaching Jesus to help her daughter was like a drag queen approaching a bunch of teenagers on a street corner for change to call 911 after her sister has been beaten. Her act required courage and the willingness to go against stereotypes and current understandings of how the world was and necessitated a belief that individuals could rise to the occasion of helping another human being and would not always act out of hatred. Maybe it was because of her desperation, maybe it was because of her fundamental belief in the goodness of others, but she goes to Jesus and asks for his help, in spite of the historic and ethnic tensions between them.

Not only does she approach Jesus, but she refuses to leave him alone. She pesters him. She will not take no for an answer when he initially ignores her. She is so persistent that she makes the disciples uncomfortable. They go to Jesus and beg, "Send her away, for she is crying after us." They are so overwhelmed by her that they go to Jesus to get him to fix it, to send away this person who will not politely give up and leave and who does not see that she is not wanted.

Jesus answers, "I was sent only to the lost sheep of Israel." He was saying, in effect, "I'm sorry, you're not covered in our mission statement," or "We don't serve your kind here." Maybe Jesus was just exercising appropriate boundaries and doing effective self-care, realizing, "Hey, we can't help everyone. Resources are tight right now. We can't do everything." We have heard these words spoken out of good intentions and bad, but all to the same effect: "Go away." Maybe he was just uncomfortable; he wasn't sure how to act with someone of a different culture. We've all been there, too.

Even if Jesus did need time away, even if he was caring for himself, that does not explain his behavior. Ignoring those who come to us for help and ask for our mercy is not our best response, nor was it Jesus'. It seems that in Jesus' ministry, as it has been in mine, people's needs do not always come at the most convenient times and sometimes present themselves at the very worst times. God's timing is often not the same as ours. Those inconvenient moments can reveal the most important connections of ministry and call upon us to reach into our depths to offer compassion, care, and the love of God. Sometimes people come to us—people we do not understand and are not comfortable dealing with—and yet these are often the people in whom we discover the spirit of God.

The Canaanite woman is not put off by Jesus' rebuff, no matter why he said it. She does not go away. Her care for her daughter drives her to continue, "Help me." Jesus still is not swayed. He says, "It is not fair to take the children's bread and throw it to the dogs." The "dogs" is a racial epithet used by Jesus' people to put down the Canaanites. It was a slur. Commentators have jumped on this, saying things like, "Christ was not a racist.... There is no doubt that it was his purpose to have mercy. He delayed in order to bring out a great lesson."[1] Or maybe, just maybe, he believed it. Perhaps the limitations of his human nature demonstrate here a lack of expansiveness in his vision of the world. We will never know the exact answer. But we do know that too often people resort to an epithet or stereotype: "Look, I tried to tell you politely—you freaks are not wanted here."

Whatever Jesus' reasons for saying this, the woman is not deterred. Not at all. She knows who she is, and she doesn't stoop to argue with his slurs. She knows what she needs. She talks back to Jesus: "Even the dogs eat the crumbs that fall from the table." She knows there is enough for all, with nothing going to waste. She knows that God provides enough to include her, whatever this man might say to her. She knows that Jesus, with God's power, is capable of healing her daughter, whatever he might believe.

This time Jesus responds very differently and says, "O woman, great is your faith." Great was her faith in God, in Jesus, and in herself. The line between Jesus and this woman disappeared, and the barriers of race, ethnicity, nationality, and gender melted away. In that moment, when they stand face to face, her daughter is healed.

## The Woman:
## The Calling of Advocacy

It seems that this woman was convinced that Jesus was capable of more than even he seemed to believe he was. She, in fact, places more faith in the abundance of God and in Jesus' abilities to heal than he apparently does. She issues Christ an invitation to step over the barriers between them, and he in turn responds. In this encounter, both Jesus and the woman model for us the power and possibilities that are present when we face our limitations to step over and beyond them.

In reading this story, I am particularly struck by this woman's ability to take the slur that she heard and turn it into a metaphor that she uses to forward her cause. To be called a dog, and then argue that even dogs receive what they need from the Master's table, is remarkable. It takes a level head combined with a strong sense of self to pull this off. She kept herself so focused on the needs of her child that she did not waste time arguing with Jesus. She was not afraid to talk back to or challenge Jesus, but she is also a reminder that proving someone's prejudices to be wrong is more effective than arguing about them. She does not allow herself to be baited.

The Canaanite woman is very clear about her role as her child's advocate and nothing, apparently, will sway her from that mission. She is not distracted or sidetracked. She knows that Jesus' name calling will not help her child and neither will arguing with him. She does whatever is necessary to move Jesus to join her as an advocate for her child. She enlists his help in her cause. She is determined and persistent, willing to take risks.

Last year on the Internet I met a woman who deeply reminds me of the Canaanite woman in Matthew, displaying the same commitment to her child's needs, the same role as advocate for herself and her child. She is a mother who wrote to a news group for female to male transsexuals:

> My ten-year-old, David (his chosen name since age 3), will undoubtedly be a very good candidate for the type of group you host, but I don't know when that will be. At this point, David is adamant about refusing to acknowledge that there is a problem or that he will ever want to discuss being transgendered with anyone. He is living as a boy at home, in our neighborhood, at school, and in the local park sports programs. Locker rooms haven't yet become an issue. We've negotiated with the school to establish a unisex bathroom for David's classroom, and

the teachers and principals use gender-neutral or masculine pronouns when addressing him in front of other children.

I don't mean to gloss over my and my husband's years of coming to terms with this, but even before we came to realize that David is likely to need to live his whole life as a male, we were determined that he like any child deserved time and space to figure things out for himself. We didn't want anyone to try to force this child to conform to any societal stereotypes about gender.

As a result, David has had several relatively secure years of being identified as a boy by whomever he is interacting with, and, at least until puberty strikes, is unlikely to be willing to discuss these issues. I've recently begun to make some public appearances in our school system, talking about the concerns of transgendered children to teachers and health workers. David is very afraid he'll be "outed" by these activities, so I use pseudonyms for him and myself when I tell our story.

Again, thank you for writing me. I hope David will seek out support from other FTMs [female-to-males] when the going gets rough, but for now, he insists he doesn't want to talk about it. I am very much interested in lining up as many reliable resources as possible in the meantime.

I particularly want to be prepared when and if David wants to transition. It's not something I can decide for him, but I want to have safe, reputable options available whenever we may need them. The age requirement in the Harry Benjamin standards does concern me, given the enormous physical changes that come with puberty. But I suppose we must experience puberty to be absolutely sure that this child is a boy. What do you and your list members think?

Thanks again,
Elizabeth[2]

This is unconditional love. Like the Canaanite mother in Matthew 15, David's mother has had to fight for the wholeness and well-being of her child. She, too, brings to our world a message of radical inclusion and challenge to those who say that those who are not like everyone else should just go away. She reminds us of the spiritual significance of self-determination, that her child has as much right to determine how he will live in this world as any other human being. She accepts her child on his own terms. Both of these mothers step outside the bounds of the usual way of doing things in order to protect and meet the needs of their children. Both of these mothers remind us that we are called to be advocates, for ourselves and for one another, to display the same kind of determination and willingness to take risks.

From these two mothers, I have taken new courage as an advocate for myself and for others. No matter what names someone may want to call me, no matter what others think of people like me, no matter what stereotypes are thrown at me, this text is a reminder to me to stay firm in who I am and what I am doing. It is a lesson in staying calm and focused in the face of opposition, not to allow myself to be baited or swayed by someone else's discomfort or prejudice.

The unnamed Canaanite mother is a reminder to me not to give up on someone, that we are called to turn enemies into allies and to risk doing so. But she also reminds me that she does not sit back and take it. She talks back to power, and she answers prejudice. We too can talk back, with the power of our lives as well as with our words. I am proud of the strength and courage that I have needed in order to transition, to stand up against other people's ideas of who I am, and to define myself. I find excitement in the discovery of who God created me to be, beyond the obvious physical answer, to the inward most parts of my being. I am able to celebrate my own transformative powers: the power to make the changes that I have made thus far in my life and those that are still ahead.

The most important changes, it seems to me, are not physical but spiritual and emotional. We live our promise as a people of faith when we act as these mothers do: with unconditional love, accepting people on their own terms, with their own definitions and their own time frames, free from the burdens of demons or prejudices. We live our promise when we acknowledge our struggles to accept others but own them as our struggles, our problems. We live our promise when we advocate for those who do not fit, looking to the future, accepting that there will be both struggles and joy. We know that others are needed on our journeys as companions to support us, advocate for us, and uphold us.

During Advent, as we prepare to celebrate the birth of Jesus, we read the words of the prophet Isaiah,

> Comfort, O comfort my people,
> 　says your God. . . . A voice cries out:
> "In the wilderness prepare the way of the LORD,
> 　make straight in the desert a highway for our God.
> Every valley shall be lifted up,
> 　and every mountain and hill be made low;
> the uneven ground shall become level,
> 　and the rough places a plain.
> Then the glory of the LORD shall be revealed."
> 　　　　　　　　　　　　　　　　(Isa. 40:1, 3–5a)

We comfort God's people and reveal God's glory when we are part of preparing that highway, when we make the rough places of life plain for each other, when we bring down the mountains and walls that divide us, when we lift up those who are low in the valleys. Advocacy, for ourselves and for each other, prepares the way for God's actions in our world.

## Jesus: The Calling of Transformation

In the course of this story, Jesus himself is transformed. How he is at the beginning of the story and how he is at the end are quite different. Jesus' ability to make a radical shift in how he interacts with this woman speaks of the depth of his relationship with God, his sense of himself, and his own expansiveness of vision. It takes a person of enormous courage to change like this, to admit that he was wrong, to do things so differently than he had done them even one minute before. A messiah who is willing to be transformed is, for me, the Messiah worth following. A messiah who changes is, for me, the Savior because my life has been a story of changes: mental, emotional, physical, and spiritual. My life has certainly included its share of mistakes and shifts in thinking. A static messiah would not provide a model of what to do when I am faced with a change or a challenge. But this Jesus does show me what change can mean at its best. He was willing to admit his mistake and change his views and actions.

This Jesus is far more powerful and far more appealing to me than a Jesus who somehow manipulated the situation to prove a point, not really thinking negatively about this woman at all. I find it frightening to think that Jesus might have simply played on the disciples' prejudices at her expense in order to make it more dramatic when he did show mercy. I do not believe that Jesus acted this way. For the story to make sense, for the story to be reflective of the Jesus I see in the Bible, Christ must have changed through this encounter.

In looking at the changes within Jesus in this story, we can let go of some of our own fears about making mistakes. If Jesus turned away a mother in need and even called her names, then the mistakes that I make, the times that I fail to act the way I think I should as a Christian, are easier for me to forgive. I know that God forgives me, but my own forgiveness has been a much harder thing to achieve throughout my life. As one called to follow Christ, this story allows me to follow him in making mistakes and growing through them. It calls us as people of faith, not to stop with or focus on the mistake, but to move forward into transformation.

Jesus also reminds me that transformation is the lifeblood of our spiritual journeys. The changes I have made in my life, whether my physical transition or any other, have enriched my life. I have done and seen things that I never would have experienced if it were not for the transitions of my life. I value deeply that I have been able to see and live my life as both a woman and as a man. By embracing such changes and experiences, we are able to hold their value.

I find irony in the fact that the gay and lesbian community—my spiritual, emotional, and physical home since I left my parent's house—has been where I have encountered outspoken prejudice and strong opposition to my transition from a lesbian woman to a gay male. It is painful every time I hear the words of homophobia reconstituted and spit back at me from the mouths of lesbians and gay men: "It's a choice; why are you doing this?" "You'll never really fit in, you know." "People like you are unstable, unhappy, and unable to hold a job." "If you just had sex with the right woman, you'd go back to being a lesbian." "You must really hate yourself to be doing this." "You're just taking the easy way out," a comment I have never understood in either context. And, of course, "It's not natural. If God had meant you to be a man, God would have created you that way." These words are nothing more than lies. When we unleash this on each other, we act no better than calling one another dogs. Prejudice in any form is just as ugly.

Looking at Jesus as the one who was transformed from using epithets to healing has helped me to remember that the name caller today can be the ally of tomorrow. It is easy to reject those who say prejudiced things as ignorant, as not worthy of my time, as irredeemable. It is safer to reject them before I have to weather more hatred from them. But the faithful response, the response that Jesus taught us, is to turn the other cheek, to hang in there with this person, to persist in sharing another perspective, and to be transformed.

In this story, Jesus shows us what it means to encounter someone quite different from ourselves. The Canaanite woman came from a different culture and practiced a different religion. While Jesus obviously noticed and commented on the difference in their culture, he also recognized her faith without trying to convert her to Judaism or to become one of his disciples. It is important that we remember this as we encounter others: that we can recognize the spirit of God moving within people who are very different than we are without trying to change them. What I long for is for the church to recognize my difference without trying to change me into a neat category of male or female, gay or lesbian, queer or straight. At the same I do not want to be a token, recognized only for my difference. I want to be encountered as a human being, a child of God.

Jesus offers us here a model of what it might mean for us to be transformed as a community of believers. A faithful response to Christ's message requires that we move beyond name calling and prejudices, beyond quick responses and judgments, beyond easy categorization, to a more mature community. It requires us to take the next step of seeing beyond the barriers of race, gender, class, sexual orientation, and the myriad of other categories into which we place people. It calls us to take the next step, having the courage to step through those barriers to see the human being on the other side.

Scientist and author Carl Sagan wrote in his book *Pale Blue Dot:*

In some respects, science has far surpassed religion in delivering awe. How is it that hardly any major religion has looked at science and concluded, "This is better than we thought! The Universe is much bigger than our prophets said, grander, more subtle, more elegant. God must be even greater than we dreamed?" Instead they say, "No, no, no! My god is a little god and I want him to stay that way." A religion, old or new, that stressed the magnificence of the Universe as revealed by modern science might be able to draw forth reserves of reverence and awe hardly tapped by conventional faiths. Sooner or later, such a religion will emerge.[3]

This is a challenge for us as people of faith. The wonder and mysteries of the universe and of the life that we see here on this planet teach us about the magnificence of God.

We worship God when we hold in reverence the wonders of God's creation. We see the glory of God in the mystery of creation. This applies not only to the galaxies and the universe but also to what we see around us every day. Imagine if we as a people of faith declared: "This is better than we thought! People come in even more varieties than we thought, many more than we were told there were—many colors, gay, straight, lesbian, bisexual, men, women, those who see themselves as no gender, those who cross genders, transsexuals, monogamous, polygamous, nonmonogamous, people with many ways of loving, people who are celibate, old, young, ageless. God must be even greater than we ever dreamed!" What if we welcomed them all? How would it affect our churches and our world if our faith celebrated all this? Or if we exploded the barriers between us? We do this, I firmly believe it, but have we taken the next step of rejoicing in our queerness, our differences, our abilities to transform our bodies, minds, and souls? Do we rejoice about what that says about the one who created us this way? We must be faithful, not to our ideas of God's creation, but to the reality of it.

A vision that sees the world only in terms of two genders and one way of living in it misses the totality and beauty of creation. Christ is an alchemist. If we affirm that Jesus lived as he died, then his life must also be a story of alchemy, transformation, and resurrection. Easter is ultimately a festival of transformation. Each Sunday worship service is a celebration of Easter reminding us that through death came life, through suffering came redemption. The apostle Paul writes, "Do not be conformed to this world, but be transformed by the renewing of your minds, that you may discern what is the will of God—what is good and acceptable and perfect" (Rom. 12:2). As people of faith, we are called to transform ourselves and our world. A transforming, learning, growing Christ is one who can guide us through that process of change.

## The Child: The Calling of Health

As a result of her mother's advocacy and Jesus' transformation, a child is healed and the demon that had possessed her was gone. We know next to nothing about this child, only these simple facts, yet she stands as a reminder of the purpose of this encounter: her healing. She reminds us that the reasons we are advocates for ourselves and one another and the reason that we transform our lives and our world is so that we and those around us can stand healthy and free in the world. It is so that we are no longer ravaged by the demons of fear, hate, shame, unworthiness, and disease unleashed on our lives.

Advocacy and transformation are not enough, in and of themselves. It is easy to get involved in causes and actions that take up all our time and distract us from the things in our lives that we would rather not address. Too many times we have fallen into the trap of thinking that if we just changed some aspect of our lives—our location, our job, our spouse, whatever—that we would finally find happiness. Those are myths. When we remember why we are advocates and why we engage in the process of transformation, when we are focused on bringing health to our lives and the lives of others, then we fulfill our calling and find that for which we are looking.

The child in this story reminds me of why I am going on this journey. I have transitioned from female to male because in this journey I have found healing and wholeness. That's the purpose for me, plain and simple. It is easy to get wrapped up in change for change's sake. It is easy for me to get distracted fighting injustices and unfairness. Crucial to both of those processes is the focus on health. If we truly act to bring healing and wholeness to one another and if we are willing to be changed in the process, there we will discover the risen, transformative Christ in our midst and in our lives.

This story is, for me, a profound statement about the abundance of God. There is enough to feed all of us, for even the dogs eat the crumbs that fall from the table. God provides enough so that all are fed. The Canaanite woman turned around Jesus' metaphor of taking the children's bread and feeding it to the dogs to make her statement that there was enough of Jesus' healing power and God's love for her daughter, too. I believe her point was that in God's economy there is no such thing as scraps and no one who is unworthy to receive food from the table. One person's crumbs is another's bounty; one person's bounty may be another's crumbs. Her daughter did not receive the scraps of God's healing; that concept is meaningless. Humans may give stature and rank; God does not. Humans may call other people "dogs"; God does not.

Jesus, too, turns this around, calling her claim on the table crumbs a sign of a great faith. That which is small and insignificant becomes the symbol for that which is great, a motif repeated often in the Bible. Several chapters later in the book of Matthew, Jesus states, "So the last will be first, and the first will be last" (Matt. 20:16).[4] If her claim of the crumbs symbolized a great faith, then the small crumbs themselves can indicate an abundance of love.

God's love is not restricted to one category of people, those who choose one way of living or being in this world. There is enough for all. This is God's promise to us. Abraham looked to the heavens, and God told him that his descendants would be as many as the stars. God never promised that all of those stars would be the same. Science tells us that each of those stars is unique. That, too, is part of God's promise. God created us each individually, with boundless creativity and provided enough for us all. We are those descendants, numerous as the stars and just as different one from another. God is faithful to all of us.

God calls us to expand our thinking and our ways of being. There is more than enough for everyone—gay, lesbian, bisexual, transgendered, straight— however we define ourselves. There is more than enough for every one of God's children who knows that their sexuality and spirituality are connected and for every one who needs to know that. There is more than enough for everyone who needs to know God's love that is more permanent than the mountains, more abiding than anything that ever was or will be. May we be a people of advocacy, transformation, and health.

## Notes

1. George Arthur Buttrick, ed., *The Interpreter's Bible* (New York: Abingdon/ Cokesbury Press, 1952), 7:441–42.

2. *Harry Benjamin International Gender Dysphoria Association's: The Standards of Care for Gender Identity Disorders.* The latest (5th) version can be viewed online in the *International Journal of Transgenderism* 2, no. 2 (April–June 1998): http://www.symposion.com/ ijt/ijtc0405.htm.

3. Carl Sagan, *Pale Blue Dot: A Vision of the Human Future in Space* (New York: Random House, 1994), 52.

4. This theme is repeated twice: in Matthew 19:30 and Matthew 20:16.

*Part 2*

# TAKING BACK
# THE HEBREW SCRIPTURES

## 5

# The Garden of Eden and
# the Heterosexual Contract

### KEN STONE

*Queer cultural criticism has impacted a number of humanities disciplines: liter-
ature, history, music, art, political science, and religion. It has also impacted the
academic reading of biblical texts. Ken Stone, a seminary professor of the Hebrew
Bible, applies queer criticism to the so-called heterosexual contract in the Garden
of Eden story. He does not try to read the text as queer affirming; rather he presents
a strategy that emphasizes the contradictions and the tensions within the text. He
troubles or problematizes a heterosexual reading of the garden story. Stone's essay
represents a queer strategy for deconstructing the heterosexual privilegizing of the
biblical texts.*

### I

Queer interactions with the Bible often focus on a handful of passages that
refer to, or can be interpreted as referring to, same-sex sexual contact.
Because these passages are frequently used as proof-texts to condemn homosexuality, careful attention to them is both easily understood and justifiable.[1]
Yet such a focus also carries with it certain risks. For example, by working
continually over texts that seem actually to refer to homoeroticism, queer
readers may ignore other texts that simply presuppose that sexual relations
between women and men are socially normative and divinely ordained.

Consider, in this context, the frequency with which one hears such statements as "God created Adam and Eve, not Adam and Steve." Although it is
tempting to dismiss this sort of statement with scorn, the appeal to such an
"argument" underscores the need for reflection on the ways in which biblical texts that do not refer to same-sex sexual activity at all are nevertheless
characterized by what we might call, borrowing a phrase from Teresa de
Lauretis, "heterosexual presumption."[2] I use this term, "heterosexual," with

some hesitation here since the term often carries with it certain assumptions about identity that should not be imposed anachronistically upon the
ancient world.[3] Nevertheless, there is plenty of evidence that many cultures
and societies (including those that produced the Bible) have valorized the
sexual relation between women and men, especially in terms of its reproductive potential, and have stigmatized to varying degrees other forms of
sexual contact.

In a series of provocative essays, Monique Wittig has argued that this
valorization of heterosexual relations and sexual reproduction is in fact already implicit in the binary sexual differentiation of humankind. According
to Wittig, the division of the human species into male and female is a historical and social phenomenon accomplished through language rather than
a self-evident biological fact, but it is often mistaken for the latter. "And although it has been accepted in recent years," she adds, "that there is no such
thing as nature, that everything is culture, there remains within that culture
a core of nature which resists examination, a relationship excluded from
the social in the analysis...which is the heterosexual relationship. I will
call it the obligatory social relationship between 'man' and 'woman.' "[4] Wittig insists that "the categories 'man' and 'woman'... are political categories
and not natural givens."[5] As her use of the adjective "political" indicates,
such categories are, in Wittig's estimation, not innocent. Rather, the binary
categories of sex are defended with such vehemence precisely because they
constitute the foundation upon which the heterosexualization of society and
the imperative of sexual reproduction rest. In Wittig's words, "[t]he category
of sex is the political category that founds society as heterosexual."[6]

Wittig's discussion suggests that binary sexual differentiation works to the
disadvantage of those whose lives do not conform to conventional expectations about sex, gender, and sexual behavior—for example, lesbians, gay
men, bisexuals, and transgendered persons. Indeed, careful attention to the
lives of transgendered persons in particular reveals the inadequacies of the
rigid binary systems of sexual categorizing that Wittig attacks.[7] But Wittig
also argues that the category of "sex" is detrimental to all women inasmuch as it "conceals the political fact of the subjugation of one sex by the
other" while grounding heterosexual relationships in the order of nature itself.[8] Building upon Jean-Jacques Rousseau's notion of the "social contract,"
Wittig goes on to refer to the system of assumptions and institutions that
rests upon binary sexual division as "the heterosexual contract."[9]

In the wake of Wittig's argument, the attraction of such statements as
"God created Adam and Eve, not Adam and Steve" becomes more apparent. Once the binary sexual division of humanity is attributed to God
and located at the moment of the creation of humankind, endless arguments over the explicit biblical attitude toward homoeroticism can appear

to be somewhat beside the point. The emphasis can now fall, not so much upon the occasional biblical condemnation of same-sex sexual activity, but rather upon the divine imperative to have sexual relations with the opposite sex. And since the binary sexual differentiation upon which this imperative rests does appear to be presupposed throughout the Bible, the fact that the Bible has so few explicit references to same-sex sexual contact becomes less problematic for the proponents of the heterosexual contract. What is important is that the Bible does promote, naturalize, and sanctify a particular "obligatory social relationship between 'man' and 'woman.'"

The present essay considers certain aspects of this problem in relation to the Genesis creation accounts. I will argue that the structure and content of these accounts makes them especially attractive as rhetorical supports for the heterosexual contract. After a brief discussion of the first biblical creation account (Gen. 1:1–2:4a) and its reception, a discussion that underscores some of the problems raised for queer readers by this text, I will turn to the second biblical creation account (Gen. 2:4b–3:24). Although this text, too, can be (and often has been) read as a foundation for compulsory heterosexuality, I will argue for the importance of a reading that focuses upon the instability and incoherence of this textual foundation. While such a rereading can never turn Genesis into a queer manifesto, it may reveal potential openings for queer contestation of the heterosexual contract or, in any case, of biblical justifications given for that contract.

## II

The creation account in Genesis 1:1–2:4a (generally referred to as the "priestly" creation account) moves, as has often been noted, in an orderly and progressive fashion. From its beginning in a time of watery chaos to its conclusion on the day of God's rest, the narrative constructs a picture of the process whereby God creates the ordered structures of the cosmos. Although it incorporates mythological themes that appeared throughout the ancient Near East, the story was probably written to foster confidence in Israel's God in the wake of the Babylonian Exile.[10] By representing Israel's God as the creator of an orderly cosmos, the priestly writers hoped to encourage trust in the power and might of that God at a time when such power and might seemed to have been called into question by the events of history.

At a crucial point in this story, God creates humankind. The priestly creation account notes at the first appearance of humanity its twofold sexual division: "So God created humankind (*'adam*) in his image, in the image of God he created it, male and female he created them" (Gen. 1:27).[11] The binary sexual differentiation of humankind seems, therefore, to be part of God's orderly cosmos from the beginning. While this initial statement says nothing about sexual relations, such relations are implied in the verse that follows. There we find God's first commandment to the new human beings: "Bear fruit, and increase in number, and fill the earth" (Gen. 1:28). The commandment is concerned with procreation and not with sexual ethics, but sexual intercourse between males and females is obviously presupposed.

Now there is a great deal of historical and comparative evidence indicating that readers should proceed with caution when interpreting this commandment. Sexual relations with members of the opposite sex were not always understood to be exclusive of same-sex sexual contact in the ancient world, as studies of Greek and Roman attitudes and practices reveal.[12] Thus, we cannot simply assume that an ancient imperative to produce offspring (and, hence, to participate in opposite-sex sexual intercourse) was necessarily understood to imply a *prohibition* on all forms of same-sex sexual contact.

On the other hand, neither should we underestimate the effects of this representation of the creation of humanity or ignore the possible relations between that representation and a hostility toward homoeroticism. Because the linguistic structure of Genesis 1:27 does underscore a binary division of humankind ("male and female he created them") and moves immediately to an emphasis upon reproduction, the text easily lends itself to interpretations that valorize the relation between woman and man and make that relation key to the understanding of human ontology and vocation. Indeed, it is not difficult to find such interpretations. Karl Barth, for example, made the following comments in his discussion of creation in the influential *Church Dogmatics:*

> Men [*sic*] are simply male and female. Whatever else they may be, it is only in this differentiation and relationship. This is the particular dignity ascribed to the sex relationship.... [A]s the only real principle of differentiation and relationship, as the original form not only of man's confrontation of God but also of all intercourse between man and man, it is the true *humanum* and therefore the true creaturely image of God. Man can and will always be man before God and among his fellows only as he is man in relationship to woman and woman in relationship to man.... The fact that he was created man and woman will be the great paradigm of everything that is to take place between him and God, and also of everything that is to take place between him and his fellows.... In all His future utterances and actions God will acknowledge that He has created man male and female, and in this way in His own image and likeness.[13]

Notice the rhetorical drift of this passage. Barth seizes upon the fact that human binary sexual division is juxtaposed in Genesis 1:27 with an affirmation that human beings are created in the image of God. Thus, within the course of a few sentences, Barth can imply a direct link between these two, arguably distinct, phenomena: sexual dimorphism and the image of God. The "image and likeness" of God in humankind seems in fact to consist in Barth's discussion, at least in part, in humanity's having been created male and female. And, just in case Barth's reader has not read Monique Wittig (and so remains oblivious to the possibility that an emphasis upon binary sexual difference underwrites the heterosexual contract), Barth returns to this theological interpretation of humanity in a later volume of the *Church Dogmatics*. Raising the specter of "the malady called homosexuality . . . the physical, psychological and social sickness, the phenomenon of perversion, decadence and decay," Barth reminds his reader once again that "humanity . . . is to be understood in its root as the togetherness of man and woman."[14]

I will leave it for others to decide whether any of the theological points that Barth wished to make with such statements can be redeemed for a nonheterosexist theological project.[15] In the present context, I am more interested in noting how the structure of Genesis 1:27 with its juxtaposition of a reference to binary sexual division, on the one hand, and a reference to the "image of God" in humankind, on the other—encouraged such a reading. Indeed, this juxtaposition has led other sorts of readers, working on very different types of projects, to make remarkably similar arguments.

Consider, for example, the influential feminist study by Phyllis Trible. Trible also suggests, on the basis of a close literary analysis, that "'male and female' correspond structurally to 'the image of God'" in Genesis 1:27.[16] Humankind, Trible argues, "is the original unity that is at the same time the original differentiation." The differentiation to which Trible refers is, of course, binary sexual differentiation: "From the beginning, the word 'humankind' is synonymous with the phrase 'male and female.'"[17] And, by taking her reader through a consideration of parallelism, tenor, and metaphor, Trible can conclude from Genesis 1:27 that "'male and female' is the finger pointing to the 'image of God.'"[18] The binary division of humankind into two sexes, male and female, thus becomes for Trible as for Barth an indicator of what it means to be created in "the image of God." Trible, of course, in distinction from Barth, deploys this argument strategically toward the goal of constructing nonpatriarchal communities of faith, a goal that I share. Yet it has to be recognized that her argument veers perilously close to the rhetoric of "gender complementarity" that is so often used in support of heterosexist positions.

It is worth pointing out here that the readings put forward by Trible and Barth have not always been accepted within biblical scholarship. On the contrary, a number of biblical scholars have argued that the phrase "image of God" in Genesis 1:27 probably does not refer to binary sexual division (which is apparently shared by humans with the animals, which are also commanded to "be fruitful and multiply" [Gen. 1:22]).[19] The primary point I wish to make, however, is that whatever the original authorial intentions behind Genesis 1:27 might have been, the structure and content of the text as it stands do seem to encourage interpretations that grant a foundational status to binary sexual division as a crucial defining feature of humankind. Thus, when we compare the interpretations of Barth and Trible with Wittig's argument, we become aware of the extent to which Genesis 1:27 lends itself to readings that buttress the heterosexual contract.

### III

Wittig's response to the problems presented by the heterosexual contract seems to involve some sort of movement beyond such categories as "sex" and "gender" altogether. As she puts it, "[t]he refusal to become (or to remain) heterosexual always meant to refuse to become a man or a woman, consciously or not."[20] Since compulsory heterosexuality and patriarchy establish themselves through the continued inscription, by way of language and ideology, of binary sexual difference, it is important in Wittig's opinion to refuse the categories "woman" and "man" upon and through which the heterosexual contract is constructed.

Judith Butler, however, in an important study that is greatly indebted to Wittig's analysis, argues nevertheless that Wittig grants too much success to the role of sex and gender categories in establishing compulsory heterosexuality and patriarchy. Butler agrees with Wittig that the naturalization of sex and gender categories needs to be exposed as an attempt to ground the heterosexual contract, but in Butler's view it is not sufficient to reject the categories of sex and gender altogether in hopes of moving beyond them to some utopian space. Even when categories of sex and gender are deployed, they seldom succeed in reaffirming what Butler calls the "heterosexual matrix" of society in quite so total a fashion as Wittig seems to imply. Hence, Butler emphasizes the *instability* of the norms and categories of sex and gender, an instability that allows them to be contested in a fashion "that robs compulsory heterosexuality of its claims to naturalness and originality."[21] It is this instability, of course, that leads to Butler's influential "performative" theory of gender.[22] Transposing this philosophical discussion into the present context, however, we might say that if Wittig's work encourages us to look with suspicion at biblical texts that undergird the heterosexual contract,

Butler's work encourages us to focus upon instabilities and ambiguities in those texts, instabilities and ambiguities that might represent weak spots in the biblical foundation of the heterosexual contract and, hence, openings for a queer contestation.

With that encouragement in mind, let us turn to the second or "Yahwist" creation account. This text, generally considered older than the priestly account, can also be seen as serving the interests of hegemonic hetero-sexuality—it is here, after all, that we find Adam and Eve rather than Adam and Steve. The text serves in fact as a sort of explanation for the origins of opposite-sex marriage, an attempt to explain and perhaps jus-tify that institution by narrating the way in which it came into existence. Hence, after recounting an operation on the original human being that results in two humans, one male and one female, the narrator is care-ful to note that "therefore a man leaves his father and his mother and clings to his woman [or "wife"], and they become one flesh" (Gen. 2:24) At a later point in the story, God's response to the transgressions of the human pair in the Garden of Eden includes decrees that—particularly in the case of the woman—consolidate the reproductive imperative. From now on, God insists, the woman will desire her man (or "husband") in spite of the fact that the pain associated with childbirth has been increased. Thus, the story as a whole seems not only to insist upon binary sexual difference but also to underscore the inevitability of sexual reproduction (with partic-ular consequences for the woman), to affirm the subordination of women to men, and to highlight the importance of desire (at least in the case of the woman) for the opposite-sex partner. In all of these respects, the Yahwist creation account serves as a paradigmatic example of Wittig's heterosexual contract.

Yet there are certain features of this text that make its support for the heterosexual contract somewhat more problematic. It is interesting, for ex-ample, that the text needs to specify in 3:16b that the woman's "desire" or "longing" will be directed toward her husband and that this specification of heterosexual desire occurs in a list of those features of human existence that result from the pair's transgressions. What are we to make of this sur-prising and often-ignored statement? A reader might very well conclude that heterosexual desire on the part of the woman is a consequence of—or even a punishment for—the woman's misdeeds rather than an original com-ponent of her nature. Perhaps it is true, as some scholars have suggested, that the writer of this story simply assumed that Adam and Eve had sexual relations with one another already in the Garden of Eden.[23] But it is never-theless striking that the text seems to display a certain amount of insecurity about the woman's desire for the man, having to insist upon that desire as something that God ordains while also recognizing that it is a consequence of her rebellion, a consequence that might not have been any more certain than such other consequences as, for example, the woman's increased pain in childbirth, the man's having to toil and labor as he works a recalcitrant earth, or the snake's having to crawl upon its belly. Moreover, this statement about the woman's heterosexual desire is followed immediately by the infamous recognition that, from now on, her husband will "rule" over her. The conjunction of these two statements almost makes it sound as if the text recognizes, with Wittig, that women might have good reasons for refusing to submit to the terms of the heterosexual contract, so the text has to insist upon the installation of heterosexual desire as a guarantee of such submission.

Moreover, the Yahwist creation account, in distinction from the priestly text that precedes it, makes no reference to sexual division at the initial creation of humankind. Rather, the text simply states that "Yahweh God formed '*adam* from the dust of the ground '*adamah*), and breathed into its nostrils the breath of life" (Gen. 2:7). A single creature is produced here rather than a pair, a creature referred to as '*adam*. To be sure, Genesis 2:7 has often been read as a reference to the creation of a specifically male creature named Adam. It is therefore frequently said that God created man before woman, and this interpretation has sometimes been given (e.g., in 1 Tim. 2:13) as a justification for the subordination of women to men. In recent years, however, the obviousness of this interpretation of Genesis 2:7 has been called into question, especially by feminist literary analyses of the Bible.[24] Such readings point out that the word '*adam* functions within the Hebrew Bible not only as a proper name but also as a generic term for humanity. The word is in fact used in precisely this sense in the previous priestly creation account (Gen. 1:27). The sexually differentiated terms '*ish* (man) and '*ishah* (woman), on the other hand, do not appear in the Yahwist text until Genesis 2:23, after the creation of the second creature. Is it legitimate, then, to read binary sexual difference into the text prior to this moment?

There are, in fact, some logical difficulties raised by any interpretation that would argue that '*adam* is male prior to the appearance of the woman. Just what exactly does it mean to have a single "male" creature prior to the creation of a female one? Is he "male" by virtue of his genitalia? If so, what functions might we imagine to have been served by these genitalia at a time when sexual reproduction or sexual contact with any other human creature was impossible? And if we close off this uncomfortable question (to which I return below) by arguing (though without textual support) that specific biological and anatomical features associated with sexual reproduction were not yet present, then we have to ask ourselves whether there is any sense in which it remains meaningful to speak of the first creature as male.

Such feminist readers as Trible and Mieke Bal suggest, therefore, that it is preferable to think, not of God's having created Eve out of Adam, but rather of God's having created Adam *and* Eve by dividing a single androgynous being, *'adam*, into two creatures, *'ish* (man) and *'ishah* (woman). Since the word *'adam* is clearly used in Genesis 2 in the context of wordplay with *'adamah*, "ground" or "earth," from which *'adam* is taken, Trible offers the translation "earth creature" for *'adam* and notes that this creature is not yet sexually differentiated.[25] This understanding coheres in certain respects with the interpretations of early Jewish readers who, by reading the second creation account in light of the references to sexual difference that already appear in the first account, also concluded that *'adam* was an androgynous creature.[26]

Now there are obviously some attractive features of this reading of *'adam* as an androgynous "earth creature" rather than a man. From a feminist point of view, it gives the reader a biblical text with which to combat the attempt to ground male supremacy in the secondary creation of the first woman. In the context of the present article, it also presents us with a countertext to the priestly creation narrative, a countertext in which it is not self-evident that binary sexual division is assumed from the beginning of human existence.

On the other hand this interpretation, too, runs into problems that make it difficult to accept without qualification. For example, the term *'adam* continues to be used with reference to the male character even after the creation of the woman, implying perhaps that *'adam* was already understood to be male prior to that time. Moreover, the speech of *'adam* in 2:23 does seem to indicate a continuity of identity between *'adam* and the "man" (*'ish*) when it notes that "woman" was taken "from man" just after verse 21 has specified that God caused *'adam* to fall asleep and then took "one from his ribs" in order to create the second human. Furthermore, the man who is punished in 3:17–19 is assigned agricultural tasks, just as *'adam* was assigned agricultural tasks by God in 2:17, prior to the creation of the second creature.

So in spite of the literary and linguistic features that lead some readers to argue that the first creature is androgynous or sexually undifferentiated, there are other features of the text that lead other readers—even other feminist readers—to reject this interpretation and identify the first creature, *'adam*, as already a male creature.[27] Hence, as several perceptive commentators have noted, the Yahwist creation account as it now stands is riven with tensions and contradictions, problems of logic that cannot be completely resolved but that the story attempts to paper over in an attempt to account for human existence as experienced and understood by the story's male authors.[28] Such a conclusion underlies the argument of David Jobling, for

example, who—reflecting upon the implications of his structuralist reading for feminist analyses—resists the conclusion that "'positive' features"
of the story's female character result from a nonpatriarchal consciousness
underlying the text:

> Rather, they are the effects of the patriarchal mind-set tying itself in
> knots trying to account for woman and femaleness in a way which *both*
> makes sense *and* supports patriarchal assumptions. Given that there
> must be *two* sexes, why cannot they be *really* one.... In the face of
> the irreducible twoness, the text strives for a false unity by making
> maleness the norm, and accounting for human experience by making
> "humanity as male" its protagonist; but it fails in this, for "humanity
> as male and female" inevitably reasserts itself as the true protagonist.[29]

Now I agree with Jobling that the text as it stands is characterized by tensions and contradictions related to sex and gender and that these tensions
and contradictions result from the social ideology that generated the text. I
would like to suggest, however, that the situation is even more complex than
Jobling's analysis indicates and that what we find "tying itself in knots" in
this text is not *simply* "the patriarchal mind-set" but, rather, the heterosexual
contract upon which patriarchy relies. Instead of suggesting that "humanity
as male and female" has to "reassert" itself here, I propose that it is precisely the goal of this text—as it is also the goal of the priestly creation
account—to buttress the heterosexual contract by sketching the etiology of
"humanity as male and female." In order to do this, the Yahwist text—in
distinction from the priestly account—attempts to speak about a moment
prior to the establishment of binary sexual difference, but it does so from
an ideological position (inhabited also by most of the subsequent readers of
this text) that both presupposes and promotes compulsory heterosexuality
and patriarchy. It is this difficult project of trying to imagine a moment before the establishment of an institution—the heterosexual contract—which
is nevertheless everywhere presupposed, that leads the Yahwist to formu-
late a text with interpretive problems that continue to vex readers to the
present day.

Let us think further about the bind in which this text consequently finds
itself. Given the fact that the Yahwist text was certainly written (as Jobling
recognizes) in a thoroughly, if not uniformly, patriarchal society,[30] it is possible that the author of the text actually *does* wish to assert the temporal
priority of male over female, and perhaps also the closer (because prior)
relationship between the male creature and the God who creates him. This
wish, however, leads to an uncomfortable situation: the man is, by virtue
of being a man, presumably sexed but without an appropriate partner prior
to the creation of the woman. God has created neither Adam and Eve, nor

Adam and Steve, but simply Adam, who stands alone in the garden with no one but God. For whom, then, are the man's sexual components intended? God is only then represented as noticing the lack of a partner or "helper" and as searching for one, first of all by assuming naively that the animals will serve this role and only then by creating a second creature out of the first one. What is striking is that God's search implies a recognition that God alone is not a sufficient companion for the man.[31]

At precisely this point in the text it might be productive to read Genesis in dialogue with the recent work of Howard Eilberg-Schwartz. In a fascinating (if somewhat speculative) interpretation indebted to psychoanalysis, Eilberg-Schwartz argues that the discourse of the Hebrew Bible is overdetermined by an attempt to deny the implications of an unconscious homoerotic relation between Israel's male deity and that deity's male worshiper.[32] Is it possible that the representation of God's searching for an appropriate partner for Adam is a reflex of a felt need, on the part of the text's writer, to preclude the possibility of this sort of homoerotic relationship? That such relations were imaginable within ancient Israel is clear from the sixth chapter of Genesis, where sexual relations between divine and human beings (albeit female human beings) are both acknowledged and condemned (Gen. 6:1–4).

I hasten to add that I am *not* trying to argue here that such a repressed divine-human homosociality can serve as the foundation for a gay-affirmative reading of the Bible. As feminist critics have noted, a certain sort of homosocial relation is implicated in, and may even help to establish, the domination of women by men.[33] My intention is simply to raise the possibility that the *discomfort* with potential homoerotic relations between male Israelites and their male deity that Eilberg-Schwartz emphasizes might motivate the *ambiguity* of 'adam's gender assignment in the Yahwist creation account. The writer refuses to specify that 'adam is a "man" ('ish) until the creation of the "woman" in order to prevent unwanted interpretive speculations. But this refusal enables, perhaps against the author's intentions, the feminist reading of 'adam as a sexually undifferentiated "earth creature," a reading that—however contested—opens a textual space from which the heterosexual contract might begin to be unraveled.

I would like to suggest in conclusion that an appropriate "queer" response to this text is, not to resolve the tensions and contradictions that I have highlighted, but rather to emphasize them. Indeed, it should be obvious by now that my goal in these "intertextual meanderings"[34] has not been to argue that the Yahwist creation account is really a queer-positive text. What I am trying to argue is that the biblical contributions to the heterosexual contract, though clearly present and certainly visible in the Genesis creation accounts, are less secure than many contemporary readers wish to admit. One legitimate and important strategy of queer "resistance reading"[35] of the Bible (though not, of course, the only one) is therefore to expose this insecurity in Genesis and elsewhere. Such exposure will never in itself be a sufficient condition for the elimination of religious heterosexism, but it may prove to be a productive contribution to such elimination. If we are able to contest what Butler calls "the regulatory fiction of heterosexual coherence"[36] by showing that the rhetorical foundations of this fiction— including the supposed biblical foundations—are never quite so coherent as we have been led to believe, we may open up spaces for the production of alternative, queer subjects of religious and theological discourse.[37]

## Notes

1. Helpful studies of such passages include Saul M. Olyan, "'And with a Male You Shall Not Lie the Lying Down of a Woman': On the Meaning and Significance of Leviticus 18:22 and 20:13," *Journal of the History of Sexuality* 5, no. 2 (1994): 179–206; Bernadette J. Brooten, *Love between Women: Early Christian Responses to Female Homoeroticism* (Chicago: University of Chicago Press, 1996); Dale B. Martin, "Heterosexism and the Interpretation of Romans 1:18–32," *Biblical Interpretation* 3, no. 3 (1995): 332–55; Deirdre Good, "Reading Strategies for Biblical Passages on Same-Sex Relations," *Theology and Sexuality* 7 (1997): 70–82. For my own comments on some of the issues, see Stone, "Gender and Homosexuality in Judges 19: Subject-Honor, Object-Shame?" *Journal for the Study of the Old Testament* 67 (1995): 87–107; idem, "The Hermeneutics of Abomination: On Gay Men, Canaanites, and Biblical Interpretation," *Biblical Theology Bulletin* 27, no. 2 (summer 1997): 36–41.

2. Teresa de Lauretis, "The Female Body and Heterosexual Presumption," *Semiotica* 67, nos. 3/4 (1987): 259–79.

3. See Jonathan Ned Katz, *The Invention of Heterosexuality* (New York: Dutton, 1995). Cf. David M. Halperin, *One Hundred Years of Homosexuality and Other Essays on Greek Love* (New York: Routledge, 1990), esp. 15–40; Daniel Boyarin, *Unheroic Conduct: The Rise of Heterosexuality and the Invention of the Jewish Man* (Berkeley: University of California Press, 1997), esp. 13–23.

4. Monique Wittig, *The Straight Mind and Other Essays* (Boston: Beacon Press, 1992), 27.

5. Ibid., 14.

6. Ibid.

7. Cf. Michel Foucault, *Herculine Barbin: Being the Recently Discovered Memoirs of a Nineteenth-Century French Hermaphrodite*, trans. Richard McDougall (New York: Pantheon Books, 1980).

8. Wittig, *Straight Mind*, 5.

9. Ibid., 32; cf. 33–45.

10. Cf. Bernard F. Batto, *Slaying the Dragon: Mythmaking in the Biblical Tradition* (Louisville: Westminster/John Knox Press, 1992), esp. 73–101; Jon D. Levenson, *Creation and the Persistence of Evil: The Jewish Drama of Divine Omnipotence* (San Francisco: Harper and Row, 1988); Robert B. Coote and David Robert Ord, *In the Beginning: Creation and the Priestly History* (Minneapolis: Fortress Press, 1991).

11. The reader will no doubt notice the use of masculine pronouns in my translation. Such usage does not reflect a resistance to inclusive language but rather recognizes the need to uncover patriarchal and androcentric assumptions when they appear in the text. For a helpful discussion of the issues, see Phyllis Bird, "Translating Sexist Language as a Theological and Cultural Problem," in her *Missing Persons and Mistaken Identities: Women and Gender in Ancient Israel* (Minneapolis: Fortress Press, 1997), 239–47.

12. See, e.g., Kenneth Dover, *Greek Homosexuality*, 2d ed. (Cambridge: Harvard University Press, 1989); Halperin, *One Hundred Years of Homosexuality*; John J. Winkler, *The Constraints of Desire: The Anthropology of Sex and Gender in Ancient Greece* (New York: Routledge, 1990); Paul Veyne, "Homosexuality in Ancient Rome," in *Western Sexuality: Practice and Precept in Past and Present Times*, ed. Philippe Ariès and André Béjin, trans. Anthony Forster (New York: Basil Blackwell, 1985); Michel Foucault, *The Use of Pleasure*, trans. Robert Hurley (New York: Random House, 1985).

13. Karl Barth, *Church Dogmatics III/1, The Doctrine of Creation*, trans. J. W. Edwards, O. Bussey, and Harold Knight, ed. G. W. Bromiley and T. F. Torrance (Edinburgh: T. & T. Clark, 1958), 186–87.

14. Karl Barth, *Church Dogmatics III/4, The Doctrine of Creation*, trans. A. T. Mackay et al., ed. G. W. Bromiley and T. F. Torrance (Edinburgh: T. & T. Clark, 1961), 166.

15. Cf. Graham Ward, "The Erotics of Redemption—After Karl Barth," *Theology and Sexuality* 8 (1998): 52–72.

16. Phyllis Trible, *God and the Rhetoric of Sexuality* (Philadelphia: Fortress Press, 1978), 17.

17. Ibid., 18.

18. Ibid., 20.

19. See, e.g., Phyllis Bird, " 'Male and Female He Created Them': Genesis 1:27b in the Context of the Priestly Creation Account," in her *Missing Persons and Mistaken Identities*, 123–54; James Barr, *Biblical Faith and Natural Theology* (Oxford: Clarendon Press, 1993), 159–73; Levenson, *Creation and the Persistence of Evil*, 111–17.

20. Wittig, *Straight Mind*, 13.

21. Judith Butler, *Gender Trouble: Feminism and the Subversion of Identity* (New York: Routledge, 1990), 124.

22. For an important consideration of the relevance of Butler's theory for theological discourse, see Mary McClintock Fulkerson, "Gender—Being It or Doing It? The Church, Homosexuality, and the Politics of Identity," in *Que(e)rying Religion: A Critical Anthology*, ed. Gary David Comstock and Susan E. Henking (New York: Continuum, 1997), 188–201.

23. See, e.g., James Barr, *The Garden of Eden and the Hope of Immortality* (Minneapolis: Fortress Press, 1992), esp. 66–69.

24. See, e.g., the otherwise very different feminist literary interpretations of this story by Trible, *God and the Rhetoric of Sexuality*, 72–143; and Mieke Bal, *Lethal Love: Feminist Literary Readings of Biblical Love Stories* (Bloomington: Indiana University Press, 1987), 104–30.

25. Trible, *God and the Rhetoric of Sexuality*, 80; cf. Bal, *Lethal Love*, 113–14.

26. See Daniel Boyarin, *Carnal Israel: Reading Sex in Talmudic Culture* (Berkeley: University of California Press, 1993), esp. 35–46.

27. See, e.g., Susan S. Lanser, "(Feminist) Criticism in the Garden: Inferring Genesis 2–3," *Semeia* 41 (1988): 67–84; Beverly J. Stratton, *Out of Eden: Reading, Rhetoric, and Ideology in Genesis 2–3* (Sheffield: Sheffield Academic Press, 1995), esp. 102–4.

28. See, e.g., David Jobling, *The Sense of Biblical Narrative: Structural Analyses in the Hebrew Bible II* (Sheffield: Sheffield Academic Press, 1987), 17–43; Danna Nolan Fewell and David M. Gunn, *Gender, Power, and Promise: The Subject of the Bible's First Story* (Nashville: Abingdon Press, 1993), 22–38; Pamela J. Milne, "The Patriarchal Stamp of Scripture: The Implications of Structural Analyses for Feminist Hermeneutics," reprinted with a new afterword in Athalya Brenner, ed., *A Feminist Companion to Genesis* (Sheffield: Sheffield Academic Press, 1993). The original version of Milne's article appeared in *Journal of Feminist Studies in Religion* 5, no. 1 (1989): 17–34.

29. Jobling, *Sense of Biblical Narrative*, 43 (italics in original).

30. I realize that some readers will not wish to grant the predominantly patriarchal nature of both Israelite society and biblical discourse, but I see no way around such a conclusion. Cf. Milne, "The Patriarchal Stamp of Scripture"; Bird, *Missing Persons and Mistaken Identities*; Fewell and Gunn, *Gender, Power, and Promise*; J. Cheryl Exum, *Fragmented Women: Feminist (Sub)Versions of Biblical Narratives* (Valley Forge, Pa.: Trinity Press International, 1993); idem, *Plotted, Shot, and Painted: Cultural Representations of Biblical Women*, Journal for the Study of the Old Testament, Supplement Series 215 (Sheffield: Sheffield Academic Press, 1996); Athalya Brenner, *The Intercourse of Knowledge: On Gendering Desire and "Sexuality" in the Hebrew Bible* (Leiden: E. J. Brill, 1997); and the various contributions to Carol A. Newsom and Sharon H. Ringe, eds., *The Women's Bible Commentary* (Louisville: Westminster/John Knox Press, 1992).

31. Cf. Fewell and Gunn, *Gender, Power, and Promise*, 27.

32. Howard Eilberg-Schwartz, *God's Phallus: And Other Problems for Men and Monotheism* (Boston: Beacon Press, 1994).

33. See, e.g., Eve Kosofsky Sedgwick, *Between Men: English Literature and Male Homosocial Desire* (New York: Columbia University Press, 1985), esp. 1–20.

34. I owe this term to Teresa de Lauretis, "Eccentric Subjects: Feminist Theory and Historical Consciousness," *Feminist Studies* 16, no. 1 (spring 1990): 139.

35. The term is offered by the Bible and Culture Collective to refer to "different readings that resist the oppressive use of power in discourse" in their *The Postmodern Bible* (New Haven: Yale University Press, 1995), 302. I would argue that the strategies outlined in this volume are crucial for a queer reading of the Bible.

36. Butler, *Gender Trouble*, 136.

37. For my argument in favor of the production of queer theological subjects through alternative practices of biblical interpretation, see my "Biblical Interpretation as a Technology of the Self: Gay Men and the Ethics of Reading," in *Bible and Ethics of Reading*, Semeia 77, ed. Donna Nolan Fewell and Gary Phillips (1977): 139–55.

# 6

# Outsiders, Aliens, and Boundary Crossers

## A Queer Reading of the Hebrew Exodus

### MONA WEST

*Coming out remains a significant event for many queers. Mona West reads the Hebrew Exodus account as a story of coming out, exile, and transformation. The Exodus tradition reminds queers that the "silence of the closet does equal death" and that the dominant culture tries to cut queers off from their past by rendering them invisible and silent. Like the fleeing Hebrews, many queers have faced the challenge of journeying into the wilderness, accepting exile from their religious enslavement and oppression. The wilderness becomes a revelatory location of spiritual renewal and transformation. Just as the ancient Israelites retold the story anew to each generation and made themselves the subjects of their own history, West notes that it is the retelling of the stories of our own coming out and wilderness transformations that ignites subversive memories of movement of queer lives from enslavement to freedom, from death to life.*

The story of the Hebrew Exodus has been read from a variety of social locations. In the political history of the modern Western world the biblical Exodus has functioned as a story of revolution. It was central to the communist theology of Ernst Bloch, used in a defense of Leninist politics, and invoked in liberation theologies of Latin America.[1] For African Americans it is a story of deliverance and liberation. Reading the same Bible that their slave owners read, African Americans used their experience to find themselves in the story of the Exodus and have continued to construct a way of reading and appropriating the biblical text that grows out of their particular worldview and social experience.[2]

From the social location of American Indians, however, the Exodus is a text of terror. Inevitably the God of liberation becomes the God of conquest. American Indians read the entire narrative of Exodus/Conquest from the perspective of the Canaanites, who were driven from their homeland and annihilated and whose religious heritage was an abomination in the liberator God's eyes.[3]

For those who identify with the Israelites, at the core of these readings of revolution, deliverance, and liberation is the realization that Exodus is ultimately a story of transformation. Yahweh claims that this group of slaves Moses has led out of Egypt has become Yahweh's treasured possession, a priestly kingdom, a holy nation (Exod. 19:1–6). Indeed the experience of exodus and wilderness wanderings transforms the *habiru*—known in the ancient Near East as the aliens, the strangers, and the marginalized—into a people with a common religious history and experience of God. Walter Brueggemann points out that the word *habiru* is related etymologically and sociologically to the biblical term "Hebrew." From the root *abar*, meaning "to cross over," the Hebrew is "one who crosses over boundaries, who has no respect for imperial boundaries, is not confined by such boundaries, and crosses them in desperate quest of the necessities of life. The Hebrew is driven by the urgent issue of survival."[4] It is these *habiru* that would eventually be transformed into the nation of Israel.

Bernhard Anderson has called the Exodus Israel's creation story. It is the crucial event by which Israel "became a self conscious historical community."[5] Exodus was an event that gave Israel an identity, and it was an event around which Israel ordered the past and anticipated the future.

In essence, Exodus is a coming-out story. The *habiru* risk the security of their closets of slavery in Egypt (Exod. 16:3; Num. 11:5–6) in order to come into their full identity as God's people. This identity did not happen at the crossing of the Red Sea. The story tells us that they wandered in the wilderness for forty years. During this time of trial and rebellion, they discovered more fully what it meant to embrace this new identity.

Once in the promised land, the Israelites found that their journey to self-discovery as God's people had not ended. No longer oppressed and enslaved, Israel was challenged to live fully and responsibly out of this new self—this new identity called forth by God. Compromising that identity eventually led to exile—the loss of promised land and a fragmentation of the work God had begun in them so long ago.

What follows is a queer reading of the Hebrew Exodus. From the social location of gay and lesbian Christians, the Hebrew Exodus is indeed a coming-out story. Ken Plummer, in his book *Telling Sexual Stories: Power, Change, and Social Worlds*, claims that gay and lesbian coming-out stories exhibit elements of "grand stories" that have to do with journey, enduring suffering, engaging in a contest, and establishing a home. He states, "Certainly, over the years, from fieldwork, interviews and reading I have heard within the elements of these narratives over and over again the substance of the lesbian and gay coming-out stories. Here are men and women engaged on a voyage of discovery to be true to their inner self."[6] The themes of enslavement, exodus, wilderness wanderings, promised land, and exile parallel the stories of queer Christians who risk the security of their closets to find wholeness in relation to God and the believing community. Just as the Exodus was a crucial event for the Israelites, "the most momentous act in the life of any lesbian and or gay person is when they proclaim their gayness."[7]

A queer reading of the Exodus will also consider the Exodus tradition. The Israelites kept the story of the Exodus alive through its telling and retelling so that future generations could participate in its power and reality. Queers also tell their coming-out stories to keep their history alive and make way for existing and future generations to enter that history and identity.

## Enslavement and Exodus: Silence Equals Death

> Now a new king arose over Egypt, who did not know Joseph. He said to his people, "Look, the Israelite people are more numerous and more powerful than we. Come, let us deal shrewdly with them, or they will increase and, in the event of war, join our enemies and fight against us and escape from the land." (Exod. 1:8–10)

Queers identify with the nature of the oppression experienced by the Hebrews found in the first chapter of the book of Exodus. The dominant culture (the Egyptians) fears them because of their otherness and because of their numbers. Queers hear echoed in the words of the pharaoh such phrases as "don't ask, don't tell," "love the sinner, hate the sin," "self-avowed, openly practicing." When we come out of our closets, we make our pharaohs nervous. We become too many. We become a threat to national security. When we come out of our closets, we experience the threat of genocide. There is a calculated effort on the part of the dominant culture to "deal shrewdly" with us—to get rid of us. Queers experience this in the form of physical violence, hate crimes, and denied access to goods and services.

When the pharaoh's plan of increased labor and oppression does not work, he resorts to infanticide. In the face of the pharaoh's efforts to rid himself of the Hebrews at any cost, queers are left wondering what our pharaohs will attempt if a gay gene is discovered and a person's sexual orientation can be determined in utero. But the pharaoh does not have the last word. The Hebrews refuse to be silent. They cry out, naming their pain and suffering, refusing to accept things the way they are. Yahweh hears and responds. Ultimately they are delivered from their enslavement by risking coming out of the closet of Egypt.

Joretta Marshall defines closet as "a descriptive word that corresponds to the dynamics of hiding a part of one's self-identity or choosing carefully to be open and out."[8] In gay and lesbian experience, closets isolate, enslave, and eventually kill us physically as well as spiritually. Because the Exodus is the crucial event in the formation of the identity of Israel, it is appropriate to draw the parallel that to stay in Egypt would be to stay in the closet. In their encounters with Moses at the very beginning of the story and throughout their experiences in the wilderness, the Israelites were constantly faced with the decision to accept Yahweh's offer of liberation, which meant coming into their full identity as the people God intended them to be. Walter Brueggemann claims, "It is important that this people now formed in covenant was not originally an ethnic community. They were in fact 'no-people.' Yahweh evoked and convened a community of people that did not exist until that hour. They are, until then, only Hebrews, *habiru*, socially marginal masses without status or identity."[9]

Queers are aliens and outsiders in a hostile environment. Because of sexual orientation, queers are excluded from the rites and sacraments of the church. As "openly practicing, self-avowed homosexuals," queers are refused ordination, denied participation in the eucharist, and often excluded from the worshiping community. The church or the state does not sanction queer unions. Queers are made outsiders and kept outsiders by the dominant culture through demonization as sexual outlaws. Much as in biblical times, rules of religion, purity, access to goods and land, and access to God are formulated and regulated by those in power. Those who do not conform pose a threat to the dominant culture. They are alienated, kept on the outside, considered an abomination. Queers are the twentieth-century equivalent to the *habiru* of the ancient Near East: the strangers, the boundary crossers, the ones who cross over in order to survive.

"Silence equals death" is a powerful adage in the queer community. It speaks of the necessity to be made known in a culture that denies queer existence. Unlike race and gender, sexual orientation is not visibly identifiable. Queers can "pass" as members of the dominant culture since it is assumed by the dominant culture that everyone is heterosexual. Many queers choose to pass in this culture, to keep their sexual orientation hidden—closeted—for fear of rejection by family and friends, job loss, and physical violence. This closeted experience produces death, not only death to the existence of a queer community but also death to the individual. Maintaining a dual identity kills many. Queers die through the crushing of their spirits and the splintering of their wholeness. Queers die through addictions and often at their own hands when the only way out of the closet is suicide.

Coming out of the closet is a powerful, liberative act for queers. It is life giving. It is risky. It is the ultimate act of boundary crossing. Queers have refused to be silent. Like the Hebrews, queers cry out against the dominant culture, refusing to accept outsider status. In the act of coming out, queers cross over and discover a new identity and a new name for God. Like the *habiru* of the Exodus, who go on to experience wilderness, promised land, and exile, queers embark upon a lifelong journey when deciding to come out. It is a journey that is often dangerous and exciting, and ultimately life giving and transforming.

If the *habiru* of the Exodus had not trusted in God and had not risked their passage into freedom, they would have died in Egypt. When queers risk the passage out of the closet, risk trusting in God, a new self is discovered that is able to enter into relationship with a God who was thought to regard queers as an "abomination."

## Wilderness Wanderings: The Paradox of Freedom

The whole congregation of the Israelites set out from Elim; and Israel came to the wilderness of Sin, which is between Elim and Sinai, on the fifteenth day of the second month after they had departed from the land of Egypt. The whole congregation of the Israelites complained against Moses and Aaron in the wilderness. The Israelites said to them, "If only we had died by the hand of the LORD in the land of Egypt, when we sat by the fleshpots and ate our fill of bread; for you have brought us out into this wilderness to kill this whole assembly with hunger." (Exod. 16:1–3)

The wilderness wandering has both negative and positive connotations for the Israelites. On the one hand, wilderness is the place where they experience hunger and thirst. It is a place of rebellion and struggle, a place of fear and grumbling. On the other hand, wilderness is also the place of covenant and the sustaining power of God. In the wilderness Israel experienced the paradox of freedom. While the Israelites have left behind an old way of life characterized by bondage and oppression, they have difficulty embracing this newfound freedom. On the heels of the crossing of the Red Sea and with the song of Miriam still ringing in their ears, at the first sign of difficulty they long for the life they knew in Egypt. They realize being free is one thing, living free is quite another. In the words of Bernhard Anderson, "freedom in the desert was a poor substitute for slavery in Egypt."[10]

In their boundary crossing as the *habiru*, the Hebrews left behind the familiarity of an old identity, the false security of a well-known closet, and the structures of life in Egypt. On the other side of the Exodus, they find themselves faced with the vastness of the wilderness, that ambiguous place of middle passage. It is a time of great vulnerability and a time of trust.

They learn that claiming a new identity requires a journey that is liberating but also painful because it requires a letting go of the old in order to find the new.

Brueggemann claims that the aliens of the Exodus become citizens of a new community through the covenant they make with Yahweh. The strangers, aliens, and outsiders gain new status as covenant partners.[11] Through the lens of their experience of oppression, the Hebrews have the opportunity as covenant partners with Yahweh to create a community in which the stranger will be welcome. It will be a community characterized, not by rules of the empire and the dominant culture, but by justice and righteousness as they are articulated in covenant living.[12]

In his exploration of exodus and wilderness as biblical symbols of coming out for gay and lesbian people, John McNeill states the following about the paradox of passage from Egypt to the desert: "The central paradox of a passage is always both loss and gain; in a time of passage we become vulnerable to both personal loss and unexpected grace. Every passage begins in disorientation and the threat of loss. It matures into a second stage as we allow ourselves to fully experience and to name the loss. In the reluctant, gradual letting go of the old self and gingerly admitting in of the new self, we are losing ourselves and finding ourselves."[13] Gay and lesbian people experience a paradox of freedom when they choose to come out of the closet and begin to embrace their queer identity. They have spent lifetimes constructing closets that would shield them from an oppressive heterosexist society or allow them to survive within it. Like life in Egypt for the Israelites, queer closets become familiar, small enough to control yet ultimately constricting and limiting. When this constructed identity is left behind and queers are faced with the vastness of the freedom of the wilderness, there is often desire to go back into the closet because of the pain of dealing with family and religious systems that will not acknowledge the truth of their existence. At the first sign of difficulty some gays and lesbians want to return to Egypt. In the midst of navigating this new identity, even in the midst of outright rebellion, God is present, providing sustenance along the way and exhibiting a willingness to struggle with the people to give birth to this new identity.

The coming-out process for gay and lesbian people is often a forty-year wilderness experience. Therapists and theologians have noted that there are stages in the coming-out process that move one through a sense of loss and grief and ultimately to integration and transformation.[14] Part of the coming-out process involves an awareness of the larger gay and lesbian community. As queers come out of their closets and traverse the wilderness of their newfound freedom, they realize they are not the only ones—there is a larger community with the shared experience of coming out.

While covenant making in the wilderness is a unique experience for the Israelites and their relationship to Yahweh, parallels can be drawn for queers with regard to their conscious participation in a larger community with shared values. For gay and lesbian Christians, wilderness wanderings are often about reconciling their queer identity with their religious tradition—a tradition that more than likely has taught them that being queer is sinful and an abomination to God. Part of the "covenant" process for queer Christians at this stage in their journey is coming to a place of inner peace about their spirituality and their sexuality. When queers are able to embrace both of these as essential parts of themselves and good gifts from their Creator, they are indeed transformed from aliens and outsiders into covenant partners with God.

Many live out their covenant relationships in the context of reconciling or More Light (open, affirming) congregations in mainline denominations or the Universal Fellowship of Metropolitan Community Churches, which is the world's only denomination founded solely for gay and lesbian people. These communities of faith are indeed shaped by the experience of oppression and a passion for justice that welcomes the stranger.

## Promised Land and Exile: Destinations That Fuel the Journey

Then the LORD said, "I have observed the misery of my people who are in Egypt; I have heard their cry on account of their taskmasters. Indeed, I know their sufferings, and I have come down to deliver them from the Egyptians, and to bring them up out of that land to a good and broad land, a land flowing with milk and honey, to the country of the Canaanites, the Hittites, the Amorites, the Perizzites, the Hivites, and the Jebusites." (Exod. 3:7–8)

Promised land is integral to the story of liberation told in the Exodus. It is the destination that fuels the journey. The promise of land keeps the Israelites (and the story) moving forward to a literal place that will complete their journey begun in Egypt. The realization of this promise is also key to the establishment of their new identity as the people of God.

Roy May, in his book *The Poor of the Land*, points out the significance of land in the Bible and in the struggle for liberation in Latin America. Land is more than physical dirt. Although it is a material reality, it is also "a place, an identity, a history and a future.... It signifies physical and existential well-being and security."[15] Promised land as a place of physical well-being and security for the Israelites meant that those who were once aliens, outsiders, and boundary crossers become insiders, grounded, landed, the ones who establish boundaries with the making of homes and communities. Security and well-being exist in the ability to survive through the production of food and offspring. Eventually Israel becomes a great nation in the land, able to offer the security of military protection as well as the influence of a world empire.

The land is also a place where Israel is grounded spiritually as well as physically. It is literally the place from which they worship Yahweh, and it is a place that continues to call forth an identity in relation to Yahweh. Now that Israel is in the land, they must live responsibly as Yahweh's covenant people.

In the story of Israel's coming out, promised land becomes a reality, but for queers it is still hoped for, at least from the standpoint of physical well-being and security. Gay and lesbian people are still longing for a place of security to be totally out of the closet without the fear of physical violence—a promised land beyond gay ghettos. Queers long for a land where gay and lesbian relationships are granted equal status under the law so that they may become grounded, establish homes, and enjoy the security of spousal benefits, inheritance rights, and family privilege in medical decisions. In the midst of this longing, gay and lesbian people are able to experience the existential well-being and security of promised land through their transformation into covenant partners with God. Coming out, crossing over the boundaries of silence and homophobia, gay and lesbian Christians come home to God. Promised land continues to be integral to stories of queer liberation. Its reality is the destination that fuels the journey toward a society of true liberation.

A word should be said here about the conquest traditions that have been troublesome to interpreters of the Exodus story. According to some of the biblical traditions, the Canaanites had to be annihilated in order for Israel to take the land. There are other theories of gradual settlement of the land that can also be supported from the biblical text. Some years ago Norman Gottwald posited a theory of a peasant revolt, which claims that the Israelites provided the religious impetus for a revolt of those Canaanite peasants who were being exploited by the Canaanite city-state structure. In essence, the pharaoh's fears of Exodus 1 come true for the Canaanite overlords. This theory "softens" the conquest narratives and makes the Exodus story more palatable for those who would identify with the Canaanites, but as Robert Allen Warrior reminds us, this theory does not solve the narrative problem: "People who read the narratives read them as they are, not as scholars and experts would like them to be read and interpreted."[16]

In a queer reading of the Exodus, it is important for gay and lesbian people to caution against becoming the oppressed-turned-oppressor. When persons begin to experience some measure of freedom and liberation, that "privilege" is often used to oppress others. In marginalized communities this is called "lateral violence." Gay and lesbian people know all too well the abuse of those who read biblical narratives as they are. Like the conquest traditions, Genesis 19, Leviticus 18:22 and 20:13, Romans 1:26–28, 1 Corinthians 6:9, and 1 Timothy 1:10 have been read without the benefit of historical-critical scholarship, which indicates these texts do not address homosexuality and sexual orientation as we understand them today. Instead they have been read "as they are" and used as "clobber texts" that fuel hate and violence against the queer community.

In the land, Israel faced the biggest challenge of all: living as a true community of justice and righteousness. The prophetic books of the Hebrew Bible report that ultimately Israel fails to meet the challenge and eventually loses the land and is exiled—made to live in a foreign land, enslaved once again. Yet, in the midst of exile there is the hope of restoration and a new promise of a future characterized by God's righteous rule.

Scholars of the Hebrew Bible have noted that while the Exile signaled loss of the land and posed a crisis for Israel in terms of the people's relationship with Yahweh, it was also a time of great creativity and change. It was during this period of Israel's history that most of the canon of the Hebrew Bible took its final form and new theological ideas such as vicarious suffering and resurrection of the righteous dead began to take shape. Life on the margins caused Israel to see the world and Yahweh with different eyes.

John Fortunato uses exile as a biblical symbol for gay and lesbian spiritual renewal. He claims that part of the coming-out process involves letting go and grieving the heterosexist ideal of marriage, kids, a great job, and a house with a picket fence. Because queers do not fit into this myth of the dominant culture, they are exiles. When gay and lesbian people are able to break free of this myth and embrace exile as a place of spiritual renewal, true transformation occurs.[17] Melanie Morrison claims that for gay and lesbian Christians, exile can be a revelatory place on the margins. Life at the margins "can be a place of ferment and creativity, a place in which to discover a sustained urgency to imagine new structures, new ways of relating, new forms of speech."[18]

## Conclusion:
## Exodus and the Power of Telling the Story

"A wandering Aramean was my ancestor; he went down into Egypt and lived there as an alien, few in number, and there he became a great nation, mighty and populous. When the Egyptians treated us harshly and afflicted us, by imposing hard labor on us, we cried to the

LORD, the God of our ancestors; the LORD heard our voice and saw our affliction, our toil, and our oppression. The LORD brought us out of Egypt with a mighty hand and an outstretched arm."

(Deut. 26:5–8)

Not only is the Exodus a coming-out story for queers because it articulates an event of liberation and transformation; the Exodus also functions as a coming-out story because it keeps a tradition alive for future generations. Walter Brueggemann has identified Exodus as a dynamic text that demands a fresh hearing from every generation. He claims that it is a liturgical text, shaped, remembered, and appropriated in its telling. In its telling, the text makes oppressed persons subjects of their own history.[19] In the telling and retelling of the Exodus event, future Israelites were able to claim that liberative event as their own and participate in the covenant community. The telling and retelling of the story made it possible for other Israelites to know about their history and their ancestors' faith. This function of the Exodus tradition is much like the function of queer coming-out stories. Queers tell their stories so that their history will stay alive. Queers tell their stories so that others may be strengthened and encouraged to risk coming out. Ken Plummer quotes Adrienne Rich in her foreword to an anthology entitled *The Coming Out Stories:*

Cultural imperialism . . . [is] the decision made by one group of people that another shall be cut off from their past, shall be kept from the power of memory, context, community, continuity. This is why lesbians, meeting, need to tell and retell stories like the ones in this book. In the absence of the books we needed, the knowledge of women whose lives were like our own, an oral tradition—here set down on paper—has sustained us. These stories, which bring us together and which also confirm for each of us the path and meaning of her individual journey, are like the oldest tribal legends: tales of birth and rebirth, of death and rebirth; sometimes—too often—of death without rebirth."[20]

The Exodus tradition reminds the queer community that indeed silence equals death and to claim the power of their stories makes a way for life. It takes the stories of everyone to shape a tradition that makes oppressed persons the subject of their own history. The Exodus tradition reminds queers that they are on a lifelong journey that is dangerous and exciting. The Exodus tradition reminds queers that the dominant culture will try to cut them off from their past, that silence will not protect, and that it is their stories that will sustain them.

## Notes

1. Michael Walzer, *Exodus and Revolution* (New York: Basic Books, 1985).

2. James Earl Massey, "Reading the Bible as African Americans," in *The New Interpreter's Bible*, vol. 1, ed. Leander Keck et al. (Nashville: Abingdon Press, 1994).

3. Robert Allen Warrior, "A Native American Perspective: Canaanites, Cowboys, and Indians," in *Voices from the Margin: Interpreting the Bible in the Third World*, ed. R. S. Sugirtharajah (Maryknoll, N.Y.: Orbis, 1991).

4. Walter Brueggemann, "Welcoming the Stranger," in *Interpretation and Obedience: From Faithful Reading to Faithful Living* (Minneapolis: Augsburg Fortress Press, 1991), 292.

5. Bernhard W. Anderson, *Understanding the Old Testament*, 3d ed. (Englewood Cliffs, N.J.: Prentice-Hall, 1975), 8.

6. Ken Plummer, *Telling Sexual Stories: Power, Change, and Social Worlds* (London: Routledge, 1995), 55.

7. Ibid., 82.

8. Joretta L. Marshall, *Counseling Lesbian Partners* (Louisville: Westminster/John Knox Press, 1997), 100.

9. Brueggemann,"Welcoming the Stranger," 298.

10. Anderson, *Understanding the Old Testament*, 76.

11. Brueggemann, "Welcoming the Stranger," 298–99.

12. Ibid.

13. John J. McNeill, *Freedom, Glorious Freedom: The Spiritual Journey to the Fulness of Life for Gays, Lesbians, and Everybody Else* (Boston: Beacon Press, 1995), 62.

14. Craig O'Neill and Kathleen Ritter, *Coming Out Within: Stages of Spiritual Awakening for Lesbians and Gay Men* (San Francisco: Harper, 1992).

15. Roy H. May Jr., *The Poor of the Land: A Christian Case for Land Reform* (Maryknoll, N.Y.: Orbis, 1991), 49–74.

16. Warrior, "A Native American Perspective," 290.

17. John E. Fortunato, *Embracing the Exile: Healing Journeys of Gay Christians* (Minneapolis: Seabury Press, 1982).

18. Melanie Morrison, *The Grace of Coming Home: Spirituality, Sexuality, and the Struggle for Justice* (Cleveland: Pilgrim Press, 1995), 18–19.

19. Walter Brueggemann, "Exodus," in *The New Interpreter's Bible*, ed. Leander Keck et al. (Nashville: Abingdon Press, 1994), 1:683.

20. Plummer, *Telling Sexual Stories*, 82–83.

# 7

# When and Where I Enter,
# Then the Whole Race Enters with Me

## Que(e)rying Exodus

IRENE MONROE

*African American males from various Christian denominations and the Nation of Islam have interpreted Exodus from the "endangered black male" perspective. Irene Monroe challenges that reading since it excludes African American women and translesbigays, thus legitimizing misogyny and phobias of sexual minorities. She proposes a more inclusive and liberative reading of Exodus from an embodied and sexual praxis.*

Of the many liberation motifs used in the African American biblical canon, none is so central as the Exodus narrative. In analyzing the Exodus narrative in light of the struggle for black freedom, the trials and tribulations of the Israelites under Egyptian domination parallel those of African Americans under the reign of white supremacy in the United States. From the hermeneutical perspective that God's liberating actions for the oppressed take place in history and as history, African Americans' appropriation of the Exodus motif functions as a historical account of God's omnipresence in black life. As permanent outsiders to American mainstream society, the Exodus narrative affords African Americans the social location of privileged insiders in the scriptural drama for liberation.

However, as a liberating paradigm for African Americans, the Exodus narrative has never been fully exegeted in the context of black physical bondage. Just as it was for the Israelites during Egyptian slavocracy, American slavocracy was the working and controlling of racialized subjugated bodies and sexualities. Forced into compulsory heterosexuality for the economic purpose of replenishing an enslaved labor force, both black men and women were subjected to the vagaries of a racialized system of gender and sexual domination. The Exodus narrative has always been a coming-out story for all African Americans. It is a story about coming out from the fetters not only of racial captivity but also of physical and sexual captivity. Because both black heterosexual male Christians as well as Muslims construct the Exodus narrative around a narrow racially gendered discourse on the "endangered black male," the narrative remains in both gender and sexual captivity. As an African American lesbian feminist my struggle in fully coming out and being accepted in the black community, as the Exodus narrative calls for, is inextricably tied to the liberation of all my people, because when and where I enter into the struggle for black liberation both within my community and within the dominant culture is where the whole race enters with me.

Although this appropriation of the Exodus motif is touted as being liberating and inclusive to all black people, from the social locations of women and lesbian, gay, bisexual, and transgender people in the black community, this reading has been nothing but a ball and chain around our necks. By unhinging the Exodus motif from its patriarchal theme of the "endangered black male," as this essay attempts to do, the traditional Africentric male narrative becomes inclusive and emancipatory for all people in the African American community to freely come out of the closet of gender and sexual slavery.

The Exodus narrative is the first of stories in the African American biblical canon that sets the stage for African Americans to come out of black physical bondage. Ever since 1619, when the first cargo of enslaved Africans was brought to America, liberation from racial oppression was and continues to be a central theme and necessary preoccupation for the livelihood and survival of black people. With over two hundred years of slavery followed by a provisional emancipation in 1865 due to both hegemonic ideologies and legislative edicts of Jim Crowism, segregation, and now reverse discrimination, liberation for African Americans in this country has at its best been nominal and has at its worst been blatantly denied. Given America's tenuous commitment to black freedom, African Americans sought out an authority that would give them both an unwavering spiritual succor and an unshakable earthly foundation: the Exodus narrative.

As the formation and framer of a black world order, the Exodus narrative has iconic status and authority in African American culture. With constitutional rights not guaranteed to African American citizenry in this country, the Decalogue handed to Moses on Mount Sinai and the civil and religious laws called the Covenant Code (Exod. 20–23) functioned as our very own Declaration of Independence and our Bill of Rights through the labyrinth maze of America's unyielding racism. Intended by slavers to make Africans, not better Christians, but instead better slaves, the Bible was the legitimate biblical sanction for American slavery. However, my ancestors, enslaved Africans, turned this authoritative text, which was meant to aid them in acclimating to their life of servitude, by their reading of Exodus into an incendiary text that fomented not only slave revolts and abolitionist movements but also this nation's civil rights movement. As a road map for liberation, the Exodus narrative told African Americans how to do what must be done. And in so doing, Nat Turner revolted against slavery, and Harriet Tubman conducted a railroad out of it.

The clarion call for all Israelites to come out of physical bondage, and by extension for all enslaved Africans, is heard in Exodus 5:1, when both Moses and Aaron went to the pharaoh to relay God's message, which said, "Let my people go." So commonly heard in sermons, protest speeches, and spirituals by African Americans, and in the refrain of the best known of all the spirituals "Go Down, Moses," "Let my people go" was one of the first calls for black revolt. So stirring and electrifying were the words that singing the spiritual was prohibited on many plantations, especially since it was believed the song was composed to honor insurrectionist Nat Turner, whose slave revolt in Virginia in 1831, the bloodiest of the 250 slave revolts, first introduced America to the meaning of black rage and tore asunder its myth of the docile slave.

"Let my people go" is a command from God to come out of physical bondage. The command calls for all enslaved black people to come into their bodyselves. In the African American folktale of High John de Conquer, he espouses a command to come out of physical bondage and into our bodyselves when he ordered the slaves, "Just leave your worktired bodies around for him [the master] to look at, and he'll never realize youse way off somewhere, going about your business."[1] By claiming our bodyselves African Americans can then reclaim their bodyrights and sexualities. Since our bodies and sexualities have been demonized by white culture, the reclaiming of black bodyrights and sexualities has to begin with self-love, which in the African American community has been in short supply. Baby Suggs in *Beloved* invites a self-love of black bodies and sexualities when she said:

> Here ... in this place, we flesh: flesh that weeps, laughs; flesh that dances on bare feet in grass. Love it. Love it hard. Yonder they do not love your flesh. They despise it. . . . And O my people they do not love your hands. Those they only use, tie, bind, chop off and leave empty. Love your hands! Love them. Raise them up and kiss them. Touch others with them, pat them together, stroke them on your face 'cause they don't love that either. You got to love it, you! ... And all your inside parts that they'd just as soon slop for hogs, you got to love them.[2]

Unfortunately, black bodies and sexualities are just as repugnant to many African Americans as they are to white Americans. To be trapped in undesirable bodies creates a hatred for all sexualities because, as Christine E. Gudorf states, "Sexuality is who we are as bodyselves—selves who experience the ambiguity of both having and being bodies."[3]

Whereas the black community executed God's injunction of "Let my people go!" against the dominant culture, it has not been obedient in executing the injunction within its community. By incorporating the Judeo-Christian mind/body dualism coupled with a history of both physical and sexual abuse due to slavery, African Americans are cut off not only from their bodies but also their sexualities. With a strong embrace of fundamentalist Christianity that has embedded in its tenets an asexual theology, African American bodies and sexualities, which were once systematically usurped by white slave masters, are now ritualistically harnessed by the black church.

God's words "Let my people go!" is a command to come out of physical bondage to not only reclaim our bodies but also to rebuild a broken black humanity that includes lesbians, gays, bisexuals, and transgender people. By creating an interpretation of Exodus that is imbued with either the tenets of racial essentialism or of black nationalism, we see that the metal chains from physical bondage left black bodies after slavery, but the mental chains remained intact. Racial essentialism purports that there is a monolithic "black experience," and therefore, it views women, queers, and their sexualities as inauthentic representations of the race. Black nationalism puts "the race" or "the nation" above individual gender and sexual identities; therefore, it views feminists, lesbians, gays, bisexuals, and transgender people as counterrevolutionary to the cause of black liberation for all people.

Since both racial essentialism and black nationalism are dismissive of the lives of people who experience multiple forms of oppressions—that is, women, lesbians, gays, bisexuals, and transgender people—they promote a black male heterosexuality as the icon of racial suffering and for black liberation. Combining the icon of racial suffering and racial liberation into the sole image of the black heterosexual male creates a gendered and sexual construction of black racial victimhood that has come to be known as "the endangered black male." Kristal Zook states that "the Endangered Black man narrative speaks to the very real assaults on the material well-being of black men. But it is part of a larger myth of racial authenticity that is cultivated in ghettocentric culture, a myth that renders invisible the specific contours of living in female, working class, gay and lesbian black bodies."[4]

An important antecedent that gives rise to the belief that the African American heterosexual male is an endangered member in his community who must be saved in order to liberate his entire people is the gender and sexual biases in African American Muslim and Christian appropriation of the Exodus motif. As a central paradigm for liberation and leadership, the Exodus narrative has shaped African American Christian and Muslim theologies and has called both groups to social protest and action.

Just as the curse of Ham in Genesis 9:25–27 was used as the legitimate biblical sanction for slavery, in the African American Christian and Muslim communities Exodus 1:22 is the legitimate biblical sanction for heterosexism, expressed in terms of the "endangered black male." The early biblical roots about an oppressed male's life being endangered derive from this text. The narrative opens with Moses' life precariously floating on water because of the pharaoh's edict in Exodus 1:22, which is to "take every newborn Hebrew boy and throw him into the Nile, but let all the girls live." The subversive acts of the midwives, pharaoh's daughter, and Moses' mother and sister, all working in concert, saved Moses' life and defied the pharaoh's infanticidal decree on Hebrew males. Unarguably, Israel's liberation from Egyptian bondage had its beginning with these women. However, the female-centered narrative abruptly moves to and remains fixed as a male-centered narrative, consequently focusing solely on the oppression of the Israelites and the election of Moses as their divine leader. The uncritical use of the same interpretation and images over and over again keeps the narrative in patriarchal captivity. Therefore, what we miss in the Exodus narrative is the fact that women make possible the survival and growth of Moses, that they refuse to cooperate with the Egyptian pharaoh's decree because their obedience to God takes precedence, and that there is strength in females bonding against patriarchal oppression. However, what we derive from the fixed interpretation of the narrative is imbalanced gender relations between men and women: women who act independently against male authority are ignored, and women are excluded from leadership positions. Nevertheless, when interpreted within the patriarchal constraints of the African American experience the Exodus narrative tells African American women that only their men's lives are endangered. As women we are to nurture, save, and protect our men for the survival of the race. As men they have the ordained right to lead our liberation movements, and we are to organize and follow them. As Michael Dyson states, "Reducing black suffering to its lowest common male denominator not only presumes a hierarchy of pain that removes priority from black female struggle, but also trivialized the analysis and actions of black women in the quest for liberation."[5]

Although the African American appropriation of the Exodus narrative is no different from that of most white Christian churches nationwide, our enactment of it has spearheaded social and political movements such as the abolitionist movement, the Garvey movement, the civil rights movement, and the black theology movement. These movements have all showcased male leadership. Our Moses figures in history have been male, from Nat Turner to Martin Luther King, with the exception of one: Harriet Tubman, conductor on the Underground Railroad.

Although Tubman was an exception to the rule, she neither negates nor disrupts the androcentric thought and base of African American leadership from slavery to the present day. Many African American men have argued that it doesn't matter that Tubman was female because they are "gender blind" when it comes to her leadership role in the emancipation of African American people during slavery. Others have argued that they see her as female but ostensibly in a male role. Her husband, a free black man during slavery, saw her as a disobedient wife. He attempted to dissuade her from fleeing for her freedom, but Harriet Tubman, nonetheless, went north. When she returned home months later to get him, she discovered that her husband had taken up with another woman. As one who had transgressed the prescribed gender role for African American leadership, Tubman paid a heavy price: her marriage.

The Exodus narrative assumes a heterosexual orientation not only because Moses is the icon of the black endangered male but also because the narrative is one of the pillars that upholds and institutionalizes male leaders in the black church. If the Moses narrative did not exist, the black church would have had to invent it.

In the Nation of Islam, the Exodus narrative is one of the central motifs in its theology and its social protest and action. It is buttressed by both a selective interpretation of scripture and an Africentric creation myth of the Original Man. In the Original Man story, African men were the original inhabitants of the earth. As descendants from the tribes of Shabazz, these thirteen tribes constituted an African Nation united by black skin color, the Islamic religion, and reverence for Allah, a supreme black man among black men. The creation of the white race was an experiment in human hybridization by a brilliant but demonic African scientist named Dr. Yakub. Derived from the Original Man sprang forth a race of "blue-eyed devils," known as the Caucasian race, who were genetically programmed to promulgate evil in the world. The Original Man story is basic to the Nation of Islam's fundamental premise of reclaiming for all men of African descent their central place in the creation and leadership of the universe. Former minister of the Nation of Islam, the Honorable Elijah Muhammad stated, "When the world knows who the Original Man is and only then wars will cease. For everything depends on knowing who is the rightful owner of the earth."[6]

The creator of the Original Man story was Wallace D. Fard, a mysterious but charismatic door-to-door salesman in an African American neighborhood in Detroit, who told his followers in the 1930s that "I come from the Holy City of Mecca. More about myself I will not tell you yet, for the time has not yet come. I am your brother. You have not yet seen me in my royal robes."[7] Fard's purpose as the self-proclaimed Supreme Ruler of the universe and the incarnation of Allah was "to bring freedom, justice and equality to the black men in the wilderness of North America" and "to reconnect with his lostfound nation [to] raise from among them a messenger."[8] Thus began the Islamization of the "endangered black man" theme through appropriation of the Exodus story.

To explain the upcoming demise of white world supremacy, the Nation of Islam's theology of the Original Man inscribes the Exodus motif into the New Testament apocalyptic narrative, the book of Revelation. Fard argues that because white domination throughout the world "became too morbid and bestial...Allah himself was touched by the suffering and decided to send a mulatto prophet Moses in 2000 B.C.E. to assist in reforming the white race and free it from the clutches of barbarism."[9] Reascendancy of the Original Man will begin with a global conflagration of the Caucasian race and the death of Christianity and Judaism in the year 2000. Keeping consistent with the theme of the "endangered black man," the end of the black man's plight begins with the second advent of Fard. Before being forced out of town because of police harassment, Fard promised to return in order to deliver his "lostfound" African brothers in the wilderness of North America from the yoke of white oppression. His parting words to his crying followers outside the Temple of Islam, which he founded, were, "I am with you; I will be back to you in the near future to lead you out of this hell."[10]

Whereas Fard was the creator of the Original Man myth, the Honorable Elijah Muhammad, who headed the Nation of Islam from 1934 until his death in 1975, was its messenger. Louis Farrakhan, on the other hand, is now the sustainer of the Original Man theme. Mattias Gardell states that "Moses is Elijah Muhammad, who prepared to go and meet with God [Fard] and assigned Farrakhan to be his Aaron, leaving the Nation and his legacy in his charge."[11]

The Million Man March was a rearticulation of Farrakhan's theme of the "endangered black man" by a ritualized production of African American-male uplift. The belief that an emasculated African American-male image is to be salvaged by reinstitutionalizing black patriarchy with black puritan mores only affirms heterosexual male domination and control over women, children, lesbians, gays, bisexuals, and transgender people. It creates a gender and sexual hierarchy that keeps women, children, and queers subordinate to heterosexual men and subject to patriarchal violence should they step out of their prescribed gender and sexual roles.

Many out-of-the-closet gay men attended the Million Man March to make their presence visible and to stand in defiance against Farrakhan's homophobic pronouncements. The march's theme of articulating the racial problems of African American men impelled many African American gay men to go and to stand in gender solidarity with their heterosexual brothers, hoping the issues of sexual orientation and AIDS would be addressed. However homophobia prevailed because last-minute decision changes due to "time constraints" and "priority factors" canceled the only openly gay speaker. Nonetheless, the clarion call for African American men to save and to liberate the African American community echoed across sexual orientations because it also spoke to some gay men's belief that they too are to lead in correcting the entire African American community's problem. Keith Boykin, former executive director of the National Black Gay and Lesbian Leadership Forum, stated, "And who is better suited to lead the long overdue revolution against patriarchy and violence against women than black gay men."[12] Of course, replacing heterosexual patriarchy with homosexual patriarchy replicates the same male power dynamics that Farrakhan espouses. Boykin's statement shows how the foundation of African American leadership is rooted in an Africentric messianic male tradition.

In carving out a racial essentialist or black nationalist identity with the Exodus narrative, African Americans have done it at the expense of leaving their bodies and sexualities behind. The theme of the "endangered black male" within the Exodus narrative has turned a liberation motif into a policing one because it keeps all African Americans—heterosexuals and queers, males and females—in both gender and sexual captivity. The African American interpretation of Exodus, from its inception to present day, has been merely the ritualization of black heterosexist patriarchy, which is modeled after and in competition with white male supremacy. The liberation of black bodies and sexualities using the Exodus motif is as impossible as the liberation of black bodies under the domination of white male supremacy. Both racial essentialism and black nationalism vie for the social ordering and policing of black bodies and sexualities. African Americans have always been in the closet about sexuality, especially as it relates to sexual abuse, and both maintain the two salient features that shape black sexuality: sexual exploitation and sexual violence because of its scapegoating of women and queer sexualities. Also, both maintain the cultural hysteria and iconography of black sexuality as "other."

When unhinged from the patriarchal theme of the "endangered black male," the Exodus narrative is a liberation story about the renewal of black life and the healing of black relationships to the world and to each other. Having been bombarded with a history of stereotypes, violence, and abuse, neither whites nor African Americans know what black sexuality is. African Americans' silence speaks volumes of that history. Our fractured relationships between and across genders and sexualities in the black community are testimony to the pain and confusion. Policing women, lesbians, gays, bisexuals, and transgender people gives black heterosexual men what they could not have during slavery and what they only have nominally today: power.

As a coming-out story, Exodus is about the celebration of being freed from black physical bondage. It is the discovery of our bodyselves and bodyrights that allows for the affirmation of black bodies and the validation of black sexualities within our community and in the world. In talking about human freedom, African American philosopher Cornel West states, "We must be strong enough to resist the prevailing forms of bondage yet honest enough to acknowledge our weaknesses.... This honesty about our weaknesses is itself a supreme form of strength that precludes paralysis and impotence."[13]

When the African American community owns up to weaknesses by dismantling its dominant belief that racism is the only and ultimate oppression African American people face in this country, then the community can begin to address the sexism and homophobia within its fold. In order for African American leadership to be both effective and inclusive, we must implement a new emancipatory reading of Exodus that encompasses a comprehensive analysis of race. Since racial oppression is the common reality that all African American females, males, gays, lesbians, bisexuals, and transgender people confront every day of their lives, we clearly need a model of leadership that articulates simultaneously the multiple oppressions of race, class, gender, and sexual orientation. Because race links us across and between various identities, a racialized understanding of how class, gender, and sexual orientation are linked to the pernicious and intricate patterns of white male supremacy would liberate us from the myopic view that only African American males are the endangered members in our communities.

Until we dismantle this hierarchy of oppressions, which makes people fight among themselves and believe that one oppression—their oppression—is greater than any other oppression, the black liberation movement in this country will not cease to function in a Sisyphean pattern. The struggle against racism is only legitimate if we are also fighting anti-Semitism, sexism, classism, etc. All of these isms are merely tools of oppression, which will continue to keep us fractured instead of united toward the common goal of a multicultural democracy. Bernhard W. Anderson stated that "those who followed Moses in flight from Egypt, as we have seen, were a variegated company, a 'mixed multitude' as we are told specifically (Exodus 12:38), who were held together primarily by their common desire to be free from slavery."[14] As an African American, my liberation is tied to the freedom of my people, but my liberation is also tied to the struggle of women and queers everywhere the integrity of their bodies and sexualities is compromised.

The Exodus narrative calls us all to come out of whatever bondage enslaves us. For African Americans, our bodies and sexualities are in as much need for freedom as our skin color is. The controlling of racialized bodies and sexualities in this country requires an embodied reading and praxis of Exodus in our future social protests and speeches about liberation. As an African American lesbian, when and where I enter both my body and sexuality into the struggle for black liberation is where the whole race enters with me.

## Notes

1. Garth Baker-Fletcher, *Xodus: An African-American Male Journey* (Minneapolis: Fortress Press, 1996), 61.

2. Toni Morrison, *Beloved* (New York: Alfred A. Knopf, 1987), 88.

3. Christine E. Gudorf, *Body, Sex, and Pleasure: Reconstructing Christian Sexual Ethics* (Cleveland: Pilgrim Press, 1994), 171.

4. Devon W. Carbado, ed., *Black Men on Race, Gender, and Sexuality: A Critical Reader* (New York: New York University Press, 1999), 4.

5. Michael Dyson, *Making Malcolm: The Myth and Meaning of Malcolm X* (New York: Oxford University Press, 1995), 98.

6. C. Eric Lincoln, *The Black Muslims in America*, 3d ed. (Trenton: Africa World Press, 1994), 71.

7. Ibid., 12.

8. Mattias Gardell, *In the Name of Elijah Muhammad: Louis Farrakhan and the Nation of Islam* (Durham: Duke University Press, 1996), 59.

9. Claude Andrew Clegg III, *An Original Man: The Life and Times of Elijah Muhammad* (New York: St. Martin's Press, 1997), 53.

10. Gardell, *In the Name of Elijah Muhammad*, 127.

11. Ibid.

12. Keith Boykin, "Gays and the Million Man March," in *Atonement: The Million Man March*, ed. Kim Martin Sadler (Cleveland: Pilgrim Press, 1996), 17.

13. Cornel West, foreword to *Go Down Moses: Celebrating the African-American Spiritual*, by Richard Newman (New York: Clarkson Potter, 1998), 9.

14. Bernhard W. Anderson, *Understanding the Old Testament*, 4th ed. (Englewood Cliffs, N.J.: Prentice-Hall, 1986), 84.

## 8

# The Book of Ruth

## On Boundaries, Love, and Truth

### CELENA M. DUNCAN

*Bisexual women resist the pressure to suppress their bisexual identities in a variety of ways. They frequently refuse to allow themselves to be located in the cultural code of binary categories of heterosexuality and lesbian. As prophets of the "both/and," bisexual women transgress the boundaries of constructed sexual desire to create new alternative forms of relationship and family. Celena Duncan reads the story of Ruth as a bisexual midrash, making room for inclusive possibilities of alternative desires.*

In commenting on her view of the book of Ruth, Alicia Ostriker quotes the ancient rabbis speaking of Torah, "Turn it and turn it for everything is in it."[1] Everything under the sun is in scripture, sometimes more obvious, sometimes less, but there nonetheless. That is its beauty, its richness, what accounts for its longevity. Regardless of the trappings of the society—nomadic, pastoral, or technological—scripture speaks to our hearts today, just as it did to our spiritual ancestors. The rabbis became masterful at peering intently into the depths of the clear pool of scripture, then commenting on their observations, based out of their study, their life experience, and their own interactions with God. In the spirit of rabbinic tradition, I read the book of Ruth as a bisexual midrash.[2]

First, I want to make some comments on bisexuality. While writings on the subject are increasing, there is currently still far less written and understood about bisexuality than homosexuality or heterosexuality, and there is certainly no agreement even on what late-twentieth-century bisexuality is, much less what it was in ancient times. The larger society thinks it needs, and so requires, the use of neatly printed labels by which to organize everyone into tidy categories. In identifying as bisexual, I have had the experience of erasure from both sides of the aisle. Many (not all) heterosexuals, uncomfortable with sexuality in general, have enough trouble trying to deal with issues of homosexuality; for them, a discussion of bisexuality is beyond possibility. As much as homosexuality is feared and rejected, it is at least seen as the opposite and so can be understood in terms of being one way or the other, straight or gay, but not both!

And many (not all) gays and lesbians are suspicious of bisexuals, uncritically assuming the negative message they have heard flung at themselves, instead of breaking the pattern of alienation and fear of what is different, and passing that negative message along to another group, saying, without information and knowledge, "You can't be who and what you are." Why are we so unwilling to accept the reality of forms of sexual orientation other than our own? Why are we so unwilling to believe that all sexuality is as varied and diverse as the rest of God's creation? Boundaries, pigeonholes, and labels are human constructs, and God, if we will take Jesus, Paul, and the writer of the book of Ruth at their word, loves to see all of them broken down and swept away. Biodiversity and sexual diversity are God's created norms.

I do not understand bisexuality only in terms of sexual attraction because this understanding limits human capabilities and reduces people to sexual objects, no better than the sum of their sexual organs. Beautiful and sacred though it is, the physical act of sex does not need to be the bottom line in every discussion of sexuality. My own personal experience has never been an immediate physical attraction but rather has been a slow, lengthy process over months and years of getting to know a person as a friend before there is any inkling that a physical relationship might develop. While I have only been in two long-term physical relationships, one with a man, one with a woman, my life has been enriched by a number of bisexual relationships that have had nothing to do with sex or even sensuality yet have been deeply gratifying, connections so spiritually rewarding that, like Ruth with Naomi, a bond has been formed that has gone far beyond simple friendship, far beyond concern or thought that the bond was formed with either male or female.

## Naomi and Ruth

The long-standing distrust and suspicion that existed between Israelite and Moabite have to be taken into account in this amazing story. Yet it is also clear that ancient hatreds, suspicions, and prejudices can and will die when people give themselves utterly to the voice of God within, hearing God's direction. What caused Mahlon and Chilion to contract their marriages with Moabite families? Surely theirs was not the only Israelite family to have traveled to Moab to escape the famine! Surely there was a small Israelite community in Moab from which wives could have been chosen! Yet, something (Someone?) led them to proceed with bringing two Moabite women into their home. It should have been a recipe for marital disaster. Naomi, their mother, Elimelech's widow, found herself sharing her home and household duties with two women from a nation that she had been brought up to view with suspicion and distrust. She found within herself something to overcome her ethnic prejudice.

Ruth and Orpah, likewise, learned to overcome similar prejudices, living in the same household and developing a fond friendship. It was friendship crossing ethnic boundaries and outlasting the deaths of all their husbands. In shock and grief, believing that God had deliberately dealt her a bitter and destructive blow, Naomi found the agony of her loss heightened by deciding that she had to return home. If Orpah and Ruth had not yet realized it, Naomi knew that her departure meant leaving behind not only her dead but also two beautiful young women who had come to mean so much to her.

The words were bitter to her and must have stuck in Naomi's throat: "The LORD grant that you may find security... in the house of your husband" (1:9). We can only guess what it cost Naomi to send the two young women away, and Ruth must have heard the words with utter disbelief: Ruth clearly did not want security at such cost. No doubt surprised, she found herself being drawn to the love of another woman, bonds stronger than her own with Moab. Her love for Naomi crossed ethnic and patriarchal boundaries: "Wherever you go, I will go; where you lodge, I will lodge. Your people become my people; your God is now my God. Where you die, I shall die and there be buried" (1:16–17). Thousands of lesbians have repeated these words in rituals blessing their unions. Ruth created family with Naomi. She may well have realized that they would both have a rough life ahead, two women attempting to live together without the protection of a man, and as a Moabite among Israelites, she might well expect scornful treatment.

## The Love between Women

Ruth crossed the boundaries into a deep, mature form of love by responding to what, in Naomi, compelled her. Ruth committed herself to a relationship with another woman, a deep bond that went far beyond sexuality, gender, and ethnicity and one that sought the physical, the spiritual, all the things attracting one person to another. What Ruth saw in Naomi was the elder woman's goodness, compassion, and kindness, but it was a bond of love between women that could only exist under the rubric of patriarchal marriage and family. Ruth was not deterred by Naomi's despondency. If anything, it is as if Naomi's sense of futility and emptiness made Ruth love her only so much more. She wanted to help Naomi through this difficult time, as would anyone who cares deeply for another.

Ruth was drawn to a certain, very specific relationship. Ruth entered the relationship believing she was relinquishing the one thing by which a woman's worth, value, accomplishment, and purpose were measured: her ability to bear children, in particular sons. Yet she had found a path she could not quit, a path that stirred her to make a vow. Her love for Naomi superseded her procreative responsibilities. She did not choose to follow Naomi to shock or to be different. She was drawn by her heart and could only choose in favor of what would provide her the greatest emotional and spiritual health and well-being. Not even family ties could hold her or draw her back when measured against the forward pull of her love for Naomi. Ruth's word expressed the primacy of her bond with Naomi, and she would give up everything that mattered in her society in order to stay with, as Naomi saw herself, a dried-up old woman who was out of favor with her own God and who may well have been walking back into disfavor and scorn from the townspeople in her homeland. Even so, in her silence, Naomi accepted what the younger woman offered, a bond of support, companionship, assistance, loyalty, and love. Are these not the elements of a marriage? It was a bond unbreakable by death because the God of Naomi forged it; they were both being drawn forward by God, who was weaving a grand tapestry that would forever include the names of these two humble women. God broke the boundaries that had separated the two, and who would break apart or deny what God has wrought?

*In July 1973, I was living in a major city on the East Coast and developed a real and lasting friendship with a young woman I will call Julie. We worked in the same company but in different departments. We got together with a group over lunch and breaks, started talking, liked each other, and began occasionally going to a movie, shopping, or having dinner together. Within a couple of months, we were attending church together. Nearly a year went by in this fashion. Quite unexpectedly one day, we realized that we were each seeing the other in a different way; before the day was over we had each experienced a very gentle, caring lovemaking that left us both thrilled and puzzled. Neither of us had ever even considered the possibility of a loving relationship with another woman, so it came as a surprise, as well as a joy. Both being deeply religious, we were each puzzled. Did not the Bible have something to say about this? We had never read the Bible, but we had heard enough people, including our families, talk negatively about what had just happened to us. We thought that people who engaged in same-sex relations were supposed to be perverted or dominated by a parent. We did not fit the categories of lesbians.*

*Yet it kept bothering me to the point at which my stomach was terribly upset, and I could not stop crying. I had to call in sick to work. I had no notion of where to look in the Bible, so in desperation I called my pastor, managed to stop* crying long enough to tell him that I really needed to see him. Concerned, he agreed to meet with me as soon as I could get to the church. I had been raised Roman Catholic, a faith that had supported and upheld me through all the ups and downs of my early life, and to which I remained faithful during my entire four years in the Air Force. After the Air Force, however, I felt led to seek spiritual well-being elsewhere. At God's leading, I found a wonderful spiritual home in the midst of a Southern Baptist congregation and there renewed my baptismal vows. I sang in the choir, participated in leading worship occasionally, and served on the church board. I was known and respected, yet I expected to get "the Book thrown at me" that day. But that is not what happened.

I blurted out my story, and the pastor sat quietly listening. When I was finished and just sat miserably before his desk, the pastor leaned back and said, "You know, Celena, ten years ago I would have hit you over the head with the Bible. But I can't do that now. Now I know the value, meaning, and beauty of a loving relationship, no matter whom it's with."

## Boaz and Ruth

In arriving in Bethlehem, Ruth had long since worked through her own prejudices, yet she knew that she was still likely to face anything from ac-ceptance to strained-but-polite tolerance to downright nastiness. She knew that she and Naomi had to eat, that Naomi could not do the hard work of gleaning, and that sooner or later she had to face the townspeople on her own. Ruth wanted this new life to work out well, so she went out with a positive attitude, having told Naomi that she would go to a field to glean and hope to find favor in the landowner's sight. Her immediate goal was to tip the scales of tolerance favorably toward herself and Naomi. She wanted to live in harmony with her new neighbors, and though she was not re-quired to do so, she was determined to glean only in a field in which she had obtained permission to work.

Boaz went down to see how the harvest of his fields was going. As he contentedly scanned the fields, he knew instantly that there was a new face among his people. Boaz asked who this person was, though he may have suspected. In speaking to him, Ruth carefully and formally referred to herself both as foreigner and maidservant, but he had already taken kindly to her and called her "daughter," a term that would not have escaped Ruth's attention and that spoke volumes to her about the man. Having heard about all that Ruth had done for Naomi, Boaz realized, regardless of his long-held opinions and ethnic biases about Moabites, that here was someone who did not match what he had supposed. He had already worked through much of his prejudice before he met Ruth so that when they met, he called her "daughter," having looked beyond the accidents of birth to see the unique and spiritually lovely person within the Moabite exterior. He therefore accepted her as one of his own, a good beginning indeed.

The harvest over, Boaz was working hard threshing out the crop. He ate and drank heartily that night and fell into a deep sleep on the threshing floor. Then, around midnight, he awoke feeling cold and discovered that his feet, a word often used as a euphemism for sexual organs, were uncovered. As he straightened out the covering, Boaz was startled, aware of a presence. In the deep shadows of night, he could only make out enough to tell that a woman lay close by him. Ruth identified herself and explained her mission. Boaz praised Ruth's actions, revealed the presence of a nearer relative other than himself, and promised a resolution before the next day was done. Personal disciplines and respect for each other were solidly in place, and for the remainder of the night, he was a perfect gentleman and she a perfect lady. They slept in close proximity, and having received from him another gift of barley for Naomi, Ruth left before either of them could be compromised by scandal.

The next day, Boaz hurried to the city gate to find the nearer kinsman. Having shown what a generous and gracious heart he had, having helped Naomi and Ruth far beyond what was required, Boaz amusingly and suddenly shifts gears and does only what the law absolutely required of him in transacting business with the next-of-kin, the man, caught by surprise, whose name we never know. There was no messenger sent out to request a meeting. Boaz merely sidetracked him as he passed through the gate. Then, having gathered the required number of witnesses and many onlookers, Boaz began the business, sticking to the facts yet revealing each one in a way calculated to entice and then to discourage. It was neatly done. Boaz must have gone home chuckling to himself at a job well done, not realizing that he had done God's work and done it very well.

## The Love between a Bisexual Woman and a Man

It is obvious from the text itself that suspicion of the foreigner and even of less-fortunate Israelites existed during the time of the judges. If the field workers had been welcoming and gracious toward Ruth, Boaz's careful instructions about her would not have been necessary.

Just by virtue of his being a well-to-do landowner, Boaz was a community leader. If he had been suspicious and barely tolerant of Ruth, the community, starting with his own workers, would have followed that lead. Instead, he was generous and respectful, even seating her at mealtime and bringing her food himself, a task that was surely far outside of his male status as a landowner and head of household. Boaz was fair-minded, compassionate, willing to question long-held beliefs and opinions and to step across cultural boundaries if those boundaries stood in the way of justice and loving-kindness. Boaz and Ruth were thrown together in circumstances that allowed cultural suspicions to fade so that each could see the common humanity that they shared and eventually a relationship would exist when Ruth and Boaz dropped all defenses. If asked what they each saw when looking at the other, I believe the response would have been a paraphrase of Jacob's exclamation on meeting Esau the day after Jacob's fateful wrestling match: "I have looked into the face of a Moabitess, and I have seen God!"

The scene on the threshing floor was a pivotal and critical moment. An uncertain moment became a moment of grace, and the loving-kindness of God shone through this couple more brightly than the sun at noon. Boaz praised Ruth's actions, revealed the presence of a nearer redeemer, and promised a resolution before the next day was done. I cannot but feel that their love and respect for each other grew only deeper that very night.

Boaz was clearly motivated by more than just Levirate duty, that is, the nearest male kin coupling with the widow until a male heir was produced to carry on the deceased's name and possessions. Boaz wanted Ruth, yet not at the expense of integrity, his or hers. All had to be done properly. If the nearer kin had accepted the conditions, Ruth and the land as a package deal, Boaz would have stood aside and joined the well-wishers in blessing the union. It was clear though that the nearer redeemer, whatever his reasons, was more interested in the land than in the lady. Boaz certainly did not mind acquiring the land and doing the right thing for Elimelech and Naomi, but in the end, I believe, he was more interested in the lady.

While I am not by any means an expert in the customs during the time of the judges, it seems to me that Boaz, in bringing Ruth into his home, was also willing to run the potential gossip gauntlet on behalf of Naomi, for she was certainly part of the bargain as well.[3] Where Naomi went, Ruth went. Where Ruth went, there went Naomi. They neither could nor would be parted. In marrying Ruth, Boaz was also entering into a very close, though certainly nonsexual, relationship with Naomi. Boaz did not seem to have to think it over for very long.

We have here a portrait of two very deep relationships dealing with love: one, I assert, as deep as the other. Ruth would have been hard-pressed to part from either of them, and in that sense, she was in two deeply committed relationships, both vital and precious, for the rest of her life. Boaz can be seen as a model for the words of Micah long before Micah uttered them: "What does the LORD require of you but to do justice, and to love kindness, and to walk humbly with your God?" (Mic. 6:8).

*When the relationship with Julie ceased, at her request, I was not anxious to get into another close relationship. Once again, however, the opportunity for simple, uncomplicated friendship and companionship presented itself, this time with a man. If coming to understand myself as a lesbian had been difficult, how much more astounding was the realization that I was, over several months' time, developing feelings for this man. At first, it made little sense. I had not conceived of, or asked for, a relationship with a woman, yet I had come to terms with it as valid for me. Then, believing myself to be a lesbian, I was next discovering another aspect to myself that seemed to negate the relationship with Julie. It took a long while to work out that both relationships were valid, that I was bisexual, a term I'd never heard up till then.*

In a variety of ways, bisexuality has complicated my life immensely since many heterosexuals both reject and challenge its validity. I have not chosen bisexuality any more than heterosexuals choose to be heterosexual or any more than homosexuals choose to be homosexual. I did not ask to be bisexual; I simply am. What arises within, naturally and unbidden, is the ability to appreciate equally both male and female beauty and very occasionally for that attraction to develop into sexual expression. It has happened only three times in my life.

## The Community

The whole town was stirred up because of them. While glad to see Naomi, the townsfolk were abuzz with gossip, uncertain, watching from afar the foreigner in their midst, seeming to be disinterested yet most likely aware of her every move. At the start was an attitude of tense, whispered xenophobia. The servant in charge of Boaz's reapers allowed Ruth to glean, though one wonders how grudging he was. In fairness, he reported to Boaz, sticking strictly to the facts of Ruth's morning in the field. Yet still Boaz had to caution him and the other workers to permit her to continue, instructing them to share water with her and to even pull some sheaves out and deliberately drop them. His workers saw him offer her food and advise her to stay in his field near his female workers, for she might be harassed in another field. In chapter 3, there is growing community approval of Ruth. When Ruth went to the threshing floor and spoke with Boaz in the night, he commented, "All the assembly of my people know that you are a worthy woman" (3:11). Ruth had by then proven herself to most of the community; suspicion had given way to tolerance, and tolerance was moving toward approval. The next community interaction occurred with the business transaction between Boaz and the nearer redeemer. In watching the proceedings, the official witnesses and onlookers must have realized this woman, who could have stayed in her own homeland, had come to Israel not just to live but to contribute to the community. They saw that she was both a caring woman and a hard worker. Further, she was willing to allow herself to be used as a means to honor Israelite inheritance laws. Out of love and loyalty to Naomi, she was willing to be part of a business transaction intended to result in marriage, repeated intercourse, and pregnancy until such time as a male heir was born to carry on Elimelech's name and possessions. Was marriage a social structure that would allow the love between two women to flourish and continue? Though she did not yet know him well, Ruth trusted Boaz, but what if the nearer kin had accepted Boaz's proposal? Ruth had surely thought of the consequences and had accepted them: to marry and be used by someone she did not know at all. She would have done it, for Naomi's sake, yet her mind still must have been in a turmoil until she and Naomi heard the results of the meeting at the gate.

So impressed with the young woman were the men present at the proceedings that they blessed her, using prestigious ancestral names. These may have been customary statements at such a transaction, but here they are used in regard to a foreign woman! "May the LORD make the woman who is coming into your house like Rachel and Leah ... and ... may your house be like the house of Perez, whom Tamar bore to Judah" (4:11–12). Such high compliments in impressive terms excellently match the women's praise after Ruth had given birth to Obed, acknowledging Ruth's love for Naomi, which made possible the child who would not only keep Elimelech's line alive but who would be the grandfather of David. The women further acknowledged the primacy of the relationship with Naomi and Ruth, "A son has been born to Naomi" (4:18). The outsider was accepted as one of their own, and she was able to receive that acceptance graciously.

## Towards an Inclusive Community

What began as friendship and love between two women grew to include a worthy man and an approving community and brought about circumstances under which a child was born who would be an important link in the genealogy both of David and of Jesus. Whatever else it was, the relationship between Naomi and Ruth, along with the living arrangements, was unique. Two women living alone were vulnerable financially and could potentially have been targets for rape; further, the community would have viewed this arrangement, two women living without male protection, as scandalous. Whether it was done consciously or not, Boaz, Ruth, and Naomi worked together to bring down the false and negative boundaries thrown up in the name of ethnicity, age, race, religion, and gender boundaries that separate and divide. At the same time that those boundaries were coming down, the three, as God's agents, were erecting true boundaries—ethical and moral boundaries—that must exist if the reign of God is ever to be fully realized in the world. To the modern observer, they created a bisexual family.

For God's realm to be realized concretely on earth, at the center of one's life must be love of God, respect for self and for others, loving-kindness, responsibility, accountability, and integrity. These are boundaries by which we recognize the dignity and personhood of ourselves and of each other, by which we acknowledge our common humanity, siblings all, children of the same Parent with the same spark of the divine that runs through one and all. In the Creator of all, there is no straight or gay, asexual or bisexual, oriental or occidental, this nation or that one, old or young, not even Protestant or Roman Catholic. There is only the diversity that the Creator in wisdom, love, and grace wants to share with us, diversity that we are expected to treat responsibly and respectfully.

When I came to the realization that my same-sex relationship had been equally as valid as my opposite sex relationship, it was like a blindfold falling from my eyes. Yet the realization that I am authentically bisexual has created more problems than it solved. As a lesbian, I was accepted by the gay and lesbian community but not by everyone in the heterosexual community. When I finally understood that I am drawn to an individual on a deeper level, connecting to the person within rather than being concerned about the externals, I lost the acceptance of many in the gay/lesbian community and found that most heterosexuals were unable to conceive of bisexuality, let alone consider accepting it or at least trying to learn about it.

There are still many people who do not believe that bisexuality exists, many who think that bisexuality means that one person has many partners. Bisexual inclusion warrants a complete rethinking of human sexuality and the morality related to it. God's diversity in the universe extends even to sexuality. A lot of sexual morality is still situated in the area of the letter of the law, legislating specific acts and restricting others. Sexual morality, and our thinking about sexuality, must be placed within the spirit of the law.

## Conclusion

The power of love always defeats death. Anytime we label or fence off areas of our lives, we limit God's own possibilities, and when we limit, we deal spiritual and emotional death, besides making ourselves spiritually and emotionally small. We fly in the face of God, arrogantly informing God that what has been created cannot be, is not, right and good!

Ruth, Naomi, and Boaz caught just a glimpse of God's creational love, unbounded and all-encompassing, and they dared to do the painful work of questioning their own prejudices and boundaries. They dared to let go of long-held biases in favor of what God was revealing, and they realized how similar all humans are, rather than how different. In the foreigner, they each saw their own dreams, fears, hopes, the same longing for peace, happiness, and love, no matter our skin color, no matter our cultural oddities, no matter our dress, no matter whom we date or with whom we couple. This vision led them to estab-lish relationships that were outside the boundaries of their traditional culture.

Were Ruth and Naomi close in-laws? or friends? or sexual intimates? Labeling their relationship is to limit and diminish what they had. Spe-cial friendship does not even describe it. What I have described is, to me, precisely what bisexuality is about. It breaks boundaries of all kinds, not because one wants to shock, but because the attraction intellectually, spir-itually, emotionally, and finally physically is greater than one can resist, in the best sense. One sees God in the other, and where God is, there is re-spect, loving-kindness, and responsibility toward each other. My attraction is to the other's spirit, and the orientation is one in which I have no regard for society's boundaries and taboos. Not to shock, dissemble, or deliberately ignore society's opinion, I do not even notice, or perhaps notice only periph-erally, that the other's body bears a physical resemblance to or difference from my own. And the attraction for me occurs in the order I noted above: intellectually, spiritually, emotionally, and only finally physically.

I feel a flutter of wonder and delight in my soul every time I read Ruth's words to Naomi at a ceremony of union, and I wonder, How long, O Lord, will it be for us to catch up to you? How long before we acknowledge the words as those spoken by one woman to another and realize the implica-tions? How long before the book of Ruth ceases to be read as the story of an ancient Cinderella, noticed by the prince and plucked from the fields to live happily ever after in the castle, the mother-in-law viewed simply as a convenient plot device to bring the lovers together? How long before God's powerful message of the diversity of human relationship is acknowledged by all who call God Lord?

## Notes

1. Alicia Suskin Ostriker, *The Nakedness of the Fathers: Biblical Visions and Revisions* (New Brunswick, N.J.: Rutgers University Press, 1994), xiii.

2. For a lesbian midrash of Ruth, see Rebecca Alpert, "Finding Our Past: A Lesbian Interpretation of the Book of Ruth," in *Reading Ruth: Contemporary Women Reclaim a Sacred Story*, ed. Judith A. Kates and Gail Twesky Reimer (New York: Ballantine Books, 1996), 91–96.

3. See Mona West, "The Book of Ruth: An Example of Procreative Strategies for Queers," in *Our Families, Our Values: Snapshots of Queer Kinship*, ed. Robert E. Goss and Amy A. S. Strongheart (New York: Harrington Park Press, 1997), 51–60; June Jordan, *Out of the Garden: Women Writers on the Bible. Ruth and Naomi, David and Jonathan: One Love*, ed. Christina Buchmann and Celina Spiegel (Columbine, N.Y.: Fawcett, 1994).

# 9

# Throwing a Party

## Patriarchy, Gender, and the Death of Jezebel

### VICTORIA S. KOLAKOWSKI

*Victoria Kolakowski reads the death of Jezebel by the hands of the eunuchs from the social location of a male-to-female transsexual. She perceives "transsexual" as steering a course between exclusion and elision. She struggles with the ways transsexuals have been written about by activists and theorists such as Janice Raymond and Nancy Wilson. In her struggle for middle ground, Kolakowski finds herself drawn between the poles of exclusion and assimilation, a position similar to the eunuchs who watched Jezebel hurled to her death and fearful of siding with the losing side.*

Throughout the ages few biblical characters have more dramatically captured the imagination of readers than Jezebel, the Phoenician princess and wife of King Ahab of Israel. Throughout history, she has been vilified both as an apostate and as a whore. Her death, recounted in 2 Kings 9:30–37, is one of the most graphic and intriguing death scenes in the Bible. This story is fascinating partly because it is reasonable to argue that gender is a key element in the story. If this is so, what does this mean? Was gender used as a patriarchal persuasive tool, as an arguably sexist metaphor for religious apostasy, or for some other purpose? This story has particularly interesting implications for gay, lesbian, bisexual, and transgendered (lesbigaytrans) people because of the presence of eunuchs in the gender mix. Modern lesbigaytrans biblical scholars have drawn parallels between eunuchs and either gay men, on the one hand, or male-to-female transsexuals, on the other. The eunuchs are a wild card in the story, one that has traditionally been ignored but will be the ultimate focus of this analysis. In order to understand the role that eunuchs may play in this story, I will first provide an overview of 2 Kings 9, before entering into a deeper analysis of the text.

The story in question directly begins with the prophet Elisha commissioning an unnamed prophet to anoint Jehu, an Israelite military commander, as king of Israel. Elisha instructed the prophet in what to say and do with Jehu: the prophet was to anoint Jehu as king and then to depart swiftly. The unnamed prophet indeed found Jehu, pulled him away from a meeting, and privately anointed him as king. Instead of directly leaving as instructed, however, the prophet repeated to Jehu a prophecy of the prophet Elijah from 1 Kings 21:21–24: the house of Ahab would be destroyed, like those of Jeroboam and Basha, and Jezebel would be eaten by dogs and not be buried. When Jehu's friends/military commanders successfully pressed the strangely secretive Jehu to reveal what had happened, they acknowledged him as king, and they left to assert his claim to the throne.

Jehu went to the city of Jezreel, where Joram, the king of Israel, was recovering from war wounds. Ahaziah, king of Judah, accompanied Joram. As Jehu approached the city, Joram and Ahaziah went out to meet Jehu to determine his intent. When challenged by Joram, Jehu replied, "What peace can there be, so long as the many whoredoms and sorceries of your mother Jezebel continue?" (2 Kings 9:22).[1] Jehu then shot both Joram and Ahaziah in the back as they fled. Jehu ordered that Joram's body be thrown onto the plot of Naboth, whose land had been stolen by Joram's father Ahab at the instigation of Jezebel. Ahaziah's body, however, was taken to Judah and buried with his ancestors. Jehu then came to the city of Jezreel. Jezebel had heard of Jehu's approach and prepared herself in her finest royal garb and makeup. When Jehu entered the gate, Jezebel appeared in the window and called out to him, "Is it peace, Zimri, murderer of your master?" (2 Kings 9:31). Zimri was a previous usurper of the throne of Israel.[2]

Jehu chose to disregard Jezebel's question and instead called up to the window: "Who is on my side? Who?" (2 Kings 9:32). Two or three eunuchs looked out at him, and he ordered them to throw her down. They complied, and she died a gory death, with blood everywhere and horses trampling her body. Jehu then went in and had a party. Finally it occurred to him that her body needed to be attended to, "for she is a king's daughter" (2 Kings 9:34). They found only her skull and her hands and feet. When they informed him of this, Jehu recounted the prophecy of Elijah regarding Jezebel's death that dogs would eat her so that there would be no identifiable remains. The destruction of the body of Jezebel is recounted in graphic detail and must therefore be of some importance in the story. But what message is the author trying to convey, and how do the genders of the actors relate to this message? This has been a source of some disagreement between traditional interpretation and modern feminist analysis.

I believe that it would be fair to characterize a generic traditional interpretation of this story as follows: The prophets anointed Jehu, a godly hero dedicated to the worship of Yahweh, to be king. He was motivated by a desire to rid the nation of its corruption, as demonstrated by his reply to

Joram that there would be no peace while the "whoredoms and sorceries" of Jezebel continued. He killed Joram and had his body delivered to the plot of Naboth, as revenge for Ahab's (Joram's father) theft of the land. He then confronted Jezebel, whose foreign harlotry and apostasy had corrupted the entire nation. She was defiant and possibly hoped to awe Jehu with her appearance. She caustically likened Jehu to Zimri, a previous usurper who killed his master. She was so wicked that even her own servants despised her and eagerly answered Jehu's call to throw her down. Her gory death and dismemberment were a fulfillment of Elijah's prophecy and continues to serve as an example of the power of Yahweh and the impotence of Baal. Jehu went on to defend Yahwism, doing what Yahweh desires.[3] Gender is therefore irrelevant in this story; all that matters is whether one follows Yahweh's commands, without regard to whether one is male or female. Some feminist commentators reject the notion that gender is irrelevant in this story. Why is Jezebel portrayed in such a negative light, especially when her acts are compared with others in the Deuteronomistic history, all of whom were probably men? Isn't there really an underlying patriarchal agenda to this story?

One such critique came from Danna Nolan Fewell and David M. Gunn in *Gender, Power, and Promise.*[4] Regarding Jezebel, they argue that "in all of Kings it is hard to find any deeper hostility than that expressed against this woman" and describe her gory death and dismemberment as the most severe in the book of Kings.[5] What do they believe to be the source of this hostility? They contend that "as the quintessential foreign woman of power she is for the patriarchal Subject the quintessential Other, to be feared and blamed."[6] They challenge the traditional view of Jezebel as being particularly wicked and argue that the Deuteronomistic historian's true concern was religious apostasy.[7] Fewell and Gunn proceed to develop an argument regarding patriarchy, marriage, and apostasy.[8] The relationship between Yahweh and Israel is compared to that of husband and wife. To serve Baal is to serve another master/husband, and to serve Asherah is dually disturbing, as it suggests both authority for the female as well as lust of a woman for a woman. Hence, worshiping these gods is a form of adultery and sexual perversion by the people of Israel. Jezebel thus transformed Israel into whoring women.

Fewell and Gunn further elaborated on the purportedly connected themes of whoring and apostasy, arguing that women are vilified because men are displacing their own illicit sexual and spiritual desires onto the object, thereby shifting blame to women while supporting increased patriarchal male control over women. Indeed, they note that Solomon's own apostasy is blamed on his wives and that he himself does not suffer such a fate as Jezebel. Only the queen of Sheba, who, they argued, played the patriarchal game by ultimately submitting to Solomon and Yahweh, escapes the misogynistic wrath of the author(s) of the Deuteronomistic history. In summary, Fewell and Gunn argue that Jezebel is despised because she was a strong, independent woman, unwilling to be subservient to a monotheistic framework that subjugates women. As a result, she becomes the scapegoat for all of Israel's apostasy, and Yahweh requires her utter destruction.

Is this a convincing reading of the text? Clearly, there is a scriptural basis for viewing the major concern as apostasy and for reading an analogy between the covenantal relationship between Yahweh and Israel and that of man and wife. It does not necessarily follow, however, that saying that the men of Israel are acting like illicit women must result in blaming women for the problem. What does logically follow is that saying that the men of Israel are acting like illicit women means that they are not acting like men.

Fewell's and Gunn's analysis raises important questions about the role that gender played in the reading of this story and about whether Jezebel is indeed the monster that tradition presents. Viewed objectively, her "sins" do not appear to be so outrageous as to warrant such an extreme death story. Hence, there may be something else acting in the story, not a vilification based upon a large number of actions but upon something in Jezebel's character that is intrinsically offensive to the hearers of this story. Given that there may be such a character interpretation, I suggest that what matters here is the way that the intended audience would hear and interpret this story. This makes sense because the story was meant to communicate some important principles that would be understood by that particular audience, which was rooted in a specific culture. One of the most powerful cultural forces is that of gender. Since this story has characters who are male (Jehu, Joram, Ahaziah, and many supporting characters) and female (Jezebel) and some who are ambiguously in-between (the eunuchs), gender probably played a major role in how the characters were perceived by the original audience.

Hence, I would raise a different critique of the traditional interpretation of this story, one based on the interplay of gender in the story itself. I will examine the gender roles of the various actors in this story and the ways that these gender roles interact. I believe that this sheds some light on the story and is much deeper and subtler than any of the previously cited commentators have considered. In general, the character of Jehu is not fully addressed either by the traditional interpretations or by the feminist counterinterpretations. How does Jehu measure up, particularly from the point of view of ancient patriarchal notions of manliness? First, he attempts to hide his anointing by the prophet. Next, he encounters Joram and Ahaziah; he personally shoots Joram in the back and orders Ahaziah shot in the back (the reason for this killing is not made explicit in the text). Then he finds Jezebel, orders her eunuchs to throw her down from the wall, and proceeds to dine, while the dogs dine on Jezebel.[9] Was this really intended to be a model of a "man of God"?[10] Jehu does not confront any of these people in face-to-face, hand-to-hand combat; instead he and his men shoot the two kings in the back, and he orders the eunuchs to kill the queen mother. While this story clearly shows Jehu is in charge, does it really show him to be the hero? Is he any better a man than Ahab, who was supposedly manipulated by Jezebel and thereby politically emasculated?

How does gender play out in the death of Jezebel? First, I think that Jezebel's influence over Ahab, and later her son Joram, was probably viewed as diminishing the masculinity of those kings. A true "manly" king would rule on his own, based on the precepts of Yahwism. But seductive foreign women, like Jezebel and the wives of Solomon, lead men astray. This diminishes their manhood, rendering them figuratively impotent.[11] In such a view, the control of women is not, as Fewell and Gunn suggest, an aim in itself. Rather, the control of women is necessary for men to retain control of themselves, a view that Fewell and Gunn recognize but treat simply as projective. I suspect that this element is more central than they acknowledge. This is where another gender element in the story comes in, which all of the commentators that I have reviewed ignored. I see the eunuchs of this story as mediators of the gender play between the defiant, seductive, and strong Jezebel and the dubiously manly Jehu (the manliest among wimps).

The problem is in interpreting how that ancient audience would have perceived the characters' roles in the story. Understanding references to eunuchs themselves in the Hebrew Scriptures is complicated by the ambiguity of the words used for them. The Hebrew term most commonly used for eunuchs is *syris*, which is accepted as being derived from Akkadian for "he who is chief" or "he who is head" (to the king).[12] As a result, it is often unclear whether the reference is specifically to a castrated male or generically to the high official of a foreign king or queen.[13] However, this appears to be a case in which the eunuchs in question were most likely castrated men.[14] The people of Israel had strong rules prohibiting the castration of both animals and humans. Leviticus requires that animals for sacrifice not be castrated.[15] Similar laws regarding castration existed for humans, with eunuchs being considered unacceptable for admission to the assembly or the priesthood.[16] Hence, there would likely have been a strong negative association with the castrated nature of the eunuchs in this story.[17]

Given this understanding of eunuchs, let us review the death scene again. As Jehu approaches, Jezebel adorns herself and goes to the window. The adornment has been viewed in many ways: the proud last stand of a valiant, strong woman,[18] a crafty attempt at seduction, and a haughty attempt to awe Jehu.[19] The appearance at the window itself is a common motif, which some suggest represents the powerless woman looking out on the world of men.[20]

As noted above, Jezebel then makes the comparison of Jehu to Zimri, which either serves to point out Jehu's perilous position or indicates Jezebel's lack of understanding of Yahweh's role in the usurpation. Her comment goes unanswered by Jehu. Is this a case of ignoring the Siren's call, a model for how men are to regard the taunting cries of women such as Jezebel? Could a response suck Jehu into losing his resolve? Or does her comment cut him more deeply than we are led to believe?

Jehu's response is to call for help. And his call is answered by two or three eunuchs. Jehu orders them to throw her down, and they follow his orders immediately. Is this more than just a few eunuchs hating their wicked mistress so much that they wish her dead, as some contend?[21] Or is this an example of eunuchs acting as holy agents?[22] Or, as none suggest, are they merely fearful of Jehu's wrath and attempt to be on the obviously winning side?

I would suggest that there may be alternative readings of this story. First, if indeed Jezebel figuratively emasculated Ahab and the men of Israel, then for the eunuchs the impotence was more than figurative. By casting down Jezebel, the root source of their impotence, these eunuchs may be viewed as symbolically regaining their masculinity. In a dramatic reversal, we see Jehu restoring the masculinity to the impotent men under the domination of Jezebel. By allowing the eunuchs to kill Jezebel, the eunuchs are empowered by Jehu, and indirectly by Yahweh.

Or is there still another way of viewing the role of the eunuchs? Has Israel's manhood been so diminished that it is impotent to kill Jezebel, to remove the seductress from the nation? Do the men of Israel need the assistance of half-men, most likely foreigners? Is Jehu, the purported hero of the story, still less than a full man himself? Perhaps part of the literary agenda was to show the audience that the nation had degenerated. Perhaps this story shows that the monstrous eunuchs, abominations created by Jezebel, in the end turned on her as a form of poetic justice for her defilement of men. Perhaps even Jezebel couldn't totally reduce men to impotent slaves, as the Greek mythical Circe reduced men to animals.

I suspect that at some level all of these readings are operating in this story. While I personally would like to think of this story as validating and support-ing eunuchs as divine agents, I am left wondering whether eunuchs are once again viewed merely as pawns in the patriarchal oppression of women or as a tool for belittling men. Clearly, the presence of this third gender element, the eunuchs, produces the possibility for a variety of alternative readings heretofore ignored even by feminist scholars. The gender play among Jehu, Jezebel, and the eunuchs may very well be key in understanding this story. Unfortunately, the reading one obtains may say more about the reader than about the author, and the text itself does not resolve the question of the true meaning, if there is but one, of this gender interaction.

Modern attention to eunuchs has come primarily from lesbigaytrans scholars, who see parallels between the ancient eunuchs and (selected) elements of the modern lesbian, gay, bisexual, and transgender community. The way that eunuchs are viewed reflects at least as much the specific author's political agenda as it does anything about the eunuchs themselves.

Lesbian author and pastor Nancy Wilson argued in *Our Tribe* that "[e]unuchs and barren women, I believe, are our gay, lesbian and bisexual antecedents."[23] She cites John McNeill's seminal book *The Church and the Homosexual* in arguing that the term "eunuchs from birth" refers to gay and lesbian people.[24] Wilson sees eunuchs as performing two special roles in the Bible. First, she argues that eunuchs were shamans and magicians, who acted as mediators between heaven and earth. Second, she argues that eunuchs "act as a kind of palace double agent."[25] It is in this second role that Wilson sees the eunuchs of this story: "Two or three eunuchs throw the wicked Queen Jezebel out of the window to her death! They act as agents of God and the prophet Elijah."[26]

Hence, Wilson's interpretation of this story is essentially the traditional interpretation. This position is consistent with Wilson's role as a lesbian Christian apologist, who has devoted much energy to gaining acceptance for gay and lesbian Christians in the wider Christian community while trying to use her Christianity to provide support and meaning for gay and lesbian people.[27] In my previous work I have argued for a different understanding of eunuchs in modern times. I have argued that a more reasonable interpretation of eunuchs would be transgendered persons and that any analogies to gay, lesbian, and bisexual people would be through a commonality of experience as gender and procreative subversives with transgendered people.[28] I have tried to be balanced in recognizing that biblical discussions of eunuchs are mixed, with both positive and negative views of eunuchs expressed in the Hebrew Scriptures. Nevertheless, I have presented a primarily upbeat view of eunuchs and used that to argue for transgender inclusion. This is consistent with my own experience as a transgender person seeking acceptance not just within the larger Christian community but also within the gay and lesbian community.[29]

Feminist ethicist Janice Raymond in her critiques of transsexuals, particularly lesbian-identified male-to-female transsexuals, has expressed a very different understanding of eunuchs. In *The Transsexual Empire*, Raymond wrote:

Furthermore, the deceptiveness of men without "members," that is, castrated men or eunuchs, has historical precedent. There is a long tradition of eunuchs who were used by rulers, heads of states, and magistrates as keepers of women: "Will every lesbian-feminist space become a harem?" Just because transsexually constructed lesbian-feminists are not only castrated men, but also have acquired artifacts of a woman's body and spirit, does not mean that they are un-men, and that they cannot be used as "keepers" of woman-identified women when the "real men," the "rulers of patriarchy," decide that the women's movement (used here as both noun and verb) should be controlled and contained.[30]

I see a strong similarity between Raymond's feared betrayal of the lesbian-feminist community by the nouveau eunuch transsexuals and the betrayal of the strong Jezebel by the eunuchs of her own court. Could such stories be one source of this fear? I do not pretend that Raymond or Mary Daly, her partner in promoting this particular view, is directly concerned about this story. I present this argument however for two reasons. The first relates back to Wilson's analysis. Part of the value of presenting meaningful stories such as those in the Bible as gay, lesbian, bisexual, and transgender affirming is their power to overcome oppression through biblical interpretation. Just as the African American communities spun the Exodus story to be one that fed those communities in times of great trial and to overcome biblical interpretations condemning their very existence, queer-affirming biblical stories can also redeem and liberate us. However, we need to be sure when we choose an "affirming" reading that we know whom or what we are affirming.

Fundamentally, Wilson and Raymond are relating almost the exact same story. For both, eunuchs are spies in enemy territory, ready to spring into action when the Master calls. It is just that for Wilson the Master is a loving God, while for Raymond the Master is a cruel patriarch. Raymond has made me aware that before we blindly accept Wilson's reading of this story, we need to critically engage it and make sure that we really know which Master we are serving. Wilson's and Raymond's spinning of eunuchs shows the landscape within which I, as a transsexual lesbian-feminist scholar, have to navigate in my own interpretation. I am thoroughly grounded in a faith community and a political setting that influences the very questions that I ask. Do I accept Wilson's view that eunuchs are divine agents, and thereby claim a respectable role in God's plan? And if so, am I committing the very act that Raymond fears, that is, throwing the strong, subversive woman out because the patriarchal keeper demanded that I do so? If I reject Wilson's interpretation and argue that this story is indeed one of betrayal of the subversive woman by the assimilationist queer, whether gay male or transsexual, am I accepting Raymond's conclusion that my own inclusion into the lesbian-feminist world is a threat to women?

In the final analysis, I am left to choose which group(s) to support and which to offend from among the following: the (patriarchal) establishment, the gay and lesbian mainstream (which seeks acceptance from the establishment for their homosexuality), the lesbian-feminist separatists (who find power and voice in Daly and Raymond), and the transgender community, of which I am an emerging political and spiritual leader (and which struggles with all of the above but particularly dislikes being demonized by Raymond). This analytical process is like trying to have deep self-reflection while juggling balls in the air. One's attention would be very scattered, even if one became facile with juggling. I struggle with finding myself and my own power while balancing the power that these groups may have over me against my own desires to ingratiate myself to them, despite my knowledge that not one of them really thinks of me as "one of us." Issues such as these usually operate in the background as we begin to travel new ground in queer biblical interpretation. This is also the danger of ideological critical interpretation: that the true agendas underlying our readings are unstated and usually not critically engaged. I see this failure to engage our own locations as potentially leading to sloppy reasoning and intellectually disingenuous results.

I need to acknowledge that I am completing this essay well past the deadline, partly because I was paralyzed by fear. At what cost to my own (patriarchal institutional) prestige do I write material such as this! Will a patriarchal power system appreciate my analysis? Will critiquing Wilson, who is an emerging dominant queer-friendly thinker and who is very powerful in my denomination, undermine my own acceptance by gay and lesbian Christians? Will Raymond be happy that I find her fears partly supported by this text? Will she be more likely to accept me into her circles? Will other transgendered people view me as a traitor for even acknowledging that Raymond's fears, while misguided, are grounded in reality? My own confusion makes me wonder how many eunuchs stood by and watched their queen being hurled from the window, fearful of siding with the obvious loser in the power struggle. I think that this story represents for the modern gay, lesbian, bisexual, and transgender person the ever present tension between assimilation (which embraces apologetics for increasing acceptance in the "mainstream") and queer-identity (which dances between the "tribal" pole and the separatist pole in terms of the need for "mainstream" acceptance). I believe that my, albeit unenthusiastic, willingness to stand separated and to challenge the legitimacy of the apologistic model demonstrates that Raymond's fear is fundamentally misplaced. It has been my experience that separatists do not challenge women who are born with women's bodies the way that they challenge those of us who aren't. But whom would they rather have engaging these issues, Wilson or Kolakowski?

Ultimately, I think that true assimilation is an unachievable goal and has been the focus of far too much energy. In the Jezebel story, the eunuchs were not given great honors. Jehu just went off and partied. Dominant power does not thank others for submission; submission is presumed. Submission is a survival technique, and as long as that is necessary, then there is no real incorporation at all. In spinning new stories and meanings for ourselves, we need to question whether we are doing so to thrive, or merely to survive. I'm tired of merely surviving, and so I am looking for still further stories, new stories, that can empower and affirm my people and me. Wilson is correct in seeing the power of a belief system, such as Christianity, in developing a "tribal" identity, as Wilson describes what is indeed nation building. I agree that this is needed, and I applaud that aspect of her work (and my own previous work as well).

However, the intersection of gender and power are key parts of nation building, as the need for this story about Jezebel in this nationalistic sacred text demonstrates. We are conducting this nation building, not in a vacuum, but in a complex, fundamentally unbalanced social power structure (over-simplistically called "patriarchy"). Far more critical work is needed into such issues (gender, sexuality, nation building, ideology, spirituality, etc.) and into how this ancient collection of texts supports or undermines not only our own "tribal" identity but also what the emerging "tribe" would look like.[31] I am afraid that without this type of analysis we may unintentionally succeed, not in creating a proud and independent "tribe," but instead a colonized nation that embraces the values of the oppressor in that (perceived) need to survive. That would be a tragic loss. If our journey is indeed like the great Exodus story, I don't want to go back to that figurative Egypt, no matter how hard the desert may seem.

## Notes

1. See M. Beeching, "Jezebel," in *New Bible Dictionary*, ed. J. J. Douglas et al., 2d ed. (Wheaton: Tyndale House, 1982), 596; Jo Ann Hackett, "Jezebel," in *The Oxford Companion to the Bible*, ed. Bruce M. Metzger and Michael D. Coogan (New York: Oxford University Press, 1993), 368.

2. For a discussion of Jezebel as a negative female image, see Tina Pippin, "Jezebel Revamped," in *A Feminist Companion to Samuel and Kings*, ed. Athalya Brenner (Sheffield: Sheffield Academic Press, 1994), 196–206.

3. See 2 Kings 10:30 for scriptural support for Yahweh's approval.

4. Danna Nolan Fewell and David M. Gunn, *Gender, Power, and Promise: The Subject of the Bible's First Story* (Nashville: Abingdon Press, 1993), 164–86.

5. Ibid., 165.

6. Ibid., 167.

7. Ibid., 168.

8. Ibid., 169.

9. An interesting discussion of a possible biblical connection between dogs and gay men is made in the chapter "The 'Dogs' or Homosexual 'Holy Men,'" in Tom Horner, *Jonathan Loved David: Homosexuality in Biblical Times* (Philadelphia: Westminster Press, 1978), 59–70. If, indeed, dogs have some sort of an unconscious association for this community with gay men, then my argument that this story can be read as being about assimilationist betrayal of the sexually different is strengthened. Also interestingly, this story would have representatives of deep struggles with lesbianism (see the apostasy argument of Fewell and Gunn), male homosexuality (the dogs), and transgendered people (the eunuchs). It is precisely this sort of sexually conflicted imagery that makes this story a fascinating subject of analysis.

10. T. R. Hobbs does not paint a flattering portrait of Jehu, whom he calls a tyrant. T. R. Hobbs, *2 Kings*, Word Biblical Commentary 13 (Waco, Tex.: Word Publishers, 1985), 113, 118–20.

11. Pippin cites a number of sources regarding the masculinity of Jezebel and the powerlessness of men ("Jezebel Revamped," particularly 197).

12. Robert North, "Palestine, Administration of (Judean Officials)," in *The Anchor Bible Dictionary*, ed. David Noel Freedman (New York: Doubleday, 1992), 5.86–90, 87; R. J. A. Sheriffs, "Eunuch," in *New Bible Dictionary*, ed. J. J. Douglas et al., 2d ed. (Wheaton: Tyndale House, 1982), 356.

13. The foreignness is often stressed. See North, "Palestine," 87; Gerhard A. Krodel, *Acts*, Augsburg Commentary on the New Testament (Minneapolis: Augsburg, 1986), 168. Officials of queens were commonly eunuchs.

14. Castrated eunuchs were commonly used as guards for queens, most likely because they posed no threat as potential mates to the queens. The paternity of children would not be in question, and the oft-used method of ascension to challenging the throne by seizing the king's harem would be effectively unavailable.

15. Leviticus 22:24–25. While this prohibition applies only to sacrificed animals, it is believed that it was generalized to all animals. This prohibition is undoubtedly connected to the value of the animal as a sacrifice—only the best unblemished offerings were to be given to Yahweh—the most valuable and not the castoffs.

16. "No one whose testicles are crushed or whose penis is cut off shall be admitted to the assembly of the LORD" (Deut. 23:1). See also Leviticus 21:16–23 regarding the prohibitions on castrated men serving as priests.

17. Different nonexclusive reasons are cited for this Hebraic prohibition on castration. First, there is the strong emphasis on reproduction. See Jerome Kodell, "The Celibacy Logion in Matthew 19:12," *Biblical Theology Bulletin* 8, no. 1 (February 1978): 19–23, 19. From the early command in Genesis 1:28 to "be fruitful and multiply, and fill the earth and subdue it" to later rabbinical literature, there was a strong emphasis on the necessity of marriage and of procreation. Dale Allison, "Eunuchs because of the Kingdom of Heaven (Matthew 19:12)," *TSF Bulletin* (November–December 1984): 2–5, 2; Kodell, "The Celibacy Logion in Matthew 19:12," 19; Francis J. Moloney, "Matthew 19, 3–12 and Celibacy: A Redactional and Form Critical Study," *JSNT* 2 (1979): 42–60, 51; Johannes Schneider, "eunouchos," in *Theological Dictionary of the New Testament*, ed. Gerhard Kittel (Grand Rapids: Wm. B. Eerdmans, 1964), 2:765–68, 767; F. Scott Spencer, "The Ethiopian Eunuch and His Bible: A Social-Science Analysis," *Biblical Theology Bulletin*, 22 (1992):

155–65, 157. Second, it implies a connection to external religious traditions and following other gods. See Karl Rengstorf, "apokoptoo," in *Theological Dictionary of the New Testament*, ed. Gerhard Kittel (Grand Rapids: Wm. B. Eerdmans, 1964), 3:852–55, 854; Schneider, "eunouchos," 766. Third, eunuchs could not be circumcised. Spencer, "The Ethiopian Eunuch and His Bible," 157. Finally, all that is imperfect or blemished is unfit for worship of Yahweh, just as with the castrated animals discussed above. Rengstorf, "apokoptoo," 854.

18. Claudia V. Camp, "1 and 2 Kings," in *The Women's Bible Commentary*, ed. Carol A. Newsom and Sharon H. Ringe (Louisville: Westminster/John Knox Press, 1992), 96–109, 103–4.

19. Edith Deen, *All of the Women of the Bible* (San Francisco: HarperSanFrancisco, 1988), 129.

20. E.g., J. Cheryl Exum, *Fragmented Women: Feminist (Sub)versions of Biblical Narratives* (Valley Forge, Pa.: Trinity Press International, 1993), 47.

21. Deen, *Women of the Bible*, 130.

22. See Nancy L. Wilson, *Our Tribe: Queer Folks, God, Jesus, and the Bible* (San Francisco: HarperSanFrancisco, 1995), 282.

23. Ibid., 124.

24. Ibid., 129.

25. Ibid., 126.

26. Ibid., 282.

27. Wilson has served for many years as one of the seven elders of the Universal Fellowship of Metropolitan Community Churches, a predominantly gay and lesbian denomination, and worked unsuccessfully for years towards UFMCC membership in the National Council of Churches (NCC). References to her experiences in working with the NCC are scattered widely throughout *Our Tribe*. One of the more extensive discussions is at 77–79.

28. Victoria S. Kolakowski, "The Concubine and the Eunuch: Queering Up the Breeder's Bible," in *Our Families, Our Values: Snapshots of Queer Kinship*, ed. Robert E. Goss and Amy A. S. Strongheart (New York: Harrington Park Press, 1997), 35–49.

29. Ibid.; and Victoria S. Kolakowski, "Toward a Christian Ethical Response to Transsexual Persons," in *Theology and Sexuality* 6 (1997): 10–31.

30. Janice Raymond, *The Transsexual Empire: The Making of the She-Male* (Boston: Beacon Press, 1979), 104–5. A related argument was made in Mary Daly, *Gyn/Ecology: The Metaethics of Radical Feminism* (Boston: Beacon Press, 1978), 67–68. Daly discusses Raymond's argument in 432 n. 56.

31. I am indebted to Isabel E. Velez for her insights on the intersection of gender, sexuality, and nations and for challenging me to examine critically these issues in this context.

## 10

# Nehemiah as a Queer Model
# for Servant Leadership

### MICHAEL S. PIAZZA

*The Cathedral of Hope was founded in Dallas in 1970 and has become the first gay and lesbian megachurch in the world. Like the great cathedrals of Europe and major metropolitan cities, it serves as a regional spiritual center with a growing national presence, in this case for queer Christians. Michael Piazza, the senior pastor, engages the prophet Nehemiah as a prototype, a person whom God called to rebuild Jerusalem in the midst of hostility. Nehemiah, a eunuch, receives local criticism for his vision of a new Jerusalem. The prophet becomes a model of servant leadership for the queer Christian community and for the queer community. Nehemiah rebuilt a community wounded from the Exile. Many queer Christians have been excluded from their churches or have been forced into exile from their denominations because of their sexual orientation. The Cathedral of Hope has been welcoming of the unchurched and exiled queer Christians. Piazza, a modern-day Nehemiah, has embarked upon building a twenty-million-dollar structure to seat several thousand people driven from their denominations.*

One never reads scripture objectively. In addition to our theological perspective and educational background, the reality of life at the moment seems the most powerful lens through which we read. For many years now I have been reading biblical stories and interpreting them with the people of the Cathedral of Hope. The most common label applied to this faith community is "the world's largest lesbian and gay church." While that is true, in as far as it goes, it does not begin to reveal the amazing reality of this congregation.

The Cathedral of Hope is one of the largest churches of any kind. Yet it has an intense experience of intimate community. It is a place where spiritual realities are encountered by the heart not just the mind. Hundreds of people risk their jobs to worship in this visible and out church, in one of the most conservative cities in America. Despite this fact, or perhaps because of it, the congregation continues to grow in number. Although we offer six weekly services, there are still many times when all the people who attend cannot be squeezed into the sanctuary, which seats over eight hundred. What is this about? Why is one of the fastest growing churches in America a queer congregation in a homophobic setting?

The worship is remarkable and traditional. The weekly readings are assigned by the common lectionary, but the sermons, music, and liturgy invite people to encounter the ancient text in their daily lives. Somehow it happens. The proof is that people return each week wondering what word God might have for them that day.

Although it seems almost a cliché, people's lives are genuinely transformed as they encounter the Book, which many had assumed was only a tool of their enemies. Lesbian and gay people at the Cathedral seem to be genuinely surprised and joyful that the Bible has something to teach them. They are feeling the challenge to be a part of God's redeeming work in the world. As a result, this community of faith has generated thousands of volunteers and millions of dollars to care for those who are hurting and in great need.

More and more people seem attracted by what God is building and want to be a part of it. The congregation decided to build a multimillion-dollar cathedral designed by openly gay, world-acclaimed architect Philip Johnson. This building will not only house this extraordinary congregation, but it will serve as an ever visible symbol of the reality that God's family includes lesbian and gay people.

Like Nehemiah's work this project has not been without its critics and its enemies. Like his work the funding for the project will come from outside the community it is designed to benefit. Like his work the project itself has the power to build the community in ways that are hard to anticipate. Like Nehemiah's project this one looks impossible, but already the walls are going up, and we are too busy building to come down and argue with our critics.

## Nehemiah as a Model
## for Queer Servant Leadership

Nehemiah led the rebuilding of Jerusalem, the city of God. Perhaps he can teach us some principles about rebuilding our lives as the children of God. Whether you are rebuilding from scratch or simply remodeling a room or two, I think the ancient story has something to say to modern lesbigay people.

After the death of King Solomon, the nation of Israel split into two parts. Ten of the original twelve tribes followed one king, while the other two tribes followed a different king. The nation was weakened, and many people began to abandon the faith that had once united those from diverse tribes into a strong nation. As a result of this division, they were easily invaded and conquered by many of the neighboring countries and peoples. Eventually the Babylonians conquered them, burning the Temple and tearing down the walls of the city. The destruction of the Temple took away that which gave them unity. The destruction of the walls took away their security. Then, as was the custom in those days, the Babylonians took hundreds of people away into exile. They forced the brightest and best to move to Babylon to use their skills and talents for them. The Exile left Jerusalem depopulated and hopeless.

Ultimately, the Persians conquered the Babylonians and became the latest dominators of the Hebrews. The Persians did begin to allow some of the Jews to return to their homeland. A man named Zerubbabel led the first group back. Then eighty years later the priest Ezra led the second wave back to Jerusalem. The story of Nehemiah picks up thirteen years after that second wave of Hebrews had arrived back in Jerusalem. Nehemiah was one of the Jews still living in exile. Quite likely he had been too young to go with Ezra and the last group who went home. Eventually word came to Nehemiah about how desperate the situation was back in Jerusalem. Without a wall around the city it was vulnerable to all types of marauders. It was constantly being attacked, impoverished, and diminished. Between attacks, people lived in fear and with the shame that often becomes the irrational companion of victims. The city was in disrepair, and the people were disheartened, discouraged, and afraid. Constant attacks poisoned them and tore them down from the inside. And the Temple's destruction left them without a place to renew their faith.

Unfortunately the condition of Jerusalem and its people serves as an all-too-accurate analogy of what has happened spiritually to the lesbian and gay community. Too often we have had our place taken from us, and we have been left vulnerable to the repeated attacks of radical fundamentalists. We may claim that we know God's grace includes us, but the assaults have a toxic effect on our souls.

When word of the terrible condition of his sisters and brothers came to Nehemiah, he himself became very depressed. In the midst of his depression he seemed to sense God calling him to do something about it. It may seem to be a strange call. Nehemiah was not a politician, soldier, priest, or leader of any kind. In fact, according to the ancient text, he was the cupbearer of Persian king Artaxerxes.

If you have ever waited tables, you know it is a lot harder than it looks, but still it doesn't exactly qualify you to rebuild a nation. Add to that the fact that Nehemiah was living the good life. What God was calling him to do was dangerous and likely to be unpopular in many circles. Surely Nehemiah recognized that not everyone would want to see the Jews strong, healthy, and secure. In fact, as it turns out, many of the Jews had a substantial investment in keeping their own people fragmented and powerless.

Nehemiah's job as the cupbearer of the king allowed him to live in almost the same luxury as the king. His job was to taste everything the king ate or drank. There are two interesting things about Nehemiah's job. First, his role was to keep the king from being poisoned. As a result, every time the king got hungry or thirsty, the cupbearer risked his life for the king. This daily routine led to a close relationship between the two men. According to one historian, cupbearers were always the most attractive men and were often closer intimates of the king than the queen herself.[1]

Well, I'm not going to touch that line except to note that the servants and slaves who served the royal household were most often eunuchs.[2] Others before me have done a great job of explaining the parallels between the situation of the eunuch and the translesbigay person. John McNeill and others have gone so far as to suggest that it is more than just a parallel. They propose that the Bible refers to three types of eunuchs, one type being in fact the homosexual man. In Matthew 19:10–12, Jesus referred to those who were "made eunuchs," that is, those who were castrated; those who were born eunuchs, that is, those who were born homosexual; and then those who choose to be eunuchs for the sake of the realm of God, that is, those for whom celibacy was a spiritual calling.[3] In most eras of ancient Judaism all eunuchs were treated as spiritual outcasts (Deut. 23:1). Jesus, however, did not distance himself from the eunuchs. He himself may have been called a eunuch; then his statements in Matthew 19:10–12 are a response to that accusation. At the very least we have a picture of how Jesus felt about those who were considered sexually queer by his society.

Perhaps Jesus recalled Isaiah's record of the promises of God to those who were eunuchs. In Isaiah (56:3–7), God promises a special place in the household of God for the eunuchs. Also promised is a name "better than sons and daughters." Though it is unlikely that Nehemiah knew of this prophecy, he still seemed to be one who claims that reality in a way that empowered him. Though a eunuch in exile he refused to see himself as a powerless victim of an unjust society. Usually royal households used homosexual eunuchs in order to insure the safety of the queen and royal daughters from rape. It is quite likely that what we have in the story of Nehemiah is historical evidence that God called a man sexually attracted to other men, or at the very least a sexual outcast. God was calling a member of the queer community to lead the rebuilding of the city of God and rebuild the people of God.

Nehemiah was someone living a comfortable, prosperous life of material ease. Then God came along and called him to do something requiring sacrifice and self-denial. It would require a dramatic change of lifestyle, but Nehemiah became an instrument of God who helped to change the world.

It is my belief that God is once more calling translesbigay people to make some sacrifices, to be willing to risk some of our comfort in order to build a spiritual home for our people, *and* to build a new life for ourselves in the process. Beyond that, I believe God is calling us to offer the modern world a new model of leadership. We might actually be the servant leaders of which Robert Greenleaf dreamed.[4] That ancient eunuch Nehemiah might be just the model for leadership in the church and within the queer community.

## Servant Leadership Is Relational

According to the ancient story, after word came to Nehemiah about the terrible conditions back in Jerusalem, he became depressed.

> In the month of Nisan, in the twentieth year of King Artaxerxes, when wine was served him, I carried the wine and gave it to the king. Now, I had never been sad in his presence before. So the king said to me, "Why is your face sad, since you are not sick? This can only be sadness of the heart." (Neh. 2:1–2)

Nehemiah's depression over the plight of his sisters and brothers in a distant land is a clear sign of the empathy that servant leaders must have. Leaders who do not genuinely feel the pain of those they lead are dangerous and usually destructive. The oppression and exclusion of queer people can leave us cynical and bitter or tenderhearted and compassionate. Fortunately for Nehemiah the effect was the later.

King Artaxerxes obviously cared about Nehemiah enough to notice that he was sad and wanted to know why. Nehemiah had endeared himself beyond simply his status as the cupbearer. When the king asked him why he was sad, Nehemiah decided to take a chance. He risked his relationship with the king in order to intercede for his own people:

> So the king said to me, "Why is your face sad, since you are not sick? This can only be sadness of the heart." Then I was very much afraid. I said to the king, "May the king live forever! Why should my face not be sad, when the city, the place of my ancestors' graves, lies waste, and its gates have been destroyed by fire?" Then the king said to me, "What do you request?" So I prayed to the God of heaven. Then I said to the king, "If it pleases the king, and if your servant has found favor with you, I ask that you send me to Judah, to the city of my ancestors' graves, so that I may rebuild it." (Neh. 2:4–5)

Nehemiah got more than permission to go back to Jerusalem and help his people. Ultimately the king gave him a blank check to secure whatever supplies he might need to do the job. What a contrast Nehemiah presents to modern queer people who have risen to positions of power and influence but have remained closeted! Many of those people have even worked against their own people.

Servant leadership begins with relationship building. When Nehemiah arrives in Jerusalem and challenges the people to work, it is always in terms of "we" and "us." He did not arrive from the palace with orders from on high. He has known too long how it feels to be queer. He refuses to compensate for his own oppression by oppressing others. Together they will rebuild their city. Together they will reclaim their faith and their place.

## Servant Leaders Have Internal Guidance Systems

Another characteristic of Nehemiah that made him an effective leader is that he was internally motivated. He didn't need to be persuaded by others to get involved. No one had to beg him to give up his comfort and take on the challenge. Perhaps this quality is so obvious in Nehemiah because it is so lacking in most leaders today. Political leaders never seem to make a decision without the latest polling figures in hand. They do not do what is right nearly as often as what is popular.

Although such behavior is easy to see in politics, it is equally true of most of us as well. We are often overwhelmed by the need to be loved and approved, which may cause us to make many of our decisions based on what others might think or say. Our judgments can then become largely externally based—despite the fact that the majority is quite often wrong. After all, the majority gave us our current batch of political leaders. The majority once supported slavery, opposed women having the right to vote, and thought homosexuality was a sin. In each case the majority was wrong.

Queer people have had to disregard the majority opinion in order to live our lives with integrity. One would think that we would have perfect internal guidance systems as a result. It is ironic that we who have been willing to risk the opinion of parents, priests, and presidents are still so immobilized by criticism. Although criticism may seem like a peripheral issue, it is something that often keeps queer folk from becoming leaders.

In the ancient story Nehemiah had his critics. At first you wonder who on earth could possibly criticize the rebuilding of the city of God. What was there not to like about this project? Nehemiah encountered significant and powerful opposition. Three people in particular are identified as his primary critics: Sanballat, Tobiah, and Geshem, all of whom are mentioned in ancient Egyptian literature. These three officials over the rural territory surrounding the city of Jerusalem were critical of Nehemiah because they were afraid that his efforts to restore the city might affect their rural enterprises. Note that it wasn't what was right or wrong, nor was it a question of what was best for people. Their guiding principle was entirely focused on what this might cost them.

It is amazing how often criticism and other negative energy can be traced back to that very thing—self-interest. Nehemiah worked building the wall around the city of God, but Sanballat, Tobiah, and Geshem stood below trying to tear it down with their words. First, they tried mockery and ridicule, which are usually the critic's first weapons of choice. Many of us grew up in families in which ridicule was a mechanism of control. Children use it effectively. Even today we are easily shattered by the threat of mockery. Listen to this ancient ridicule and see if any of it sounds familiar: "What are these feeble Jews doing?' (Neh. 4:2). They begin with name calling. Sticking a label on people is a crude but effective way to diminish them.

In the Sermon on the Mount Jesus said, "I say to you that, . . . if you say, 'Raca,' you will be liable to the hell of fire" (Matt. 5:22). The word *raca* is often translated "fool," though some scholars suggest it might be translated "sissy."[5] Jesus set a high price on ridicule because he knew it has the power to murder the soul of the vulnerable. Queers have felt its power used against us. Why would we ever use it against a sister or a brother?

"Will they restore things? Will they sacrifice?" Sanballat, Tobiah, and Geshem asked (Neh. 4:2). They ridiculed the Jew's belief that they had the power to reclaim their faith and build a place of safety, community, and worship. Sanballat was governor of Samaria. Since the destruction of Jerusalem, the Samaritans had been worshiping God on Mount Gerizim. You remember the conversation the Samaritan woman at the well had with Jesus. She talked to him about the fact that the Jews worshiped in Jerusalem and the Samaritans on the mountain. Jesus said the time was coming when true worshipers would worship in spirit and truth. That whole conversation could be traced back hundreds of years to this chapter of Nehemiah. Sanballat wanted the Jews to come to God's mountain to worship. He wanted an exclusive a corner on the God market.

Jesus went to the Temple and found people who used it for personal gain and were keeping needy people shut out. He picked up a whip and cleaned house. Then he explained what he had done by quoting Isaiah. In fact he quoted a verse taken from that same passage in which God promised eunuchs a name better than sons and daughters. Through the prophet Isaiah and through Jesus, God declared, "My house shall be a house of prayer for *all* people" (Isa. 56:7; Matt. 21:13).

Sanballat, Tobiah, and Geshem also tried to discourage Nehemiah by ridiculing how long the project was going to take: "Will they finish in a day?" (Neh. 4:2). Now, you can put up a tent pretty quickly, but the greater the building, the longer it takes to plan it, design it, fund it, and build it. Our generation is not good at long-term investing for the future. Deferred gratification is not our strong suit. We want it all, and we want it yesterday. Maybe there was a bit of that with the Hebrews because their critics tried to discourage them with how long the work would take. Your internal critic's most discouraging tool might be to point out how long it is taking you to build the strong and healthy person you long to be. It is a long slow process when what you are building is a great soul.

The final criticism was, "Will they revive the stones out of heaps of rubbish—and burned ones at that?" (Neh. 4:2). Sanballat, Tobiah, and Geshem criticized what Nehemiah had to work with. Some of the most destructive work our enemies have done has been to convince us that they have a corner on morality. Because our system of relationships is different, they have labeled us promiscuous, and too often our own people have accepted their verdict. On various levels we have allowed the voice of internalized homophobia to undermine our confidence in our own goodness and the passionate love God has for us. "You can't build a great soul, a great life, let alone be a part of building a great community. All you have to work with is rubbish." Yet look, brick upon brick Nehemiah, the eunuch, leads the people to rebuild the city and their lives. His critics kept throwing stones, and Nehemiah kept picking them up and building with them.

## Servant Leaders Are Focused

Somehow, while still sleeping in his soft bed in the palace and eating at the king's table, Nehemiah was still able to hear the call of God on his life. He saw the needs of his people and recognized the role he could play. He did not assume it was someone else's responsibility. He was unwilling to hide behind the fact that he was "only a cupbearer."

Leadership is not success, power, or popularity. In its most basic form it is getting a job done by getting others to help. This is not an easy task, and so it must be in answer to a greater call. Robert Greenleaf frequently quoted Albert Camus's lecture "Create Dangerously":

> One may long, as I do, for a gentler flame, a respite, a pause for musing. But perhaps there is no other peace for the artist than what (s)he finds in the heat of combat. "Every wall is a door," Emerson correctly said. Let us not look for the door and the way out, anywhere but in the wall against which we are living. Instead, let us seek the respite where it is—in the thick of the very battle itself. . . . Great ideas, it has been said, come into the world gently as doves. Perhaps then, if we listen

attentively, we shall hear, amid the uproar of empires and nations, a faint flutter of wings, the gentle stirring of life and hope. Some will say that this hope lies in a nation, others in a person. I believe rather that it is awakened, revived, nourished by millions of solitary individuals whose deeds and works every day negate frontiers and the crudest implications of history.[6]

Greenleaf believed that in order to be a servant leader, it would be best for one to be a servant first: "It begins with the natural feeling that one wants to serve. Then the conscious choice brings one to aspire to lead."[7]

So it was with Nehemiah. He might have longed for a "gentler flame," but he made the conscious choice to lead his people. Notice what Nehemiah said when his critics wanted him to come down from the wall and talk to them. Perhaps these words should burn within all of us because he said, "I am busy doing a great work and cannot come down" (Neh. 6:3).

Nehemiah would not be distracted. He could not be discouraged. He was fixated on a dream, a goal, a vision that was beyond him. It enlarged his life. It insured him from attacks. It gave strength and energy and courage that outsiders seldom suspect resides in the souls of queer folk of every age. Unfortunately it is strength we sometimes fail to discover in ourselves. We say, "I'm just a nurse." "I'm only a teacher." "Being a hairdresser is all I've ever done." The lesson Nehemiah offers is a summons to listen to our hearts. Listen to our God. You never know just when God might say, "Let's go rebuild a city. You look great in construction boots."

## Notes

1. Raymond Bowman, *The Interpreters Bible* (New York: Abingdon Press, 1954), 3:671.

2. Ibid.

3. John J. McNeill, *The Church and the Homosexual* (Boston: Beacon Press, 1993), 65. For other treatment of eunuchs, see Nancy L. Wilson, *Our Tribe: Queer Folks, God, Jesus, and the Bible* (San Francisco: HarperSanFrancisco, 1995). See Victoria Kolakowski's article in this volume.

4. Robert Greenleaf, *Servant Leadership* (New York: Paulist Press, 1977), 222. For views on leadership, see Laurie Beth Jones, *Jesus CEO* (New York: Hyperion, 1995); Larry C. Spears, ed., *Reflections on Leadership* (New York: John Wiley & Sons, 1995).

5. Warren Johansson, "Whoever Shall Say to His Brother Racha (Matthew 5:22)," *Cabirion and Gay Books Bulletin* 10 (1984): 2–4.

6. Greenleaf, *Servant Leadership*, 222.

7. Michael S. Piazza, *Holy Homosexuals* (Dallas: Sources of Hope Publishing, 1997).

## 11

# A Modern Psalm
# in the Midst of Breast Cancer

### IRENE S. TRAVIS

*At the final stages of writing the essay "Love Your Mother," Irene Travis was diagnosed with breast cancer. She went through an experimental and radical chemotherapy procedure. As this book goes to press, Irene is cancer free. In announcing her diagnosis to her community of faith, Irene shared a psalm that she wrote. We have included it as a reading of scripture by all women struggling with cancer.*

Why me, O God, why me?
Why have you chosen me to live this full and wonderful life for some
     sixty years or so,
when all around the young are succumbing to accidents and illnesses?
Blessed am I among women.
Why me, O God, why me?
Why has this disease come upon me at a time in my life
when I am braced by the love of family, friends, and coworkers;
when I am to share my journey within the safety of this spiritual
     community?
This cancer could have come when I was spiritually dry and had very
     few people I called family and friends.
I am blessed among women.

Why me, O God, why me?
Why must I experience this illness today when I am in the midst of a
     beautiful long-term relationship?
I could be living alone, without my companion, lover, and dearest
     friend.
I am restored through her concern, love, and support.
I rejoice in your kindness toward me.
Blessed am I.

Why me, O God, why me?
Why have you spared me from evading the enemy by hiding at night
in the cold and frightening woods?
Why was I not the parent of one lost in the Oklahoma blast or killed
in action halfway across the world?
You have been gracious to me, O God. I am blessed.

This diagnosis of cancer is no more than many of the ills to which my
flesh is heir.
I know that I shall take this journey with you, my God, as healer,
companion, and comforter.
I rejoice in your goodness towards me.
I celebrate this life you have given me with all of its victories and
challenges.
I am most blessed among women!

## 12

# A Love as Fierce as Death

### Reclaiming the Song of Songs for Queer Lovers

CHRISTOPHER KING

*Many Jews and Christians often wonder how the Song of Songs was included in the Hebrew Scriptures. Its erotic content makes erotophobic Jews and Christians blush with embarrassment over its celebration of the sexual and social outlaw. Christopher King reads the Song of Songs from a queer perspective, noting how it celebrates transgressive eros and exalts a passionate love for the outsider. The man falls in love with a chosen outsider, the Shulamite, and their illicit love is expressed fully between equal partners. Their love reflects an ethic of intimacy rather than gender complementarity. How often queers have heard the rally cry of creationist homophobia: God made Adam and Eve, not Adam and Steve! For King, the Song affirms not only the sexual outlaw but queer ways of loving, desiring, and connecting sexually with others.*

In 1996, my partner and I celebrated our tenth year together with a ceremony of holy union and blessing, a public eucharistic liturgy to complement a simpler private ritual of covenant that we had shared in the first year of our relationship. Among the scriptural readings that we chose for the occasion were appropriate passages from the Song of Songs, the great poem of the Hebrew Scriptures praising a passionate love affair. For me, the Liturgy of the Word reached its high point with these formidable words from among those passages, words that also stand at the zenith of the whole Song of Songs:

> Bind me as a seal upon your heart,
> a sign upon your arm,
> For love is as fierce as death,
> its jealousy bitter as the grave.
> Even its sparks are a raging fire,
> a devouring flame.
> Great seas cannot extinguish love,
> no river can sweep it away." (8:6–7a)

It astonishes me even now that so few words could sum up so much of our story. The text tells of our deep sense of covenant interconnectedness ("bind me as a seal...sign"), a deeply interior unity of life ("upon your heart") that also demands public expression ("upon your arm"). Here is a love "as fierce as death." It is both the "dear love of comrades," which Walt Whitman knew to knit all queer folk together in one vast tribe and also the particular death-defying love that has given my partner and me the courage to stand together against the perils of living with HIV. "Great seas" could not swallow up our love during the years that I studied abroad. A "raging fire," a "devouring flame," perhaps even a "flame of God" (*salhebetyah*), this love urges us to live every day with passion for each other and, ultimately, for all of God's people.

What we found in the Song of Songs was an affirmation of love that matched our own experience in poignancy and power. But I must now ask difficult questions. What right did we have to seize upon this poem as a statement, even a vindication, of *queer* love? Does the Song of Songs legitimately belong to two gay men? Can the Song of Songs belong to queer people at all?

At first glance, the Song of Songs might seem to be the biblical book most friendly to a queer-positive reading. Whatever its original genre—whether love poem, covenant allegory, or hierogamic hymn—the Song of Songs builds its whole symbolism on a fervent, unashamed enthusiasm for human eros. And, indeed, when read with a fully honest, open-eyed hermeneutic, the Song of Songs yields the Bible's most potent balm for healing one of the great spiritual wounds of Christianity: the inherited fear of sexual desire. At every turn, the Song of Songs upholds embodied human eros as a genuine good, whose true measure is, not its conformity to some external standard of "nature," but only its capacity to bring joy to the hearts of man and woman.

But it is precisely on this point that the queer reader, however devoted to the Song of Songs' all-lovely lovers, must be alert to a roadblock on the way to a queer interpretation, for we must not forget that the Song of Songs' zeal for embodied, passionate love is directed entirely to that love as shared by *woman and man*. Of all the dimensions of the Song of Songs' narrative context, the one that remains most visible to us today is its situation in a world suffused with the images and reality of opposite-sex desire. Queers seem to be left entirely out of the picture. How, then, are queer believers to "take back" such a text as this?

## A Paradigm for Queer Identity and Action

The discussion will aim to show that, in fact, queer people of faith need not perceive the Song of Songs as unfriendly scriptural terrain, for as we shall see, even if the Song of Songs' two lovers (whom I shall call the Shulamite and her Beloved) are a woman and a man, the text is not principally concerned with extolling the virtues of *heterosexual* love per se. Rather, it celebrates the gift of human love itself, apart from any external measure of its worth—its procreative value, its conformity to natural law, its place in the right relationship of the sexes. Thus loosed from the fetters of an exclusive heterosexism, the Song of Songs can be seen to set forth a paradigm for queer identity and action. It only remains to be seen how this is so.

## Both Black and Beautiful:
## The Chosen Outsider and Transgressive Desire

In the first moments of the Song of Songs, a theme appears that encapsulates so much of the queer experience: the Shulamite as focus of a problem of identity, marginalizing discourses, fascination, and repulsion. The first time that the Shulamite speaks specifically about herself, she identifies herself as the object of a collective gaze that is, paradoxically, both enthralled and repelled:

> I am black and beautiful,
>    O daughters of Jerusalem,
> like the tents of Kedar,
>    like the curtains of Solomon. (1:5)

Whether the Shulamite addresses her listeners here as a dark-skinned territorial foreigner (like Moses' Cushite bride in Exod. 12), as a well-tanned worker in field and vineyard, or even as a lingering apparition of the black goddesses of antiquity, hers is an outsider's voice, speaking as a privileged alien to jealous hometown girls (the "daughters of Jerusalem"). She is as exotic and elusive as the black shelters of desert nomads ("tents of Kedar"). Yet, she has come as close to the privileges coveted by Jerusalem's social insiders as the "curtains of Solomon" are to the intimacies of the king's bedchamber.

The Shulamite enters the "daughters'" field of intense awareness only when they learn of her sexual affair with the coveted Beloved. Once initiated, this love affair alters public perception of the Shulamite. True to Foucault's model, the public "gaze" of the city daughters fixates on her most distinctive feature (i.e., her blackness), further exaggerating their perception of her as a social "other":

> Do not gaze at me because I am dark,
>    because the sun has gazed on me. (1:6a)

The Shulamite recognizes that because of her relationship to the Beloved, she has become the subject of a discourse that intensifies her experience of marginality. Having begun merely as a social outsider, she now becomes a taboo person, at once fascinating and forbidden.

The paradoxical convergence of blackness (i.e., outsider status) and beauty (i.e., desirability) in the Shulamite, then, disturbs and puzzles the "daughters of Jerusalem." Simultaneously jealous and disapproving, they cannot comprehend what drives the Beloved to pursue this dark-skinned outlander. Or, rather, perceiving the primal allure of the Shulamite with fearful clarity, they cannot risk bringing to conscious awareness its appeal for themselves. Theirs becomes deeply a problem of interpretation—how to reconcile her "blackness" with their own conflicted mimetic attraction to her beauty.

Significantly, this bedazzling blackness has also been perceived as a hermeneutical problem by the classical Jewish and Christian allegorical readings. In the Christian patristic allegories, for example, the Shulamite's "blackness" becomes a perpetual sign of her sin. Not surprisingly, this sin is frequently construed to be of a sexual kind, as spiritual *porneia* or adultery against Christ. Indelibly inked into her "flesh," into her existential density of presence, this black coloration becomes a full-body tattoo narrating her seasons of sexualized spiritual waywardness. Indeed, for Origen, the Shulamite's moral waywardness is the circumstantial cause of her "blackness." She has been deeply tanned because she has walked in crooked paths, skewwise to the rays of the divine Sun of justice. We stand in a similar danger, Origen insists: "For how can those who are crooked receive that which is straight? ... We ought, therefore, to hasten to straight ways and to stand fast in the paths of virtue, lest the Sun of Justice, who rises straight overhead, should find us crooked and turned aside, and looking askance at us, we should become black."[1] Such paths of virtue and vice do not, Origen thinks, exist outside the soul. Rather, they denote the soul's own internal processes of growth or degeneration. They are the soul's own form of life. What else does this mean except that in her infidelity to Christ, the Shulamite—as the primordially unchaste Bride of Christ—is, or rather was in some now-repented life, an ontological deviant. For Origen, the Bride was quite literally "queer" in her former lifestyle.

For the queer community, it should seem particularly apt that many Christian allegories associate the Shulamite's blackness with the disobedience of the Jews. In these readings, the Shulamite as "black" denotes the Jews as an intractable, disobedient people. As "beautiful," predictably, the Shulamite appears as the church, particularly the Gentile church, now redeemed from her particular waywardness. In this way, the phrase "black but beautiful" comes to denote two communities: a straight, righteous community of insiders and a deviant, intractable cluster of outsiders. For these allegories, the move from "black" to "beautiful" involves a conversion, a renunciation of an aberrant past.

In seeing something deviant or "queer" in the Shulamite, the Christian allegorical tradition proves its astuteness, for the Song of Songs does indeed portray her as sexually dangerous and socially "other." Yet, because this tradition sits ill at ease with the very notion of deviance, it construes the Shulamite's beauty as standing in tension with her blackness. This fact explains the Christian fathers' preference for the disjunctive rendering of the Hebrew phrase *sehorah 'ani ve-na'vah* as "black *but* beautiful." By insinuating such a contrariety into the relation between "black" and "beautiful," this interpretive tradition reinforces those dualisms that queer folk openly and vocally challenge—between sexuality and spirituality, between freedom and nature, between deviance and goodness, between outcast and insider.

Yet, in the more satisfactory reading of the verse, the Shulamite is "black and beautiful." Blackness and beauty appear as complements, not antagonistic qualities. Thus, what the classical allegories do not see, indeed what they labor to obscure, is the causal link established by the Song of Songs between the Shulamite's blackness and the Beloved's attraction to her. This "blackness," the most visible sign of her outsider status—her sexuality, freedom, and deviance—now becomes the most dazzling quality in her multifaceted beauty. The Song of Songs does not let the Shulamite's queerness vanish away into the consensus normality of the collective. It defends her "otherness" as a more sublime standard of perfection.

As a class underling or territorial alien, the Shulamite's social location as outsider makes her a prohibited object of the Beloved's erotic favor. Yet, the Beloved showers her with his passionate attention in spite of this prohibition. Indeed, he pursues her largely because of his attraction to the very feature that is the deepest sign of that prohibition. The Song of Songs, therefore, does not speak abstractly of passionate desire but of a specific sort of desire—a yearning and a pursuit whose object is not an insider but someone on the social margins, not a neighbor but the forbidden other. Thus, the romance of the Shulamite and the Beloved begins with the violation of a fixed social boundary. Their love affair, like that of all queer lovers, is essentially transgressive.

Indeed, so transgressive is the eros felt by the lovers that it propels them altogether beyond the ordinary routines of moral decision making. The Song of Songs does not portray the sexual trespasses of the Shulamite and Beloved merely as matters of individual preference. This is no "lifestyle choice" for the lovers. Why, then, do they risk the pursuit of a dangerous, socially explosive love affair? The answer is both simple and, for the Song's queer reader, manifest: *they are driven to it by the sheer desirableness of one other.*

With the Shulamite's lover, this erotic compulsion finds a poetic outlet in the language of inebriation and festal excess:

> I eat my honeycomb with my honey,
>   I drink my wine with my milk.
>
> Eat, friends, drink,
>   and be drunk with love. (5:1b)

This love not only fulfills beyond mere satisfaction. It entices the lover with its luxuriance, drawing him irresistibly into a drunken whirl.

The Shulamite, too, is tormented—but deliciously!—by a desire over which she has utterly no control:

> Upon my bed at night
>   I sought him whom my soul loves;
> I sought him, but found him not;
>   I called him, but he gave no answer.
> "I will rise now and go about the city,
>   in the streets and in the squares,
> I will seek him whom my soul loves."
>   I sought him, but found him not.
> The sentinels found me,
>   as they went about in the city.
> "Have you seen him whom my soul loves?"
> (3:1–3)

The Shulamite's longing eros for her Beloved brings on an acute delirium, a "fever" or "faint" (5:8) of lovesickness. It disturbs her sleep, drives her by night to the city streets, and leads her almost unwittingly into those dangerous brushes with the law (the "sentinels").

Standards, rationales, social norms, codes of conduct, and reflective moral reason—all these scatter before the heat of the lovers' desire like so many clouds in the noonday sun. Nowhere in the Song of Songs does the Shulamite or the Beloved seek out any external grounds or justifications for their love affair. Nor does the Song of Songs try to interpret their love affair in light of any such rationales. The lovers ask no questions of right and wrong. Even the classical pieties surrounding fecundity, procreation, and sexual duty to the family disappear from the Song of Songs (cf. vv. 1:6; 8:5, 12). In short, the lovers altogether transcend the limits of socially constructed "nature" (as *physis*—the "way things ought to be") in pursuit of a higher "nature" that is truer to the vision enlivened by their desire.

In the final analysis, the Song of Songs presents us with an insight already known and spoken out loud by queer folk: *Reciprocal desire is a law unto itself.* In the Song of Songs, neither "nature" nor gender can finally lay claim on the allegiance of truly well-ordered desire. Only a mutually beheld allure, an attractiveness that opens up the possibility of a coequal response between lovers, holds the last word in matters of love, sexuality, and human eros. Ultimately, then, eros—passionate yearning for union with the beauty of another—reigns supreme in the moral universe of the Song of Songs. When true to its own energy, eros requires no justification and needs make no defense for its movements.

## My Beloved Is Mine, and I Am His:
## Subversive Equality and Erotic Autonomy

The Song of Songs does not uniquely grace the Shulamite with beauty, nor is it only the Beloved who expresses a desire for union with such beauty. Rather, the fervent love of the Shulamite and her Beloved is fueled by a real parity of desire, an erotic symmetry arising from their reciprocal share in a loveliness that is irresistible. Each lover is, in other words, drawn to a "sameness"—an essential similarity—seen in the beauty, the sexiness, of the other. The dynamism might be heterosexual, but its structure is definitely homoerotic: *an attraction of sames*. By unveiling this "queer" dimension in the love life of the Shulamite and the Beloved, the Song of Songs not only champions the dignity of queer passion but upholds it as a model for any love worth pursuing.

The Song of Songs lets us witness this deep reciprocity, this "sameness," in the exchanges of the lovers themselves. The Shulamite, for example, says of her Beloved:

> Let him kiss me with the kisses of his mouth!
> For your love is better than wine, ...
> therefore the maidens love you....
>    rightly do they love you. (1:2–4)

> His appearance is like Lebanon,
>    choice as the cedars.
> His speech is most sweet,
>    and he is altogether desirable. (5:15b–16)

Concerning the Shulamite, we hear the Beloved say:

> If you do not know,
>    O fairest among women,
> follow the tracks of the flock
>    and pasture your kids
> beside the shepherds' tents. (1:8)

> You are beautiful as Tirzah, my love,
>    comely as Jerusalem,
>    terrible as an army with banners.

Turn away your eyes from me,
for they overwhelm me! (6:4–5a)

How fair and pleasant you are,
O loved one, delectable maiden! (7:6)

The mutual likeness of beauties is one of the emphatic themes of the Song of Songs. Each lover acknowledges the other's beauty to be all-surpassing. And each holds out this beauty as the deepest proof that the desire is legitimate.

This attraction is seen where the Beloved and the Shulamite, drawn in desire to one another's beauty, are caught up in an exchange of mutual adoration. The Song of Songs is largely a record of this dialectic, and it reaches a particularly brilliant visibility in passages such as these:

Ah, you are beautiful, my love;
ah, you are beautiful;
your eyes are doves.
Ah, you are beautiful, my beloved,
truly lovely. (1:15–16)

As a lily among the brambles,
so is my love among maidens.

As an apple tree among the trees of the wood,
so is my beloved among young men. (2:2–3)

In a circling dance of acclamation, the lovers declare their pleasure in one another's beauty. In this way, their mutual attraction flows like an alternating current from the fundamental "sameness" of their shared desirability. So intense, indeed, does this mutual perception of "sameness" become that the Shulamite and the Beloved begin to see one another as "brother" (8:1) and "sister" (4:9–12; 5:1–2), a recognition of a shared likeness that can be expressed only in metaphors of family resemblance.

Love and lovemaking in the Song of Songs, therefore, become a "union of sames." In this union, the lovers attain an experience of synergistic merging that heterosexist ontologies usually reserve for "opposites" alone, whether genital complements or gender polarities. Certainly, the Shulamite and the Beloved do not lose their identity as female and male, but the Song of Songs refuses to appropriate this difference as a category with any ultimate social, moral, or metaphysical significance. The text thus purifies their love affair of the hierarchicalism and differences of power typical of traditional relationships between men and women. And by implication, it levels the very basis for making moral distinctions between kinds of human love, desire, and sexual relation. The Song of Songs allows us to see that, morally speaking, queer love—precisely because it is love—is the "same" as heterosexual love.

It is not surprising, then, that the Song of Songs holds up as one of its preeminent values the coequality of erotic response. In the moral world of the Song of Songs, this equality seeks its principle in the lovers' erotic autonomy, in the power to choose to live sexually as one wills. We see this autonomy in the actions and words of both the Shulamite and the Beloved.

The Beloved reveals his autonomy through his freedom of movement, a constant coming and going that signifies his independence from confinement:

> The voice of my beloved!
>    Look, he comes,
> leaping upon the mountains,
>    bounding over the hills. (2:8)

This mode of autonomy is erotic inasmuch as it allows the Beloved to visit the Shulamite by night for secret trysts ("My beloved is like a gazelle / or a young stag. / Look, there he stands / behind our wall, / gazing in at the windows" [2:9]) or to withdraw from her so as to tantalize her sexually ("I opened to my beloved, / but my beloved had turned and was gone. / My soul failed me" [5:6]).

The Shulamite, by contrast, does not enjoy this same physical liberty; she is kept at home behind walls, curtains, and lattices (2:9) and forced to tend the family vineyards (1:6). Nevertheless, she maintains a stance of inner liberty, laying bold claim to free erotic agency:

> Solomon had a vineyard at Baal-hamon;
>    he entrusted the vineyard to keepers;
>    each one was to bring for its fruit a thousand pieces of silver.
> My vineyard, my very own, is for myself;
>    you, O Solomon, may have the thousand,
>    and the keepers of the fruit two hundred! (8:11–12)

In Solomon's vineyard, the Shulamite finds a symbol of her own fecund sexuality. Yet, whereas Solomon disposes of his vineyard and its fruits as his own property, the Shulamite asserts exclusive rights to her sexual energy. Her "vineyard" with its fruits is her "very own," for herself. The Shulamite, in other words, will not allow the reader to regard her as another's sexual possession or as a mere vessel for procreation. She is, by her own strength of resolve, free to love as she chooses—free to love as she is compelled by the innate directives of her own passion.

To follow the example of the Shulamite is fundamentally a "queer" choice, for she cheerfully disregards any extrinsic norm whereby her choice to love as she pleases might be condemned. The Shulamite fearlessly and joyfully proclaims her erotic autonomy and her freedom from procreative mandates.

In so doing, the Shulamite holds out a liberating message not only for women but especially for the queer community. It is a simple message that is, nevertheless, difficult for sexism of any kind to assimilate: *When moved by reciprocal desire, men and women have the right to love as they will, whom they will, when they will, and how they will.* A more revolutionary word of sexual freedom could scarcely be spoken, yet here we find it exemplified in a sacred text that, with respect to its mystical value, lies at the heart of the biblical canon.

The erotic autonomy of the Shulamite and the Beloved does not restrict their capacity to relate to each other unselfishly. On the contrary, it enables them to recognize and freely to pursue the mandate latent in their desire for one another. It makes possible a genuine self-offering in which each belongs fully to the other:

> My beloved is mine and I am his;
> he pastures his flock among the lilies. (2:16)

> I am my beloved's and my beloved is mine;
> he pastures his flock among the lilies (6:3)

Notice the pure reciprocity in these two passages. No hierarchy or asymmetry of power can be inferred from them. If the Shulamite had said only, "I am my beloved's and my beloved is mine," some superiority in the status of the Beloved could be inferred from her word order. Yet, the Shulamite has already underscored her own prior possession of the Beloved: "My beloved is mine and I am his." Each owns the other in precisely the same degree and proportion, in accordance with their ability to honor one another's personal autonomy and erotic freedom.

The lovers' mutual exchange of desires, then, becomes a mutual gift of self-hood. Not only do the Shulamite and the Beloved give themselves to one another without holding back; they also each receive their own new and truest identity from the other's gift of desire: "I am my beloved's, / and his desire is for me" (7:10). Who does the Shulamite declare herself to be? She is her beloved's. In other words, she experiences the Beloved's desire as an activity *pro me*, an erotic grace-gift in which her new identity comes into being. The Song of Songs, therefore, presumes an etiology of the human self in which true identity grows, not from obedience to ironclad laws of natural morality, but from pursuit of one's profoundest desire for union with another.

The Song of Songs knows the queer truth that love, desire, and sexual life are given for the full blossoming of human persons, their growth unfolding in and through soul-and-body union with others whose likeness—"sameness"—they also bear. And the integrity of the developmental process, so the Song of Songs implies, depends upon all persons having the fullest

freedom to follow eros where it leads, for only unconditional erotic autonomy makes true and complete self-offering possible in the first place. It is
this liberty to love as one wills that queer people of faith must finally claim
as a fundamental principle of human well-being and, truly, of salvation itself.
With justification, then, queer men and women of faith may take heart that
the Song of Songs so completely sanctions the vision of human self-hood
and relationship implicit in queer desire itself.

## To My Mother's House: Social Oppression and the Struggle for Reconciliation

In their relation to each other, the lovers are "same," not "opposites" in
polar complementarity. They have voluntarily surrendered any differences
of power or status that might inhibit their union. Yet, paradoxically, in the
course of eschewing difference, they have made themselves "different"—
deviant—in the public eye. Pursuing a vision of equality in desire and
reciprocal self-offering, they have made themselves vulnerable to exclusion
as outsiders, as "queers." Like queer folk of today and every age, then, the
two lovers in the Song of Songs do not enjoy the benefits of public, cultural, or social sanction. On the contrary, their love is expressly forbidden
and opposed by the custodians of the social economy.

Three representatives of this public economy dominate the social universe of the Song of Songs: the city sentinels, the Shulamite's brothers, and
her mother. Each of these parties has its own reasons for disapproving of
the love affair that the Song of Songs praises as exemplary. For these civil
and familial powers, the public fictions of purity, property, and filial duty
hold greater authority than the truth articulated in the passion of lovers.
We shall examine these in turn, for each illuminates the oppression that
queer women and men face today. And in the responses of the Shulamite
and her Beloved, we find an appropriate pattern for queer response.

On the fringes of the Shulamite's social experience are certain "sentinels," night watchmen whose violence she will suffer and survive. She first
encounters these men as she roams the streets, deliriously seeking her lover
(3:1–3). When the Shulamite first describes this meeting, she innocuously
remarks that the sentinels merely "found" her. Later, though, she reveals
the more violent truth behind her euphemism:

> Making their rounds in the city,
>     the sentinels found me;
> they beat me, they wounded me,
>     they took away my mantle
>     those sentinels of the walls. (5:7)

The very men who ought to protect the Shulamite have savagely attacked her. Not only have they thrashed, bruised, and perhaps raped her, they have also stolen her outer garment, exposing her body to the physical elements and, more seriously, unveiling her shame to the elemental forces of public scorn.

But what accounts for such enormous brutality? Presumably, the sentinels have mistaken the Shulamite for a prostitute, walking the streets in search of a john. She is thus marked as a sexual outlaw and so becomes a target of the law's enforcers. Acting as guardians of public decency, then, the sentinels find in the Shulamite a fitting victim for a violence that, so the text implies, is itself sexually charged. In this way, the Shulamite becomes a scapegoat for the sexual hypocrisies of the "city" that the sentinels police; their ruthlessness merely brings to fruition the germinal envy that we have already felt simmering beneath the Jerusalem daughters' "gaze."

In the Shulamite's experience of victimization, we can find an almost exact correlate of the queer experience of "bashing," for the queer community is truly a "peculiar people," a tribe of sexual outlaws. Its members, consequently, in so many ways suffer the wrath of the collective towards those whose sexual identity it simultaneously vilifies and envies. This wrath takes its most explicit form in acts of verbal abuse and physical violence—taunts, threats, beatings, killings—but it is also endemic to the structures of heterosexist society itself. All this brutality is most often unleashed upon queer people when, like the Shulamite, we dare to reveal our sexual selves, our queer desire, in public places, on the "streets," inside the city "walls."

Queer folk must remember that by taking the Shulamite's side in these struggles with violence, the Song of Songs also condemns the agents of violence. Heterosexism with its fear, rage, and wrath will not find any justification in the Song of Songs. The Shulamite's response to this violence, moreover, is a model for the queer reader. Rather than suppressing her own voice or internalizing the shame that her attackers try to heap upon her, the Shulamite speaks her outrage "out loud." Through the Song of Songs itself, she tells every reader the truth about her mistreatment. The Shulamite never loses heart, never ceases to persist. And in spite of all her suffering, she continues to pursue her love with confidence in its perfect justice (3:4; 5:8).

If the Shulamite must endure the grave brutality of the sentinels, she must also cope with the anger of her brothers, her "mother's sons." The Shulamite's brothers are angry with their sister because she claims sole property rights over her sexual "vineyard." But her brothers do not acknowledge her prerogative:

> My mother's sons were angry with me;
> they made me keeper of the vineyards,
> but my own vineyard I have not kept! (1:6b)

The Shulamite sets the family vineyards, which she has faithfully cultivated, in ironic counterpoint to her sexual "vineyard." The family property—that she will tend well and true, but, she declares, she would rather risk incurring her brothers' anger than lose her rights over her own erotic property. Her tone is teasing, but her sense is deeply serious.

Where the Shulamite and Beloved see their love affair as a shared feast of bodies, of beauties, and of desires, the "brothers" perceive it only as a violation of the family's stake in the body and the fertility of the Shulamite. Thus, they are angry because she has not "kept" her sexual property to herself. She has offered it freely to her Beloved, in keeping with the parity of erotic power that each acknowledges in the other. Once the brothers know of this, their imagination runs wild:

> Catch us the foxes,
>     the little foxes,
> that ruin the vineyards—
> for our vineyards are in blossom. (2:15)

These "foxes" are the many lovers that the brothers fear have ruined the Shulamite's virtue and, more centrally, her value as a family commodity. The brother's anxiety is as palpable as their avidity.

The reader, of course, knows that the Shulamite is possessed by a single-minded fidelity to her Beloved. Yet, the brothers cannot conceive of a sexual liberty that is not also fundamentally promiscuous. Their response to the Shulamite's misbehavior is predictably restrictive:

> If she is a wall,
>     we will build upon her a battlement of silver;
> but if she is a door,
>     we will enclose her with boards of cedar. (8:9)

Had the Shulamite acted as a "wall" in defense of her virtue (and their interests!), the brothers would have honored and dignified her, though their honor sounds more like pedestalizing, their "battlement of silver" more like a gilded cage. Yet, they now fear that she has become a "door," opening to all comers. Their solution to this apparent problem is to "enclose" their sister "with boards of cedar." They intend, in other words, to confine her in ways that will restrict her freedom to love as she chooses.

In the interaction between the Shulamite and her brothers, queer readers will find a mirror of their own experience. The "brothers" reflect the image of all those social and cultural forces that would subdue human eros to their own interests—whether social stability, economic security, or the continuity of family lines. Queer women and men, however, have renounced the myth that these interests are ultimately compelling. We have, in fact, abandoned the very notion that eros needs to be subdued at all. It is a move that not only opens us to charges of promiscuity but that also makes us vulnerable to those regimes of control (e.g., repressive laws and customs, shame-inducing mores) put into place by those whose interests we threaten.

Finally, at the center of the social universe of the Song of Songs is the mother of the Shulamite. Throughout the Song of Songs, the Shulamite hints at her estrangement from her mother. At first, for example, she can only dream of taking her Beloved home and finding parental welcome there:

> I would lead you and bring you
> into the house of my mother,
> and into the chamber of the one who bore me. (8:2)

The Shulamite even fantasizes of having the mother's permission to share the same bed with the partner that the Shulamite herself has chosen. It is an intimate desire felt today by many queer men and women, who too often know the pain of hearing words of rejection—"Not under my roof!"

The "mother," the "mother's house," and the "mother's breast" all embody the parental blessing, the domestic security and bliss, that the Shulamite has put at risk by pursuing an illicit love affair. But why should the Shulamite fear her mother's rejection? It is because the mother prizes her daughter's purity. She is attached to it as to an ideal:

> My dove, my perfect one, is the only one,
> the darling of her mother,
> flawless to her that bore her. (6:9a)

The Beloved recognizes here that his "perfect one" (the Shulamite) is also her mother's flawless darling. She is perfect and pure to each: to the mother, because she is domestic and chaste; to the Beloved, because she is sexually desirable, available, and wild.

These two sets of reasons, however, simply cannot be reconciled. For the Beloved, the Shulamite's perfection consists precisely in the ready sexuality that, for her mother, is incompatible with the purity of a dutiful daughter. Were the mother to learn the truth about the nature of the Shulamite's desire for her Beloved—and certainly of their sexual trysts—she could never again view her daughter in the same way. "Coming out," as it were, would shatter the mother's pristine image of the Shulamite. The mother would then face a choice that the Shulamite fears; she may either reject her daughter, or she may adjust her own values and accept a new and more truthful image of her daughter.

The Shulamite presents to queer folk a model of persistence, boldness, and endurance in seeking out her love. Yet, even though she spurns and defies all social restrictions upon the free pursuit of her love, she does not

remain locked into a fixed gesture of rebellion. On the contrary, she longs
to return in reconciliation to her mother's house, hand in hand with her
beloved:

> O that you were like a brother to me,
>     who nursed at my mother's breast!
> If I met you outside, I would kiss you,
>     and no one would despise me.
> I would lead you and bring you
>     into the house of my mother,
>     and into the chamber of the one who bore me.
>                             (8:1–2a)

Given the Shulamite's social matrix and family ties, public intimacy with
her lover would make her an object of derision. Were her Beloved only
a "brother"—a kinsman with whom she may freely associate—she could
meet him in the streets, kiss him, and take him home to her mother. Their
degree of kinship would, of course, make an erotic love life untenable, but
the Shulamite's dream of public acceptance and domestic reconciliation
briefly overshadows such considerations.

At first glance, the Shulamite might appear merely to be indulging in
wishful thinking here. She shows no clear determination to pursue a definite
plan of action. But, earlier in the text—at a point that actually speaks of a
later event—we discover that the Shulamite does, at last, find the courage
to bring her Beloved home:

> Scarcely had I passed them [the sentinels],
>     when I found him whom my soul loves.
> I held him, and would not let him go
>     until I brought him into my mother's house,
>     and into the chamber of her that conceived me.
>                             (3:4)

The Shulamite's hope, then, is to win from her mother (and perhaps from
her estranged brothers, her "mother's sons") the gift of acceptance and
reconciliation. She acts boldly to fulfill her hope. Surviving the violence of
the sentinels, she lays hold not only upon her courage but also upon the
Beloved himself, leading him—against his will?—to her mother's house.

In the "mother," queer folk will see the face of all those persons and
communities—loved ones, parents, churches—whose accepting embrace we
long for and whose rejection we dread. Queer men and women know well
how painful and embittering it can be to suffer rejection by parents or by
whole communities of faith. Equally, with the Shulamite, we know how
intense can be the urgency for the "mother's" full acceptance, for full ad-

mission to the households of faith and family. The Song of Songs develops a realistic portrayal of such rejection, of such pain, and of such urgency for acceptance. And to queer readers especially, it offers a paradigm for a fearless and truthful ministry of reconciliation towards all those "mothers" whose love does not yet know how to comprehend our desire.

This discussion has only begun to explore the positive implications of the Song of Songs for queer women and men. True, the Song of Songs celebrates the love, desire, and sexual life of a man and a woman. Yet, it praises it for reasons that ought to prove deeply challenging to anyone who hopes to find in it any support for heterosexist mores, for through the words and examples of its characters, the Song of Songs sustains a moral worldview in which:

The sexual and social outlaw is a preferred object of loving desire and sexual interest.

Beauty alone is a sufficient motive for love, desire, and sexual union.

All persons have the right to love as they will according to the dictates of reciprocal desire.

An ethic of intimacy, rather than gender complementarity, ought to be central in human love relationships.

Authentic eros must be grounded in a certain homoeroticism, an attraction of "sames."

The human person is essentially erotic in nature.

Love and sexual life are most perfectly expressed in love between fully equal partners and in fully mutual self-offering of body and soul.

Persecution or oppression of the sexual outlaw is unjust and morally wrong.

The sexually marginalized person has a responsibility to work courageously and persistently for justice, tolerance, and acceptance.

The astonishing fact that the Song of Songs celebrates socially transgressive eros ought already to secure its status as a valuable biblical apologetic for queer identity. But more than this, the Song of Songs exalts a love that, like the love of queer women and men, presumes not only the inherent worth of human desire but also its moral sufficiency as a motive for the fullest union of life between human beings. Such love will, inevitably, cause social friction and discord. These difficulties, however, arise not because queer eros is inherently unjust. On the contrary, they arise because it is so acutely just that it calls the social constructions of nature, culture, and law to a painful but healing crisis.

The Song of Songs sets this eros as our ideal—a passionate love that prefers the outsider, that is entranced by sexual difference, that answers the call of beauty without vacillation, and that honors the authority of its own strength. Knowing this, queer folk have every reason to take up the Song of Songs with confidence that it affirms our own ways of loving, desiring, and bonding sexually with others. Indeed, we have every cause to take up the Song of Songs as a banner of our love, which is truly as fierce as death.

## Note

1. Origen *Commentary on the Song of Songs* 2.2.

## 13

# Insider Out

## Unmasking the Abusing God

### DAWN ROBINSON ROSE

*Battered women, rape victims, incest survivors, and others have suffered from abusing images of God. From many religious traditions, women have rejected the violent, patriarchal images of God. Dawn Robinson Rose wrestles with the Hebrew images of an abusive God who pornographically punishes the whore. She reads the pornographic texts of terror against a backdrop of her own familial experience of male violence. Like many battered women, Rose asks, If God is justice, where is God? Rabbi Rose expresses a grassroots theology of resistance and suspicion that many women and queers have of scriptural texts of terror. She finds God, not in the abusive images of the punisher of infidelity, but in personal intervention that breaks the cycle of violence.*

When my beloved slipped his hand through the latch-holes,
  my bowels stirred within me.
When I arose for my beloved,
  my hands dripped with myrrh;
  the liquid myrrh from fingers
  over the nobs of the bolt.
With my own hands I opened to my love.

(Song of Songs 5:4–6)

These are the words of the Lord God: You have been prodigal in your excesses, you have exposed your naked body in fornication with your lovers. . . . I will gather all those lovers to whom you made advances, all whom you loved and all whom you hated. . . . I will strip you naked before them. . . . I will hand you over to them. . . . They will bring up the mob against you and stone you, they will hack you to pieces with their swords. . . . Then I will abate my fury, my jealousy will turn away from You. I will be calm. . . . This is the word of the Lord. (Ezek. 16:35–43)

I will betroth you unto me forever. I will betroth you to me in righteousness and in justice and in loving kindness; I will betroth you in faithfulness; and you will know the Lord. (Hos. 2:21–22)[1]

All the time we were growing up, we kids were always aware of the imminent possibility of violence in the household.[2]

In Torah, Talmud (rabbinic writings), and kabbalah (Jewish mysticism), the relationship between God and Israel is frequently—even exquisitely—described as a marriage between husband and wife. However, in the androgynous verses of the Song of Songs notwithstanding, this biblical marriage between God and Israel was never one between equals. The theology of the Torah on this matter is straightforward: God was the master and Israel the wife; God was the Lord and Israel the vassal. The contract in simple terms was as follows: as long as Israel stayed faithful to her one God and fulfilled his commands, her villages would know peace, her grapes would grow round, and her children would be many and healthy. Should she stray, however, her jealous God would punish her by ways too horrible to speak aloud.[3] In Torahitic theology, nearly all evil events that befall Israel are thus interpreted from this cosmic worldview.

It is in the prophets after the fall of Israel that the marriage theology reaches its most graphic and violent manifestation. After all, according to the covenant, who is to blame for Israel's demise? If Israel is a wife, her sins are a wife's sins, and her punishment is in kind. The prophets do not hold back from painting the pornographic pictures of rape and abuse. Beginning with Hosea, Israel is depicted as a whore-wife who must be punished by the exposure of her genitals to her lovers.[4] Similarly, Isaiah uses such violation imagery, which begins with the focus on the actual "haughty" daughters of Zion and shifts to Zion herself, for their flagrant display of sexuality will bald their heads and bare their cunts.[5] Jeremiah, too, likens the fallen Jerusalem to an adulterous wife whose genitals are subsequently uncovered and treated with violence.[6] As J. Cheryl Exum points out, the metaphor of sexual infidelity and punishment reaches its apotheosis in Ezekiel 16.[7] Because Israel has fornicated with foreign lovers, she will be cast down, her genitals exposed. Only after she is violated, stoned, and hacked into pieces will her jealous master be appeased. One can only wonder at the extremities involved—both in terms of the actual retribution deemed necessary and in the graphic description of that retribution.

The metaphor as it stands treats Israel as a corporate (and highly corporeal) female entity. Speaking to the people as a unity, it demands the reader response of identification with the whoring woman, as Fokkelien van Dijk-Hemmes explains:

YHWH's speech to Ezekiel transforms the people of Israel and thus the target audience, males and—at least indirectly—also females, into his metaphorical wives.... The audience is forced into seeing the shameless stupidity of their religious and political behavior and the absolute hopelessness of their situation. The androcentric-pornographic character of this metaphorical language must indeed be experienced as extremely humiliating by an M (male) audience forced to imagine itself exposed to violating enemies.[8]

However, the use of the wife-metaphor also allows for certain interesting gender-specific reader dynamics that offer a radical transformation of the relational matrix: "It is exactly these androcentric-pornographic characters that at the same time offers the M audience a possibility of escape; or, more modestly, identification with the wronged and revengeful husband."[9]

Because (according to biblical understanding) both the characters in the metaphor and the readers divide into two sexes, there is still room for movement and reidentification for at least one sex. Males, initially humiliated by the feminine role (which they are forced into for reasons of transgression and punishment), can also move past this initial identification to join with the male God. (Note the insidious nature of a text that demands reader identification—but only provides one of two horrible options!) From punished whore, male readers may elevate to husband (God), most likely their "role" in the real world anyway. From there is barely a leap of the imagination to take on the role of the cuckolded husband whose righteous anger has empowered to (ab)use the offending wifely property until his anger is abated. Note how, in these actions, they become righteous "like God."

Feminist readers, such as Gracia Fay Ellwood, have found in this kind of biblical metaphor a justification for sexual abuse in marriage.[10] Indeed, the order of events is disconcertingly similar to what we know to be typical of domestic violence: jealousy erupting into an ever escalating violence until, satiated, the husband becomes calm, even conciliatory.[11] (The congruity between actual profiles of wife-beating dynamics and such biblical passages causes one to suspect the phenomena was present in the culture long before the metaphor.)

A central question here arises: If the male can escape the abusive sexual punishment by male identification with the righteously angry God, what can women do? At first glance, nothing! Trapped by gender specificity female readers are either Israel—sinful through our infidelity and liable for punishment—or we are women with the same message communicated once again: we are whores; we require punishment. As with the role of the husband, the message to the wife is not only theological; it is also personal:

As a child, I watched my father batter my mother. My father was a well-respected contractor and businessman around town. Privately, my mother went to the leaders of the community, religious and secular, for help. Alike they counseled her to bend to her husband's will. "Just don't get him angry," they said. "You must be doing something wrong." One might say we lived according to the prophet's Torah, day after day, night after night.[12]

While gendered reading of Ezekiel 16 has thus far uncovered a sinister dynamic of identification, transidentification, and divine role modeling for domestic abuse, I think a reading specific to a Jewish lesbian standpoint offers a revolutionary interpretation. In order to get at that interpretation, two basic questions must be explored: Who is a Jewish lesbian in relation to this text? And where am I (as a Jewish lesbian) within this text?

First, the fact that I am a Jew and not another religion or ethnicity is of manifest importance to my reader stance in this passage. Historically, the imagery of destruction, female violation, and rape has visceral significance for any and all Jews. The fact that mass violence by Nazis and Cossacks was accompanied by female violation and rape is well documented. Whether Roman occupation, Muslim jihad, Christian Crusades, Inquisition and Expulsion, in no way can we assume that the preceding millennia of violence and exile lacked sexual violation as well. Just as all women are liable to be violated and raped by conquering armies or slaveowners expressing their mastery, so are Jewish women. As a Jewish woman, I do not and cannot escape history. Some day I could be raped as a hate crime against my people. Whether or not God sent those conquering armies, the women of defeated Israel were raped just the same:

> (My genitals have been the object of such a sadistic display
> they keep me constantly away with the pain....
> Do whatever you can to survive
> You know, I think that men love wars....)[13]

Neither do I escape sexual abuse as woman qua woman. As are all women (and men), I am susceptible to rape as a hate crime against women, as two out of five have been.[14] And yet, despite all my vulnerabilities, I can posit that I am not in, but rather next to, that deadly relational matrix between husband and wife. A Jew and a lesbian, I am an *insider outside*.

First, I am inside and not apart from the violence as might be a Christian. Indeed, a Christian can, as many have, look upon these passage as evidence of Israel's infidelity in the face of Jesus' authenticity. They can say in regard to the problematic God of the Old Testament: "That was them over there; they were punished for their sins. Now we have a new covenant. Our God does not look like this." For a Jewish lesbian, there is no such escape. This abuse is of my people, even within my community and by our God. The relationship is ethnically, historically, and religiously specific.

As an insider, then, because these are my people and this is "my God," I am yet outside because, as a lesbian, I have no need to accept the inevitability of what Rebecca Alpert has so aptly named "male-female complementarity."[15] I do not assume women need men and men need women. Whatever that dance of violence and reconciliation and more violence that goes on before me, I have no "role." I neither lead nor follow.

I do not engage in heterosexual relationships. I am not dependent upon and have no reason to be in close proximity to that abusing male. Once struck, as long as I am an adult, I have no reason to stay. Reconciliation is not necessary if I choose otherwise. If I am a child, I have only years between me and escape from the cycle of violence. A Jewish lesbian stands outside the heterosexual matrix. From that position, I identify neither with the abusive God nor the abused whore-wife. Either I know this God of Israel is not worth my fidelity, or this is not God.

Just as a Jew may see through the façade of history saying that Israel has indeed been punished but refusing the interpretation that says it was for our sins—so also the lesbian Jew, watching heterosexual abuse, can see through the rhetoric, rejecting any suggestion that the woman deserved her treatment. I can say "That man is no god." The metaphor is unmasked as just that—a literary trope written by a man apparently steeped in cultural misogyny.

My position in the text then is one of rejection—not of the fact of punishment but at the intimation of justice therein. Israel no more deserved the Holocaust than women deserved rape. Any woman no more deserves rape than Israel the Holocaust. (That is a stunningly different statement than "That is them being punished. Now we have a new covenant.")

If I deny the intimation of justice, then I must also deny either (1) that God is just or (2) that this beast is God. Having identified this literary trope as just that—a metaphor created by a misogynist—then I must go with the latter: this beast is not God. This leaves me with a great question: Where is God in this picture? Where indeed!

If God is justice, I cannot find God in this picture—that is, not until I, or someone else, enters. God is nowhere until intervention. Thus, in a Jewish lesbian reading, the text is completely subverted, turned on its side. Read from a heterosexual reading stance, the perspective is that of an infidel nation, an unfaithful wife-become-whore. God is the active agent, entering with righteous anger to punish and chasten. The reader is asked to listen and be warned and educated—perhaps to mend her ways. Read from a lesbian Jewish stance, however, the scene is archetypical domestic violence, requiring a third party, an active agent, first to witness, then to intervene. God is the name/love/justice I invoke when I intervene between the abused woman and the false god. It is an anti-institutional God, a rebellious God, an antiauthoritarian God who guides my days and guards my nights as I live in my place on the margin of the page:

> Once as my mother lay on the floor her eye already blackening from a blow she screamed for me. I ran out of my bedroom, and, shaking horribly from fear, interposed my body between her and my father who stood raging above her. We stood there, our eyes locked in stare. And then he walked away.[16]

A lesbian who is able to recognize that "that beast is not God" need not be fooled by other phony metaphors for God and/or God's justice either. We have, by the evidence of our lives, been forced into positions of constant critique and suspicion. When the rabbi says, "This is the Torah, the laws God gave the Jews," I can already stand apart. Insider outside, I have no more reason to believe the prohibition against homosexuality than I do the justice of rape.

This posture of radical freedom might well be included in what Judith Plaskow identified as the "hermeneutics of suspicion."[17] It is also similar to the antiauthoritarian position of the adult survivor of abuse whose epistolary correspondence with Jewish theologian David Blumenthal forms a stunning focal point to *Facing the Abusing God: A Theology of Protest.* Here, the connection between God's omnipotence and the husband/father's power comes overtly from the other direction. Because her powerful, authoritative father was abusive, all power and all authority carry with them the possibility, even the inevitability, of abuse: "Authority, to me, is by definition nonbenevolent. For years I have resisted the concept of an omnipotent God because I knew that omnipotence carried with it abuse and that I would be abused."[18] Accepting the notion of an all-powerful transcendent God requires some sort of theological and personal reconciliation between abuser and abused. Rejecting that definition of God, however, leads to a new God fashioned out of intervention and action.

This is not all that a Jewish lesbian reading of the text offers. Pushing the imagery further, we find these instances of divinely inspired rape are presented as punishment in kind. The sins of Israel, having been depicted as sexual, are punished sexually. As J. Cheryl Exum explains: "In our prophetic examples, sin is identified with female sexuality, and specifically, with uncontrolled or unrestrained female sexuality.... Male control, then, is seen as necessary and desirable, and sexual abuse becomes justified as a means of correction. To make matters worse, physical assault paves the way for the abused women's reconciliation with her abusive spouse."[19]

Insiders outside, Jewish lesbians grapple with the issue of sexuality as sinful. Two primary responses may be traced throughout Jewish lesbian literature. One is beautifully expressed by Adrienne Rich:

> Your traveled, generous thighs
> between which my whole face has come and come—
> the innocence and wisdom of the place my tongue has found there—
> the live, insatiate dance of nipples in your mouth—
> your touch on me, firm, protective, searching
> me out, your strong tongue and slender fingers
> reaching where I had been waiting years for you in my
> rose wet-cave—whatever happens, this is.[20]

Although in a previously cited poem, Rich spoke of the violation of her genitalia, there appears to be no remembrance of that violence here, until you contrast the vocabulary used. "Generous," "innocence," "wisdom," and "protective"—these are the words she applies to lovemaking alongside other words like "firm" and "strong." Heterosexual sex, for Rich, is associated with violence and war. Lesbian sex not only lacks that association but actually provides healing and protection. In theological terms, then, sex associated with males equals evil and that with women signifies actual spiritual, emotional, and physical redemption.

Another response in Jewish lesbian literature is graphically illustrated by Jyl Lynn Felman in an essay in which she explores the dynamics behind her writing:

> Lurking in the background of every scene I write is a sense of the forbidden. The fact that my characters behave in ways that are politically incorrect and that my subject matter is often taboo in both the Jewish and lesbian universe can be traced to my sisters' unnatural cravings for shellfish. But what makes my stories lesbian with the emphasis on Jewish is the fact that my characters don't just imagine what eating pussy is like, they actually eat it. And eating pussy for me is just like eating treyf.[21]

Here, Felman celebrates the so-called sinfulness of lesbian sexuality as a culturally specific act of liberation. Those very religious doctrines that seek to restrain her appetite(s) are the object of her artful satire, expressed both in her art and in her very lesbian life.

It is important to note that in neither case (Rich's nor Felman's), particularly not in the case where the sinful or unkosher aspect of lesbian sexuality is embraced, does the internalization of sexuality as evil-requiring-punishment appear. Lesbians are told by most of society that their form of sexuality is "wrong," "sinful," or "perverse." Without positing that no Jewish lesbian has internalized self-hatred for her sexuality, we must recognize that lesbians, to survive the heterosexist cultural onslaught, must see through misogynist mythology surrounding female sexuality. Therefore when such propaganda is presented to me in a text, I, as a mature Jewish lesbian reader, already see through it. Just as I know my love is not "sinful," so do I understand this woman's lust cannot be sinful either. The justice myth that requires violent female sexual suppression is undone once again. This reconciliation is no reconciliation at all. Moreover and assuredly, "male control" is in no way desirable.

If we enhance the above context with the aspect of sexuality, we find the sexual woman, unrestrained, out of control, to placate the patriarchal rage and restore the natural heterosexual unit headed by the male. As a lesbian standing outside this text with my own sexuality—unrestrained by man yet hardly raging out of control—I have many things in common with this woman. We are, for one, both women. Our sexuality is considered by the same institutions to be sinful. From my life on the margins, I know our sexuality is not. However, for the Jew there may be another dimension altogether. I may more than identify with this woman qua woman and her sexuality qua female sexuality, with the attendant impulses to intervene and save her. I may in fact love this woman, yearning to express this love as a lover might. My interest in the story then changes. I become as a rival suitor, offering in my mind the kind of lovemaking I hope would heal. My intervention, informed by experience, is thus tinged by a form of self-interest. A lover's narcissism, in her do I see again myself? With the appropriate maturity, I understand the situation may require the most absolute chastity—few women running from abuse need the pressure of seduction from yet another quarter. By assisting the abused woman, I enact again the rebellion-towards-freedom/justice by which I freed myself. In offering my intervention, assistance, and love, however chastely, I express my sexuality once again—and because it is justice making, I can call that very sexuality God also.

In intervening on the part of other women, by being available as a place to run, a lesbian frees herself again and again. In saving other women, some of us save our mothers and sisters as well. In rebellion we find our God and our lives:

> When my older sister began dating, she showed a marked preference
> for hard drinking men who shouted and talked with their fists. She
> has been battered one way or another all her life. Insider outside,
> I preferred no man. I escaped my family and with it the cycle of
> violence.[22]

I found my God in the radical freedom it took to stand outside the cycle of violence. I bring my God into the world when I stand, insider outside, saying and acting, "No more."

> Late at night, my lover lies awake and dreams of raising many children. By her side I dream of raising again my sister. It would be bringing God into the world. Who was it that said, "On matters of God and justice you can't fool a Jewish lesbian? (Answer: It must have been me.)[23]

## Notes

1. This verse from Hosea is used during the laying on of *t'fillin* or phylacteries, signifying again the "marriage" of the individual Jew to God during prayer and/or study.

2. Dawn Robinson Rose, unpublished manuscript.

3. The above portion of curses are whispered.

4. Hosea 2:3

5. Isaiah 57:16–17.

6. Jeremiah 13:22.

7. J. Cheryl Exum, *Plotted, Shot, and Painted: Cultural Representations of Biblical Women*, Journal for the Study of the Old Testament, Supplement Series 215 (Sheffield: Sheffield Academic Press, 1996), 108.

8. Athalya Brenner and Fokkelien van Dijk-Hemmes, *On Gendering Texts: Female and Male Voices in the Hebrew Bible* (Leiden: E. J. Brill, 1993), 175–76.

9. Ibid.

10. Gracia Fay Ellwood, *Better My Heart*, Pamphlet 282 (Wallingford, Pa.: Pendle Hill, 1988).

11. See Lenore Walker, *The Battered Woman* (New York: Harper and Row, 1962), 36, 177; and Roger Langley and Richard Levy, *Wife Beating* (New York: Dutton, 1977), 55, 91.

12. Rose, unpublished manuscript.

13. Adrienne Rich, "I Come Home from You," in *The Dream of a Common Language* (New York: Norton, 1993), 27.

14. "A random sample of nearly a thousand women in San Francisco found that 44 percent has been subjected to rape or attempted rape at least once in their lives. Only 11 percent of these victims were assaulted by strangers; adjusted for multiple attacks, only 6 percent of the total numbers of the assaults were perpetuated by strangers. The majority of assailants were husbands or ex-husbands, friends, dates, boyfriends, acquaintances, lovers or ex-lovers, or authority figures." See Barbara Chester, "The Statistics about Sexual Violence," in *Sexual Assault and Abuse: A Handbook for Clergy and Religious Professionals*, ed. Mary D. Pellauer, Barbara Chester, and Jane Boyajian (San Francisco: Harper, 1983), 12.

15. Rebecca Alpert, "Challenging Male/Female Complementarity: Jewish Lesbians and the Jewish Tradition," in *People of the Body: Jews and Judaism from an Embodied Perspective*, ed. Howard Eilberg-Schwartz (Albany: SUNY Press, 1992), 361–77.

16. Rose, unpublished manuscript.

17. Judith Plaskow, *Standing Again at Sinai* (San Francisco: Harper and Row, 1989), 13–18.

18. David R. Blumenthal, *Facing the Abusing God: A Theology of Protest* (Louisville: Westminster Press, 1993).

19. Exum, *Plotted, Shot, and Painted*, 114.

20. Adrienne Rich, "The Floating Poem, Unnumbered," in *The Dream of a Common Language* (New York: Norton, 1978), 32.

21. Shellfish is forbidden to Jews by Jewish dietary laws. *Treyf* is the word for food forbidden by Jewish dietary law. Jyl Lynn Felman, "The Forbidden: or What Makes Me a Jewish Writer," *Hot Chicken Wings* (San Francisco: Aunt Lute Books, 1992), ii–iii.

22. Rose, unpublished manuscript.

23. Ibid.

# 14

# Ezekiel Understands AIDS

## AIDS Understands Ezekiel,
## or Reading the Bible with HIV

### JIM MITULSKI

*In the Castro at the height of the AIDS pandemic, the Metropolitan Community Church of San Francisco was the church at the center of a maelstrom. It was a place where many churched and unchurched gay men dying with AIDS found a home. There were years when Jim Mitulski, the senior pastor, celebrated over five hundred funerals. For several years, he read Ezekiel's vision about the resurrection of dry bones as a metaphor for his pastoral experience and his own HIV experience, expressing a vision of a post-AIDS era. In Dry Bones Breathe, author Eric Rofes acknowledges Jim Mitulski and likewise develops the metaphor of the dry bones for the changes sweeping a post-AIDS gay community.[1] Like a modern-day Ezekiel, Mitulski envisions a spirit of revival in this resurrection of the gay community but prophetically challenges the churches who will bury gay men but not marry them.*

In the thirtieth year, in the fourth month, on the fifth day of the month, as I was among the exiles by the river Chebar, the heavens were opened, and I saw visions of God (Ezek. 1:1)

The book of Ezekiel is about an exiled community moving from devastation to resurrection; it is the story of a community affected by HIV reconstructing its future. It is told by Ezekiel, a prophet who understands deeply the HIV experience and who sees visions of hope that sustain himself and his people through the most difficult challenge of their lives.

Reading the Bible from the social location of living with HIV has revealed treasures in the text that were previously invisible to me. The experience of living with HIV has been the greatest catalyst in my spiritual life since coming out as a gay man over twenty years ago. Although many diseases plague humankind, HIV is unique in that the disease is religiously stigmatized, and it affects religiously stigmatized people. The spirituality that has evolved in me and my community throughout the AIDS years has given me the tools to mine the biblical text for resources necessary to our survival. In some ways, it has been the HIV experience that has taught me to read the Bible as a liberating word. After identifying characteristics of an HIV hermeneutic, I will demonstrate an application of this perspective by analyzing Ezekiel 37:1–14. I believe the Bible was conceived with people in mind who share my social location. My intellectual and spiritual instincts tell me that the Bible, on some fundamental level, contains stories told by people with HIV for people with HIV and for the communities affected by it.

People with HIV understand exile. We are estranged from family and society, from church and community, because of a disease and because of how we got it. Even within the queer community, there is renewed stigmatization of people with HIV who become infected after the mid-1980s because the moral judgment is made that we should have known better. The distinction made between the truly innocent (babies) and the somehow deserving (gay men, prostitutes, and IV drug users) that characterized the early AIDS discourse has now been appropriated by our own community and applied generationally; if you got AIDS early on, it is understandable, but if you got it recently, you deserve only to be made an example. People with HIV understand what it means to be viewed as expendable. We understand the impermanence of the body and its fragility. We understand what it means to be so paralyzed by grief that we cease to care whether we live or die, whether we protect our health or the health of others, whether we take our medications on time or even at all. People with HIV understand what it means to feel ashamed, shut down, nihilistic, and reckless. We understand what it means to be fearful of giving or receiving love. We understand what it means to lose the ability to plan for the future. We understand what it means to lose faith in God, in the community, and in our selves. While not everyone with HIV experiences all these things at once, most can recall feeling these things at one time or another. I have felt personally everything I have listed here.

People with HIV also understand the innate desire of the soul and the body to overcome adversity and to survive. We understand that denial is an impediment to spiritual growth, and we know that healing comes only in the context of truth telling, even uncomfortable truth telling. Our doctors cannot help us unless we accurately depict our past and our present. We understand that resurrection when practiced daily and individually can become a collective reality. We understand the power of God to heal and to transform through hope. These insights culled from the social location of living with HIV can make the pages of the Bible come alive. They help us to see and tell our own story as part of divine revelation.

> In the thirtieth year, in the fourth month, on the fifth day of the month, as I was among the exiles by the river Chebar, the heavens were opened, and I saw visions of God (Ezek. 1:1)

Ezekiel wrote to a community of exiles, at a specific time and place. It was a community that understood itself in part to be responsible for its own situation. The HIV hermeneutic helps me to identify the many judgments against the exiles as the editorial encroachment of the religious impulse to blame the victim, just as today many churches attempt to minister to people with AIDS while condemning our sexuality. Unless we can boldly denounce the tone of judgment, attributed to the divine voice in the text, we cannot benefit from the message encoded within it. The HIV hermeneutic frees me to acknowledge this strand in the text and to remove it carefully to get to the heart of the text of hope and healing.

Ezekiel speaks to us as a person acquainted with grief. Although inextricably linked with the scientifically unsound and spiritually toxic notion that God sends illness to us as a means of teaching humanity a lesson, we can see depicted here the numbing effect of losing one's beloved to plague: "Mortal, with one blow I am about to take away from you the delight of your eyes; yet you shall not mourn or weep, nor shall your tears run down. Sigh, but not aloud; make no mourning for the dead" (Ezek. 24:16–17). When an entire community is affected by AIDS, the grief plays out in different ways at different times. When President Clinton was elected for his first term of office, his acceptance speech was broadcast live to the spontaneous party on Castro Street. His mere mention of the word "AIDS" brought forth an almost deafening shout: we imagined the whole world hearing our collective anger and grief expressed at our excitement that an elected official took notice and was unafraid to say the word. At other times, our individual and collective grief is embodied in the tearless, wordless, blunted affect the grieving Ezekiel portrays at the loss of his wife. Ezekiel would understand that it signifies profound loss to say, as many have said, "I'm not going to _____'s funeral; I'm not going to any more funerals." Ezekiel would understand why parishioners at churches like MCC San Francisco would say in the worst of the AIDS years that they needed to take a break from church because it was just too heartbreaking to hear weekly of the loss of one or two or three more fallen comrades.

It is the depth of Ezekiel's suffering and grief that gives him the credibility to talk about resurrection. His saturation with HIV-related loss is the reason he can see visions of God when the institutions and structures truly responsible for scattering the exiles have lost their ability to see visions. Perhaps it takes a prophet with AIDS to see the hope offered by a God with AIDS to a people whose survival depends on their ability to see through the lies and deceptions told to us and by us. Read the text with me, a person with HIV who has worked with people affected by HIV in churches in Greenwich Village and the Castro. Experience anew through the lens of HIV the familiar story of Ezekiel and the valley of dry bones, as told in Ezekiel 37.

> The hand of God came upon me, and God brought me out by the Spirit of God and set me down in the middle of a valley; it was full of bones. (v. 1)

God invites Ezekiel to view the battleground where his people were overcome by the Persian armies and taken into captivity. It is the site of their greatest and most bitter defeat. The bones scattered in the valley are the bones of the fallen soldiers, possibly all that remains of people with whom Ezekiel was personally acquainted. God is not cruel. God understood that Ezekiel's power to dream again requires the ability to visit the place of greatest grief. Denial of the enormity will keep him there. For people living with and affected by HIV, our transformation begins when we are willing to visit the place where we grieve the most. We cannot claim our future until we can embrace our past. We cannot marshal resources fully while photographs of loved ones remain locked in drawers because the pain they evoke is greater than the comfort they bring. The spirit of God invites us to visit these places, accompanying us as our advocate and comforter, so that we may begin again.

> God led me all around them; there were very many lying in the valley, and they were very dry. (v. 2)

Ezekiel was struck by the enormity of the loss; the repetition of "very" emphasizes the extremity of the devastation. How many? "Very many." How dry? "Very dry." Downplaying or trivializing the suffering past or present of people with HIV only cooperates in the culture of silence that makes wholesale genocide palatable. How many have HIV? "Very many," in every inhabited continent. The North American experience of AIDS is minor compared to the huge number affected in Africa and Asia. How dry are their bones? "Very dry," when we realize that even pain-abatement medication, much less HIV treatment, is not available to poverty-stricken and socially marginalized populations of these same continents.

> God said to me, "Mortal, can these bones live?" I answered, "O God, you know." (v. 3)

The rabbis speculated as to how long Ezekiel took to respond to God's question and as to what answers raced through his mind before he cagily evaded a direct response. Was there a long pause in which Ezekiel suppressed smart-aleck remarks, such as, "Nice of you to ask now, but where were you during the battle?" Is Ezekiel afraid to answer because it would reveal that he has lost faith? God poses the painful question, the one on everyone's mind. I grasp Ezekiel's hesitation. For years I faced the same groups of people, gathered week after week for funerals, waiting expectantly for a word of hope. I found Easter to be the most difficult sermon of all to prepare. I lived in between the space of posing the question and answering it. HIV demands truthful responses to difficult questions; saying "I don't know" is better than false assurance. When I asked my doctor if I could expect to live two years or three years or more, I preferred his awkward "I don't know; it's not exactly science" to a hearty promise based on the immediate desire to please.

> Then God said to me, "Prophesy to these bones, and say to them: O dry bones, hear the word of God. Thus says God to these bones: I will cause breath to enter you, and you shall live. I will lay sinews on you, and will cause flesh to come upon you, and cover you with skin, and put breath in you, and you shall live; and you shall know that I am God." (vv. 4–6)

Ezekiel stood staring at the bones, and God challenged him to image flesh. Ezekiel witnessed unforgettable scenes of violent death. God did not deprive him of these memories but recognized that Ezekiel was in a state of shock as a result of what he had lived through. Ezekiel's healing began when he was able to view dimensionally the people whom he could only recall as skeletons. When we go through the HIV experience with someone, what often remains with us is the last few weeks, the sight and sound and smells of someone's dying days. Horrible images are seared into our minds; healing begins to happen when we reclaim the nonmedical memories of our deceased friends. I know that the resurrection of the body has begun when I can remember how someone looked before illness distorted their frames and am even able to project images of them into a future we know only metaphysically but no less really.

> So I prophesied as I had been commanded; and as I prophesied, suddenly there was a noise, a rattling, and the bones came together, bone to its bone. (v. 7)

Ezekiel knew such widespread loss that he could not even remember everyone he had lost. He relied on God's memory to remember what was too enormous for him to hold. In the Great Restoration depicted here, every single bone is reunited where it belongs. I remember performing weddings for couples in hospital rooms or at home where one partner lay very close to death, barely able to say the words "in sickness and in health," and I am comforted by the image of a great wedding banquet, where bone is joined to bone for eternity. Sometimes I cannot even remember all the people I have lost; I am comforted by the certain knowledge that every lost relationship can be reconnected. It's okay if I forget because I know God will remember.

> I looked, and there were sinews on them, and flesh had come upon them, and skin had covered them; but there was no breath in them. Then God said to me, "Prophesy to the breath, prophesy, mortal, and say to the breath: Thus says God: Come from the four winds, O breath, and breathe upon these slain, that they may live." (vv. 8–9)

Ezekiel was not satisfied with a mere physical reconstruction; the body required breath in order to live, breath evoked from the four directions; matter without spirit, the flesh without the soul, life without meaning, is inadequate. We have seen our friends dwindle with mysterious weight losses, fat and muscles melting from their bodies, rendering them almost unrecognizable to us. We have watched our friends struggling for breath when stricken with pneumonia, watched and heard them drown before our eyes, wanting to breathe for them. The most terrifying experience of being ill was the ten days I spent on a respirator, unable to speak because of the apparatus, hands tied to my side, my morphine-sedated mind drifting in and out of panicky consciousness, my sole comfort the occasional glimpse of friends standing by my bedside, breathing with me through their prayers, the overwhelming anxiety abated by the touch of their hands on my body while they prayed. Learning to breathe without a ventilator indelibly teaches us never to take for granted the importance of breath.

> I prophesied as God commanded me, and the breath came into them, and they lived and stood on their feet, a vast multitude. (v. 10)

Imagine Ezekiel's joy at seeing that defeated army standing bravely at attention, filling the valley where they had been defeated. Picture our own communities, standing tall and proud, dancing in the sunlight on Castro Street, Christopher Street, 125th Street, Commercial Street, Santa Monica Boulevard, in living rooms and dining rooms and kitchens and bedrooms, on front porches and backyards, on the beach and on the farm, rooms, everywhere known and unknown where our people live.

The rabbis told many stories about this glorious moment of communal resurrection.[2] Some said in addition to the lost soldiers others were resurrected as well in that moment, including the slaves from Egypt who had slipped away before the Exodus, unable to wait for the movement led by Moses. I picture those who died in the early years of the epidemic before there were treatments or even names for their situation. This image comforts me when I feel guilty that medical situations, which routinely killed people even three years ago, are treated quickly and handily today. I know that people globally who do not have access to medications to which I have access and which are paid for by my insurance will be resurrected as part of this great resurrection, and I know that resurrection cannot be complete until their memory is vindicated by our action.

The rabbis also said that some Hebrew soldiers taken into captivity were considered very handsome by the Persian women, so much so that the Babylonian soldiers had them put to death because they were too comely. I have witnessed the death of too many about whom I can only say, they were too beautiful to live. That beauty may be physical or spiritual.

The rabbis also told another tale about this moment of resurrection. When King Nebuchadnezzar was drinking from a cup fashioned out of the skull of one of the vanquished Hebrew soldiers, as the bones rattled in that valley faraway, a fist flew out of the cup and smacked him across the jaw, and a voice rebuked him for thinking he had destroyed Israel and its army. I know that our resurrection will come in part when we really let loose our righteous and long-suppressed anger. Some years ago I performed a funeral for a man who had provided for everyone to receive a flower as they left the service. His lover said that at his own funeral, which would take place a few months later, he wanted everyone to do something that would help them express their anger. At his service, the chapel was piled high with a lifelong collection of Fiestaware, and he instructed us to break it at the end. As I stood in the chapel, in a room full of people breaking dishes, I recognized his wisdom. We don't want to live there, but there is a deep well of unexpressed rage that we must release as part of our resurrection.

> Then God said to me, "Mortal, these bones are the whole house of Israel. They say, 'Our bones are dried up, and our hope is lost; we are cut off completely.' Therefore prophesy, and say to them, Thus says God: I am going to open your graves, and bring you up from your graves, O my people; and I will bring you back to the land of Israel." (vv. 11–12)

Ezekiel was told to prophesy to the whole house of Israel, not just those defeated in the valley of dry bones and not just those in exile. People with HIV are called to prophesy to the whole church and the whole community. We are called to give hope to other people with HIV and those whose lives are affected by it, to testify truthfully to the hope we have discovered though our spirituality. We are called to prophesy to the churches and warn them to listen to what God is doing in our midst. We are called to bring to account the churches that will perform our funerals but not our marriages, who will bury us with sad and pitying faces but will not marry us proudly and openly for fear our love will defile their sanctuaries. We are called to say plainly to them that they will never learn about resurrection in the midst of AIDS as long as they foster antigay teachings and until they learn to love our queer bodies as much as our Christian souls.

> "And you shall know that I am God, when I open your graves, and bring you up from your graves, O my people. I will put my spirit within you, and you shall live, and I will place you on your own soil; then you shall know that I, God, have spoken and will act, says God." (vv. 13–14)

God promises to open our graves, and we are called to open our closets, to tell the truth about HIV, to tell the truth about sexuality and its goodness, to tell the truth about our love. We will know the promised resurrection when we learn to embody God's promise to unite speech and action. This consideration of Ezekiel 37:1–14 is an example of the HIV hermeneutic at work. It does not preclude other readings of the text, but I hope it unpacks previously unarticulated nuances. The HIV experience challenges us to take back the Word, to find its message for us. The HIV experience of time, which is more urgent for us than for people who do not live daily with it, frees us to seize what leads to healing now and to discard the rest. The HIV experience is a "quicksort" that enables us to distinguish liberating religion from the religion of oppression and provides new levels of meaning for all.

## Notes

1. Eric Rofes, *Dry Bones Breathe* (New York: Haworth Press, 1998), xii.

2. For midrashic treatments of Ezekiel 37, see Elie Wiesel, *Sages and Dreamers* (New York: Simon and Schuster, 1991), 80–98; and Louis Ginzberg, *Legends of the Bible* (Philadelphia: Jewish Publication Society, 1978).

# 15

# A Queer Reading of the Book of Jonah

### SHARON BEZNER

*In this essay, Sharon Bezner reads the story of Jonah as a modern-day queer parable in which Jonah is identified with the religious right and the Ninevites are queer people living in San Francisco. Her reading challenges all people, queer or straight, to consider the theology that shapes their lives and actions. Can we accept God's inclusive love? Just as the biblical book has a twist at the end, so does Bezner's essay—what would queer people do if called to proclaim God's love to the religious right?*

The book of Jonah is one of the twelve minor prophetic books of the Hebrew Scriptures. It has traditionally been interpreted as a parable of a recalcitrant prophet who flees from his mission and then sulks when his hearers repent. The parable has been compared to the New Testament parable of the prodigal son in Luke 15:11–31, with the forgiving father likened to the forgiving God, the prodigal son likened to the repentant Ninevites, and the resentful brother likened to Jonah. The parable has been traditionally seen as consisting of two sections, each broken into four parts.

The first part of the story is the narrative of the flight, strife, and return of Jonah, consisting of the initial call by God of Jonah and Jonah's refusal; the flight of Jonah from God to Tarshish on a boat full of people and the consequential storm at sea endangering all of their lives; the casting of Jonah off of the boat; and the swallowing by the great fish, in which Jonah stays for three days and nights before being spewed on the land. The second part of the parable is the narrative of the mission, repentance, and dissent and consists of God's second calling of Jonah and Jonah's response; the response of the Ninevites; Jonah's reaction, God's response, and Jonah's departure; and the continuing struggle between God and Jonah. The parable ends, as with the parable of the prodigal son, open-ended, leaving the reader and Jonah to ponder the final words of God.

As with all scriptural interpretation, the perspective of the interpreter plays a major role in deciphering the meaning of the text. Life experiences, cultural background, and social reality all play a part in the interpreter's understanding of the world and scriptural text. As Theodore Jennings states in *Good News to the Poor*, "things look different and mean different things, depending on where one is in the economic, social, or political system."[1] The traditional meaning and interpretation of the book of Jonah is one that has been established by the prominent theologians of the last two hundred years: white heterosexual middle-class Anglo-Saxon men. One can only wonder how the text would be interpreted by other groups of people, people whose life experiences are nonwhite, nonheterosexual, non-middle class, non-Anglo-Saxon, and non-men. What would it look like for gay/lesbian/bisexual/transgendered (queer) people to read and interpret the book of Jonah? Perhaps the first part would look something like this.

## A Queer Reading of the Book of Jonah: Part 1

Now the word of God came to Jonah, elected leader of the Christian Coalition, saying, "Go at once to San Francisco, that great gay city, and cry out against it; for their wickedness has come up before me." But Jonah set out to flee to New York, to flee from this calling of God. He went to the airport and found a plane going to New York; so he bought a ticket and boarded to go with the other passengers, who happened to have all originated on a flight from San Francisco that had stopped in Utah and was continuing on to New York City, away from the presence of God.

But God sent great winds into the air, and such a mighty wind was blowing that the plane threatened to blow apart! Then all the passengers were afraid and cried out to their god. One clung to his boyfriend, crying for him to save him; another grabbed her wallet, prepared to pay the pilot extra money to divert the flight pattern and land them in Dallas safely; two in the back of the plane got out a joint and began smoking it to calm their nerves and help them relax. They then opened the doors of the luggage compartments to allow all the luggage to drop out of the plane, to lighten it for them. Jonah, meanwhile, had gone into the back of the plane and had lain down, and was fast asleep. The pilot, also from San Francisco, came and said to Jonah, "What are you doing sound asleep? Get up, call on your god! Perhaps the god will spare us a thought so that we do not perish!"

The passengers said to one another, "Come, let us draw straws so that we may know on whose account this calamity has come upon us." So they drew straws, and the short straw fell to Jonah. Then they said to him, "Tell us why this calamity has come upon us. What is your occupation? Where do you come from? What is your state? And of what people are you?" "I am a Christian Coalition member," he replied. "I worship the Lord, the God of heaven, who made the sea and the dry land." Then the passengers were even more afraid, and said to him, "What is this that you have done!" For the passengers knew that he was fleeing from the presence of God, because he had told them so.

Then they said to him, "What shall we do to you, that the wind may quiet down for us?" For the wind was growing more and more violent. He said to them, "Pick me up and throw me out into the wind; then the wind will quiet down for you; for I know it is because of me that this great wind has come upon you." Nevertheless the pilots, at the passengers' urging, tried to fly the plane out of the wind and into calmer air, but they could not, for the wind grew more and more violent against them from seemingly every direction. Then they cried out to God, "Please, O God, we pray, do not let us perish on account of this man's life. Do not make us guilty of innocent blood; for you, O God, have done as it pleased you." So they picked Jonah up and threw him out of the plane; and the wind ceased from blowing. Then the passengers feared God even more, and they offered a sacrifice to God, passing to the front all their alcohol bottles, and made vows to go to church, to tithe, and to volunteer every week at a local AIDS service organization.

But the Lord provided a big bird to swallow up Jonah; and Jonah was in the belly of the bird three days and three nights.

Then Jonah prayed to God from the belly of the bird, saying,

> "I called to God out of my distress,
>     and God answered me;
> out of the belly of the bird I cried,
>     and you heard my voice.
> You cast me into the air,
>     into the depths of the winds,
>     and the winds surrounded me;
> all your winds and your storm
>     passed over me.
> Then I said, 'I am driven away
>     from your sight;
> how shall I look again
>     upon your holy church?'

The winds closed in over me;
　　they surrounded me;
clouds were wrapped around my head
　　at the peaks of the mountains.
I went up into the air
　　whose turbulence tossed me about forever;
yet you saved my life from the storm,
　　O Lord my God.
As my life was ebbing away,
　　I remembered God;
and my prayer came to you,
　　into your holy sanctuary.
Those who worship false idols
　　forsake their true loyalty.
But I with the voice of thanksgiving
　　will sacrifice to you;
what I have vowed I will pay.
　　Salvation belongs to God."

Then God spoke to the bird, and it set Jonah down upon the ground.

## A Queer Commentary

Jonah was an Israelite. He was one of the chosen people of God. He was the religious of his day. He was a prophet, held up by society as an upright and "holy" person. The Christian Coalition is viewed similarly today. A large section of the American population views this group as the righteous, the religious, the "holy" of modern times. They themselves believe that they are the chosen of God, the elect, the only ones who are favored by God. Therefore, it is not a far step to view Jonah as one of the Christian Coalition in a queer reading of this story.

Likewise, Nineveh was the capital of Assyria, the nation responsible for the destruction of the Northern Kingdom of Israel. At that time, the inhabitants of the Northern Kingdom, the Israelites, were scattered geographically. In their place, Assyrians, or people friendly to Assyrian control, were brought in and located in the area. Because the Assyrians were thus responsible for the Israelites losing their land, they were hated. Nineveh, as the capital of Assyria, was thus the most hated city to the Israelites.

Similarly, in modern times, the one group that is perhaps most despised by the religious right is queer people. Queers are described as a threat to the family and responsible for the "breakdown" of the traditional family unit. Queers are held responsible for the increased occurrence of divorce in heterosexual marriages. Queers are accused of being solely responsible for the introduction of the AIDS virus into the species and its spread. Homosexual hate literature is abundant and widely circulated by the Christian Coalition. Disparaging remarks about homosexuals can be heard in speeches and sermons by leaders of the Christian Coalition frequently. Homosexuals are indeed the enemy to the religious right. San Francisco, because of the large population of gay and lesbian people who live there, is often viewed as the capital of homosexuality in America. Therefore, the analogy of it to Nineveh is easily surmised.

Jonah's being sent by God to call homosexuals to repentance lest they be destroyed is a scenario that every right-wing religious zealot in America can easily envision. Jonah believed the Ninevites were sinful people, just as the religious right believes queers are sinful people. Jonah, when called to go to the Ninevites to preach the message of repentance, does not want to go and instead flees. Jonah is reluctant to preach this message to the Ninevites because he knows God is merciful and will forgive them. And, if God forgives the Ninevites, whom will Jonah hate?

Similarly, the Christian Coalition as the "representative" of the church, refuses to believe that God's love and mercy include queer people. Like Jonah, coalition members embrace a theology that includes only God's wrath. Through mistaken theology, they have backed themselves into a corner that does not allow them to reach out to homosexuals. The religious right have focused on a few passages in the Bible that they interpret as condemning homosexuality. They have ignored the context of these passages, the literal translation of the Greek and Hebrew words used to describe the act being condemned in these passages, and have ignored the fact that they do not similarly interpret other passages in the Bible—ones condemning eating pork, wearing clothes made of certain fibers, and outcasting menstruating women. Their bad theology has forced them into a situation where they must disobey God and God's call to them to preach and reach out to and include all people, including homosexuals, in the body of Christ, or else they must rethink their theology and change it. The religious right and Jonah have opted for the former.

Thus, the Christian Coalition and Jonah flee from the calling of God. They do not flee from God, for they know that they cannot, but they attempt to flee from God's word, God's call to them. They flee by running away from "those" people and their hatred of them, by refusing to look at and deal with the fear that is at the very root of their refusal to minister to homosexuals. They fear that God's love includes everyone, which means they would lose their righteous status. Instead, they attempt to calm themselves with false "sleep," the false sense of security that comes from filling their lives with "religious" actions and empty works. In so doing, they ignore the world about them and the fellow "passengers" who travel right alongside of them, teaching their children in school, cutting their hair, and treating their bodies.

However, God does not let the religious right sleep. Rather, God finds them wherever they are and disturbs their status-quo life to the point that they are aroused from their self-induced serenity. And in "awakening," they discover, in their very lives, the people they hate the most: the homosexuals. Because they are dealing with individuals though, they permit themselves to be kind, to reach out, to minister, to the few gay and lesbian people they know personally. And in so doing, they may sacrifice something of themselves: money, time, energy. However, they make these sacrifices, not for the sake of the homosexuals they are giving to, but rather again simply to continue to avoid looking at themselves and examining and rethinking the bad theology that got them into this no-win situation.

The story up till now has been based on the reality of the American situation. The remainder of the story is yet to be determined. The book of Jonah in the Bible, however, does suggest a resolution to this dilemma that faces Americans today.

## A Queer Reading of the Book of Jonah: Part 2

The word of God came to Jonah a second time, saying, "Get up, go to San Francisco, that great gay city, and proclaim to it the message that I tell you." So Jonah set out and went to San Francisco, according to the word of God. Now, San Francisco was an exceedingly large city, with thousands of queer people living there. Jonah began to go into the city, going a day's walk, saying, "Forty days more, and San Francisco shall be destroyed!" And the queer people of San Francisco believed God; they proclaimed a fast, and everyone, great and small, joined together in prayer.

When the news reached the leader of the Gay and Lesbian Alliance in San Francisco, she rose from her desk chair, removed her coat, knelt down in the street, and began to pray. Then she broadcast a bulletin over the airwaves saying: "I, the leader of the Gay and Lesbian Alliance, and all our employees, are observing a solemn fast. We will not be eating or drinking anything from sunset tonight until sunset tomorrow. We invite you to observe this fast with us. We also invite you to, during this time of fasting, examine your life and acknowledge those hurtful and harmful actions that you do, that are detrimental to yourself and to others in your life. While we have always known that our queerness does not keep us apart from God, we have failed to recognize that our lack of service to others, or hateful words to each other, and our self-absorption have kept us apart from God. We invite you to make a commitment to turn from these unhealthy areas of your life, and to replace them with actions of love and caring. Who knows? Our actions of love may save our city. God may relent and change her mind; God may turn from fierce anger, so that we do not perish."

When God saw what they did, how they turned not from their queerness but from their unloving ways of treating each other, God changed her mind about the calamity that God had said would befall them; and God did not do it.

But, this was very displeasing to Jonah, and he became angry. He prayed to God and said: "O God! Is not this what I said while I was still in my own state? That is why I fled to New York City at the beginning; for I know that you are a gracious God and merciful, slow to anger, and abounding in steadfast love, and ready to relent from punishing. And now, O God, please take my life from me, for it is better for me to die than to live." And God said, "Is it right for you to be angry?" Then Jonah left San Francisco and sat down east of the city, across the Golden Gate Bridge, and got a room at the Motel 6, for that was all he could afford. He sat in his room, looking out the window, waiting to see what would become of the great gay city of San Francisco.

God appointed one of the staff members of the San Francisco Gay and Lesbian Alliance to go to the Fairmont San Francisco and pay for room and board there for Jonah. A clerk was sent from the Fairmont to the Motel 6 to inform Jonah and take him to the new lodging. When he arrived in his room, which was the plushest suite in the hotel, Jonah was made exceedingly comfortable. Room service immediately brought him a fine meal, for he had no money and had not eaten since his arrival in San Francisco, to save him from his discomfort; so Jonah was very happy about the new lodging. But when dawn came up the next day, God appointed the clerk to go to Jonah's room and arouse him, informing him the gay man who had paid for his lodging was called out of town, to Washington, to speak before a Senate hearing against the Defamation of Marriage Act, which the Christian Coalition was backing and had been instrumental in getting introduced as a bill. Without being able to verify that he would continue to pay for Jonah's room and board, the hotel had to ask Jonah to leave. He was escorted out onto the street, where he stayed, for he had no money left. When the sun rose that August day, God prepared a sultry West Coast wind, and the sun beat down on the head of Jonah so that he was faint and asked that he might die. He said, "It is better for me to die than to live."

But God said to Jonah, "Is it right for you to be angry about the loss of your free lodging?" And he said, "Yes, angry enough to die." Then God said, "You are concerned about the free lodging, for which you did not labor; it came to you one day and was taken away the next. And should I not be concerned about the city of San Francisco, that great gay city, in which there are more than a million queer persons who do not know their right hand from their left, and also their many pets?"

## A Queer Commentary

God again gets the attention of the religious right. In the agony and pain that results from their running from God's call, they feel as if they have gone to the pit of hell. However, God brings them back. God does not give up on the Christian Coalition but continues to lead them, and again they hear the call of God to preach to queers. Well, this time they obey God's call, as Jonah did, but in a very minimalistic way. Jonah and the religious right preach the shortest sermon in the entire Hebrew Scriptures. The religious right, like Jonah, obey God but do it with the same old, tired, hateful, hesitant attitude. They preach a message of hateful repentance, "Forty days more and San Francisco will be destroyed!"

As a result of this message, however, the queer community repents. Similar to the Jonah parable, it is not the messenger that brings about the change, but rather it is the people who hear the message that bring about repentance. Like the Ninevites, the queers hear the message in a different way than it was intended and repent. They examine their lives and make changes that reflect the loving relationship with God that they are called to. Similarly, God repents of the judgment said to befall them, and they are spared. The Christian Coalition's response: ANGER! How can God not deal "justly" with these sinners? The religious right are so enraged that they would rather die than live with the reality that God shows mercy on queers who make amends with God, not for who they are as homosexuals, but rather for the lack of love that they demonstrate toward God, themselves, and each other. They are still homosexuals; are they not? Absolutely, which gives credence to the notion that being a homosexual alone does not condemn a person in the eyes of God. The religious right cannot live with this reality and would rather face death.

God, however, does not abandon the religious right. God again tries to show them the point, to make them see the truth and the calling of the church on earth. God attempts to show them, with an example, that their theology is mistaken. God provides comfort and relief for them, but just as quickly takes it away. Again they are angry, and God's question to them is, "Do you have the right to be angry?"

The book of Jonah ends with God's question posed to Jonah—and posed to the reader. It is a question that the Christian Coalition must answer for itself. It is a question that every member of the religious right must answer. And it is a question that you and I must answer. Who are we to decide whom God loves? If we are angry about how God extends God's love, and to whom, are we not making ourselves God? Isn't that the meaning of idolatry in today's society, and not the worship of statues or golden calves? And if that is the case, are not our thoughts, our beliefs, our theology, that got us to this place, in error? If so, are we not then called to examine ourselves, to do some introspective soul searching, to hear God's truth in our hearts, and to make our hearts and actions in sync with God? That's where the biblical story left Jonah, and that's were we as modern-day readers of the book of Jonah are also left.

The cryptic ending of Jonah for queers may be a challenge to examine what we would do if we were in Jonah's place and asked to proclaim a word of God's love and mercy to the religious right. Given all the violence we have experienced as a result of the rhetoric of hate spewed by the religious right, would we be on a ship to Tarshish or Nineveh? Would we be able to let go of a theology of revenge in order to embrace a theology of God's inclusive love that welcomes the religious right? How would we react if tomorrow the religious right repented and proclaimed God's love for queers? Would we rejoice with them, or would we be angry enough to die because they didn't get what was coming to them?

## Note

1. Theodore Jennings, *Good News to the Poor: John Wesley's Evangelical Economics* (Nashville: Abingdon Press, 1990), 20.

# 16

# Do Justice, Love Mercy, Walk Humbly

## Reflections on Micah and Gay Ethics

### REBECCA T. ALPERT

*Although there has been a split between activists and faith activists, faith and activism are interconnected within a Jewish perspective. Rebecca Alpert reads Micah 6:8 from a lesbian perspective with its three concerns: how to live with oneself in the world, how to establish social relationships, and how to make the world a better place. She applies these principles to lesbian Jewish life in a practical way to examine coming out, families of origin, a gay and lesbian congregation's attempt to march in an Israel Independence Day parade, and working for justice for others. Alpert makes a strong case how the narrative text becomes refigured in the texts of Jewish lives.*

It is common practice among Jewish commentators to use a biblical passage as a starting point or proof-text for contemporary ideas. The passage I have chosen as a framework for examining Jewish lesbian concerns is found in the book of Micah, the writings of a minor prophet thought to have lived in the sixth or seventh century B.C.E. Micah summarizes his understanding of "what is good" as follows: "do justice (*asot mishpat*), love well (*ahavat hesed*),[1] and walk modestly with God (*hatznea lechet im eloheha*)" (Mic. 6:8). This prophetic saying is amenable to a Jewish lesbian reading that focuses on some of the problems facing Jewish lesbians today. In addition, it offers some resolutions to those dilemmas: questions about public disclosure of our identities, our relationships to our families, and the opportunity to contribute to a more just and peaceful world from our unique position. Although this reading is specific to Jewish lesbians, it is my hope that the model created here for dealing with these dilemmas may be applied to questions faced by nonlesbian Jews as well.

Micah's threefold precept suggests these areas of particular concern: how to live with and present oneself in the world (how to walk modestly with

God), how to establish social relationships (how to love well), and how to make the world a better place (how to do justice). My interpretation inverts the order of Micah's precept. As he states it, the precept culminates with the individual's relationship with God, which is in keeping with the biblical author's theocentric worldview. From my human-centered perspective, it makes sense to begin with the individual's relationship with God, expressed through her relationship with herself. It is this relationship that enables her to love others and then to translate that love into acts of justice for all humanity, which is for me the ultimate goal.

## The Process of Coming Out

The process begins where Micah ends—with the enigmatic phrase *hatznea lechet im eloheha*. Traditionally, this has been translated "walk humbly with your God," but more recent translations have suggested it means "walk modestly" or "with decency." I interpret this statement to be about the way an individual understands her own place in the world. I assume that the way in which a person approaches her own life will determine her ability to behave ethically towards others. A central Jewish precept demands that we love our neighbors as ourselves. Commentators have understood this to mean that we can only learn to love our neighbors if we learn to love ourselves.

Walking with God is a metaphor for the way each person approaches her own life. It is a way to conceptualize one's innermost feelings and thoughts. It is not necessary to hold a traditional concept of God, or to imagine God in human form, to appreciate this metaphor. To see oneself walking with God requires a vision of God as the most important value in life, that which is with the individual always and everywhere. God may be in the image of a human being, but God could also be a power, force, feeling, idea, or anything that helps one perceive holiness in the world.

As Jewish lesbians, we begin with the assumption that we can only walk with God if we know and accept ourselves for who we are. Walking with God begins with self-acceptance and requires that we tell ourselves the truth about ourselves. This stance describes coming out, declaring oneself to be lesbian, as a necessary prerequisite to walking with God. Walking with God requires self-knowledge. Those who walk with God know their way and consciously claim a path in the world. They are guided by the understanding that all human beings are holy, having been created in God's image. They respect the mysterious process, whether it derives from nature or society,[2] that makes them women who are erotically attracted to other women and who prefer to build their lives with them.

## The Ethics of Coming Out and Outing

Accepting and acting on this erotic attraction are examples of *hatznea lechet* because they indicate self-acceptance. Jewish lesbians claim our sexual attractions as a holy pursuit. What makes our sexuality holy is not intrinsic to it; rather, it is acceptance in ourselves of our sexual joys and pleasures, of seeing our erotic lives, not as cut off from the rest of ourselves, but integral to making our lives rich and meaningful.[3] Too often lesbians, especially when our homosexuality is first awakened, feel shame about our feelings and desires. *Hatznea lechet* means accepting desire and finding creative ways of expressing it. Of course, those expressions must conform to other ethical standards of behavior towards ourselves and others, but those desires and behaviors will also unleash our creative powers and enable us to be in the world in a holy and positive way. When the connection between the sexual self and the rest of the self is cut off, we cannot walk with God. It is important for Jewish lesbians to affirm the link between our sexuality and the rest of our lives as Jews.

From this perspective, there is no holy way for a lesbian to be closeted to herself. In the closet, we relinquish the opportunity to express our own inner needs and desires. The lesbian who hides her sexual desires from herself stays still and cannot walk in the direction of self-acceptance. This is true for anyone who makes a choice that does not lead to her own self-fulfillment and growth. Coming out reminds us that God is with us, that when lesbians come out we have the support of the power in the universe that gives us strength to do courageous things.

Walking with God is not limited to self-acceptance as a lesbian in the privacy of one's own inner world. The next stages of self-acceptance suggest being out with family and friends and in the lesbian and gay or Jewish lesbian worlds. But I want to suggest that truly walking with God moves beyond this stage. The ultimate way to walk with God with self-acceptance also requires coming out publicly. The reluctance to do so may be caused by real discrimination and bigotry, the threat of losing one's job or custody of one's child. But it may also be the result of feelings of shame about one's sexuality and fear of loss of status. It is clear that the visibility of lesbians and gay men in our society has made possible civil rights and societal respect for gay people unknown in prior human history. Lesbians must be willing to write about our lives, talk about ourselves in newspaper and television stories, testify and work for laws that will increase our civil rights, be involved in test cases for the courts to expand our rights, and especially speak out in synagogues and Jewish communal organizations that want to learn about us. The more of us who speak out publicly about our commitments as lesbians and Jews, the less likely that anyone will be able deny our humanity based on the claim that they do not know anyone who is lesbian or gay.

There is another dimension to the ethics of coming out. *Hatznea lechet* also requires us to be honest people: honest with ourselves about our sexuality and honest with others in our lives. Coming out publicly keeps us from having to lie—to doctors whom we sometimes do not visit because we do not want to talk about our sex lives, to coworkers with whom we omit pronouns when referring to our partners, to acquaintances who want to introduce us to men. The lies we tell may be small ones, but they inhibit our ability to live openly and lead us into patterns of lying incompatible with walking with God. And they draw nonlesbians into our lie as well, requiring them often to deny what they see.

Not lying has another consequence. If every lesbian came out, then we would not have to lie for each other, to pretend that the rabbi, cantor, person applying to teach in the Hebrew school, or editor of the Jewish newspaper is not the same person we saw with her lover at the women's music concert the other night. The gay and lesbian community has for a long time agreed to a conspiracy of silence, never to expose a closeted gay man or lesbian outside of the gay community (although gossip of this sort within the lesbian community is commonplace). This conspiracy of silence is a burden placed upon open lesbians by our closeted friends, to the detriment of lesbian life. To walk with God requires that we stop demanding one another to keep secrets and that we persuade the closeted to come out.

The quotation from Micah suggests not only that we find a way to walk with God; that way must be modest, decent, and humble. *Hatznea lechet* does not carry with it the assumption, however, that we are not proud to be lesbians. That being open and comfortable with being a lesbian is understood as a way to walk with God should illustrate this clearly. It does imply, however, that we are not so arrogant as to assume that we can determine the right way for everyone. Walking humbly with God means self-acceptance, not requiring others to follow our example. This is not a mandate for outing others. Our humility must keep us from arrogant assumptions about who must declare their lesbian identity. This humility outweighs the burden placed on us by closeted lesbians to keep their secrets. We must be mindful of the idea that we cannot judge others until we have stood in their place.[4] Once a person has come out, it is difficult to comprehend what compels another person to remain closeted or be unable to accept their sexuality. While it is important to promote the value of coming out as exemplary of self-acceptance and an appropriate way to walk with God, not all will be comfortable enough with their own sexuality or with their family to feel safe coming out. While those who are out may wish to persuade other Jewish lesbians to come out in public ways, we must respect each person's process and decision.

I am suggesting that we encourage coming out as a value. Only by accepting who we are as Jewish lesbians can we enable others to understand
and accept us. While we cannot coerce others into being public lesbians
and Jews, we can use our powers to persuade those who can speak out. The
more Jewish lesbians who publicly acknowledge their sexuality, the easier it
will be for all of us to gain acceptance in the Jewish community, which is
a prerequisite to transforming the community. Nonlesbians will then have
the opportunity to see that we are a varied group who look and behave in
a multiplicity of ways that defy the stereotypes of lesbians. And they will
begin to understand we are Jewish in a variety of ways as well. There is no
specific way to follow the precept of *hatznea lechet.*

Walking humbly with God also has a collective dimension. Jewish lesbians
must be visible as a group in mainstream contexts as well. The experience
of Congregation Beth Simchat Torah (CBST) and the Israel Independence
Day Parade of 1993 in New York City is an example of a time when gay and
lesbian Jews were prohibited from being able to walk humbly with God. The
predominantly Orthodox organizers of the Israel Day Parade in New York
refused to let Congregation Beth Simchat Torah participate. This incident
received a great deal of publicity because of the very public struggle of gay
groups to be included in New York's St. Patrick's Day Parade for several
years prior to the event. The congregation itself was divided about how
to respond. The synagogue leadership attempted to effect a compromise,
which would have allowed them to march with the Reform movement and
include the name of the congregation on the banner, but omit the words
"gay" and "lesbian." This compromise was first accepted and then rejected
by the parade organizers. Ultimately, the congregation did not march but
held its own gathering at a Reform synagogue on the day of the parade.
Other liberal groups also boycotted the march in solidarity with the gay
congregation.

But this affair raised conflicts over loyalty. CBST members wanted to be
part of the larger Jewish community and express their support for Israel.
For some members, their investment in being part of the Jewish community made them more susceptible to compromise. Others remained angry.
This event also brought a great deal of attention to the existence of a gay
and lesbian Jewish community because it was covered extensively in the
mainstream press.[5]

But if lesbian Jews are to walk humbly with God, it is important that the
community supports every opportunity for us to be visible and to proclaim
our identity by saying the word "lesbian" in public. It is imperative that
the Jewish community take up this responsibility, since the United States
Supreme Court has denied gay and lesbian people the right to march in pa-
rades organized by other communities. Unless the Jewish community stands

up for our right to be a visible part of the community, all Jews are in effect denied the opportunity to fulfill our obligation to walk humbly with God in the Jewish community.

Walking humbly with God, individually and collectively, is prerequisite to following the other virtues that Micah suggests: a commitment to love and justice. It is only those who come to self-acceptance, including a sense that they are loved by God and by the Jewish community, who can begin to work towards creating a world of love and justice.

## *Ahavat Hesed:* Transforming Relationships

The second part of Micah's precept is about loving well. Loving is the connection we make to others, whether in intimate or social relationships. Loving in social relationships means respect for the other person; loving those with whom we are intimate involves passionate feelings and intense closeness in addition to respect. *Ahavat hesed* forms the link between individual self-acceptance (*hatznea lechet im eloheha*) and universal justice (*asot mishpat*). We cannot love others unless we accept ourselves. And we cannot bring justice to a world where people do not know how to treat others with whom they are in relationships.

While *ahavat hesed* is applicable to heterosexuals and lesbians alike, the concept raises issues that are particular to lesbian lives. There are differences in the ways that lesbians create loving networks with people around us. Lesbians also have a different perspective on coupled relationships and on the bearing and the raising of children. Looking at the subject of loving through a lesbian lens contributes a new perspective to the ongoing Jewish conversation about human relationships.

### Lesbians and Our Families of Origin

*Ahavat hesed* is often difficult for lesbians to find in our families of origin. These spaces are often a source of tension and pain for us. Coming out to our families is perhaps the most difficult dimension of lesbian existence. Jewish families often have strong expectations that children should make their parents proud by living a typical American life: settling down with a partner of the opposite sex, raising children, and living comfortably in the confines of a nuclear family. Of course, many parents get used to the idea that their child is lesbian, especially if we have children and live in what at least resembles a long-term nuclear family arrangement, but others do not.

Unique issues about achieving *ahavat hesed* arise in family settings for lesbians who may have complex relationships with their families of origin. Tensions may exist with family members who do not know about lesbian sexual orientation. How do you introduce a new partner to a cousin you have not seen in many years at the funeral of her mother, who disapproved of your life choices? Tensions also arise about public acknowledgment of your relationship. Can you and your partner come to your mother's funeral if she disapproved of your relationship? Is it all right for you and your partner to dance together at your sister's wedding when you know it will embarrass her new husband? Should you and your lover demand to have an *aliyah* (blessings surrounding the Torah readings) together at the bat mitzvah of her daughter from a previous heterosexual marriage? What if you receive an invitation to a cousin's wedding and your partner is not invited?

## Jewish Communal Support for Lesbians and Our Families of Origin

These are difficult questions. Because they arise in a Jewish setting, the Jewish community must begin to address new ways to support *ahavat hesed* for lesbians and their families of origin. The community cannot allow homophobia to be the focus for the strife and contention that exist in families.

Other situations arise that also demand new patterns of behaviors when lesbians and their families are involved. The customs and ceremonies associated with death and grief are a good example. When a lesbian dies, even if she has prepared all the necessary legal documents that will enable her partner to enter her hospital room, make decisions for her if she is not able to do so, inherit her property, and make her funeral arrangements, there is no mechanism for her partner to be recognized as a mourner within Jewish law. Only at the discretion of the rabbi who is presiding will she be allowed to stand as a mourner, rend her clothes, have her relationship to the deceased mentioned in the eulogy, sit shiva with the family, whether it be parents or children. While we hope that in most situations today the family of origin is comfortable with the relationship and the mourners grieve their loss together, it is possible that the lesbian partner's grief will not be appropriately acknowledged. While there is no remedy to this situation, *ahavat hesed* suggests that lesbians and their families discuss these issues in advance with one another and with a rabbi and funeral director with whom the family has a relationship.

Around the time of death it is most important that the families that lesbians create among their friends take up the role the biological family of the deceased would have played. If Jewish lesbians are in communities with lesbians who are not Jewish, it is important that they teach their friends about funeral and mourning customs. In their book *Cancer in Two Voices*, Barbara Rosenblum and Sandra Butler describe the rituals surrounding the death of a partner in the context of a Jewish lesbian community.[6] It is a very useful text with which to begin this discussion.

Ultimately, *ahavat hesed* requires hard work. In order to love well, we must take our responsibilities to others seriously and give careful consideration to the contribution we want to make that will enable the Jewish and lesbian communities to thrive. And in order ultimately to love well within the Jewish community, we must receive *ahavat hesed* from the community in return.

## *Asot Mishpat:* The Commitment to Justice

Having examined the commitments to *hatznea lechet im eloheha* (to walk humbly with God) and *ahavat hesed* (to love the people in our lives), I now end where Micah began, with *asot mishpat*, the commitment to justice. The commitment to do justice requires us to go beyond our own lives and look at larger issues in the world around us. In the conception of Micah's precept that I discuss here, these efforts are intrinsically interconnected. We cannot make a choice between accepting ourselves, caring for our circle of loved ones, and doing justice in the world. These efforts must be woven into one framework.

What then is the justice we seek? Our goal is to live in a world where every person has what it takes to satisfy basic human needs: food, clothing, and shelter. Where every person has the opportunity for health care, safety, education, and work. Where all people have the opportunity to participate in decisions that affect their lives. Where nations do not make war against one another. And where the planet itself and all that lives on it are treated with dignity and respect. These are the goals of a just society.

We cannot begin to envision such a world unless we have created the possibilities within ourselves and our community to work towards this plan. We begin with the idea that to walk with decency with God is measured by our self-acceptance and willingness to be visible. This is the beginning of justice. For only if we speak out about who we are, can we create the opportunity for justice for ourselves.

But this alone is insufficient: love is also a prerequisite to justice. In relation to justice *ahavat hesed* means respect not only for those whom we love particularly but for all humanity. This means figuring out how to deal with hatred that is expressed in violent words and deeds. Many acts of violence in our society are perpetrated by those who hate others whom they judge to be inferior to themselves. While hate crimes and hate speech are often committed by individuals or groups who are not powerful in our society, they are sanctioned by the powerful. And hate creates an environment inimical to a just society. We must remain vigilant to combat this type of violence and publicly speak out against the perpetration of such acts. As Jews we are mindful of the experience in Nazi Germany, which began as the hate speech of a fringe group and turned into the rule of the state. Only if we remain vigilant against those who hate difference, can we begin to speak about *asot mishpat.*

Some feminists have severed the connection between love and justice. In an effort to demonstrate the value of love, feminist philosophers like Carol Gilligan have posited that a female way of being is to focus more on intimate caring, whereas the masculine approach is to demand abstract justice.[7] This dichotomized notion demands both love and justice, but it puts them in opposition, rather than as connected parts of a single obligation as stated in Micah's words. On the other hand, Carter Heyward, a white Christian lesbian theologian, argues that justice is love. In doing justice, one is creating a loving world.[8] From the perspective of Micah's precepts, these values are not one in the same. We make distinctions between loving well and doing justice as separate but connected values. We pay attention to *ahavat hesed* among Jewish lesbians and between Jewish lesbians and the rest of the Jewish community. These are related but do not equal the efforts to bring about a just society.

For some lesbian Jews, particularly those who fit conventional gender roles and whose lifestyles are family oriented, fashioning our appeal for justice and inclusion on the basis of our similarities to other Jews has been rather successful. Jewish lesbians are very clearly part of some Jewish communities, and our presence cannot be ignored. We will not have succeeded until we are accepted by all segments of the Jewish community and not included only as tokens. But becoming part of the community is not enough! We have gained this inclusion by deemphasizing those factors that make us outsiders in the first place. Now we must focus on pursuing justice for lesbians who define ourselves as sexually different.

## Justice for Jewish Lesbians as Sexual Beings

As David Biale has suggested, Jewish women are not perceived as being sexual.[9] It is not surprising that lesbians have underplayed their sexuality in a Jewish context. Our difference is based in no small part on our erotic attraction to other women. That fact cannot be hidden in our lives in the Jewish community. We must be able to express our sexuality, flirt, and look for partners in the context of the Jewish community. Sex education in a Jewish context must include references to the ways in which lesbians are sexual with one another. Homophobia based on fear of lesbian sexuality must be confronted directly.

The sexual textures of our relationships are varied. In our dialogue with the Jewish community, we must be open about the fact that not all lesbians desire long-term, committed monogamous relationships and not all lesbians want to be parents of children. Lesbian sexuality must be acceptable even if it takes less traditional forms. Often the acceptance of lesbians in the Jewish community has been predicated on the assumption that we have no choice about our sexuality, that being attracted to women is part of our genetic makeup. But if we are truly to be accepted in the Jewish community, it must be with the understanding that many of us do understand lesbianism as a choice for us.

Most lesbians have at some time in their lives engaged in heterosexual relationships. Many of us were married to men, often happily. Being open to lesbian relationships is a choice that we made on a willingness to live life without all the privileges of heterosexuality and a desire to express our love of women in a sexual way. It means that we have opened ourselves to exploring the erotic feelings towards other women that most women experience at some time in their lives. For our acceptance in the Jewish community to be based on the assumption that lesbians are incapable of engaging in satisfying heterosexual relationships and therefore have no choice but to be in relationships with other women is not an acceptance based on justice. We cannot accept the assumption that heterosexuality is superior and that lesbianism is only for those who cannot succeed in heterosexual relationships. Without true acceptance of the choices that make us different, we will never be partners in the Jewish world.

## Jewish Lesbians Work toward Justice for Others

Working towards achieving our goals for justice for Jewish lesbians is not sufficient. While it is important for us to be able to articulate what others must do for us, that cannot be our only concern. We must also talk about the justice that affects other Jews in our community and everyone in the world. There is no more important thing for Jewish lesbians to do than work on issues that make justice possible not only for us but also for others who are not like us.

Jewish lesbians have not taken up this responsibility sufficiently. Our inability to focus our efforts on an ethic of doing justice is related to the understanding of oppression from which our existence as Jewish lesbians originated. Many Jewish lesbians have focused on the ways in which we have been oppressed in society as Jews and as lesbians. While oppression theory argues that we must empower ourselves in the world, it is often the case that we retain and perpetuate our status as victims.

Doing justice must be based on a new understanding about the role of victims and oppressors. Micah's invocation is to do justice. That means that we take an active role in creating opportunities for justice in this world. *Asot mishpat* means that we cannot persist in perceiving ourselves as victims, or in perceiving the world split between the oppressed and the oppressor. This kind of dualistic thinking keeps us forever focused on the ways in which justice has not been done to us and limits our ability to take power into our hands. This position makes it impossible to engage in the task of doing justice.

From the position of victims we underestimate our own power to do justice. When we identify as victims, we do not think about how to change power relations to bring about a more just world. All we see are the ways in which we are not being treated fairly ourselves. Claiming the role of victim creates a situation that leads groups such as Jews and lesbians to pity and not respect ourselves. It also fosters comparisons of oppression. Despite our best efforts to avoid doing so, we focus on the ways in which our suffering compares to that of others. The problem is most clearly illustrated by Jews in North America who live in relative comfort, free from oppression. We still cling to images of the Holocaust, claiming the status of victim. We are wounded deeply by any and all expressions of anti-Semitism. No doubt, hatred of Jews is real in the United States. But we often focus our energies on claiming our victimization and ignore our own responsibility in the world for doing justice.

Ashkenazi Jewish lesbians forget the ways in which most of us are privileged because of the color of our skin in this country. We may be so engaged in seeing our own victimization that we forget the ways in which we contribute to the victimization of others. We cannot build coalitions if we do not acknowledge the difficult relationships between us. We also cannot build coalitions based on oppression alone; they must be built on a common view of a just society, of *asot mishpat*.

We need new categories to think about the possibilities for justice. In rethinking these questions, we may be able to put an end to the self-fulfilling prophecy of victim status and create new understandings of the ways in which groups in a multicultural society interact. We can maintain our integrity as diverse groups and at the same time begin to work together to end injustice for all. It is time to stop viewing this world through the lens of oppressor and victim, for it has not enhanced our ability to do justice in the world.[10]

Instead we should look for opportunities to build coalitions with others whose goal is to create a just society and to challenge injustice for others within the Jewish community. When we work for justice, we do it as Jewish lesbians. It is important that we maintain our cultural heritage and identity and bring the wisdom that this heritage provides into our work in the world. We cannot neglect our own rights while we work for the rights of others. Of course it is easier to focus exclusively on our own problems and tempting to argue that no one will address our concerns if we do not take up our own cause. But the goal of doing justice is to be present for others and by example to support the principle of working together toward the goal of a just society. Of course, there cannot be a just society unless all groups are treated fairly. So in this model, Jewish lesbians must have our needs met at the same time as we support the needs of others.

All of these issues lead us to the conclusion that *asot mishpat* requires the Jewish community to question its assumption that heterosexuality is normative and desirable for everyone. Rather, heterosexuality should be seen as one among many options, not the standard by which all else is judged. Acceptance of lesbians and gay men cannot be predicated on ignoring our sexuality, assuming that we do not choose our sexual identities, and denying differences like bisexuality and transgendered existence. A rigorous and serious look at heterosexuality and its meaning within the Jewish community is the next step in dialogue.

Guided by Micah's precept we have a set of goals to work toward: begin with self-acceptance, continue with love within our close communities, and reach beyond ourselves to demand and create a world within which there is justice for everyone. These goals are not for lesbian Jews only. This is a model for the transformation of Judaism from a lesbian perspective that derives from our interpretation of the biblical text.

## Notes

1. The concept of *ahavat hesed* is difficult to translate. The standard translation is "love of mercy," but this is inadequate. *Ahavat hesed* is love that is based on kindness. Perhaps it is the love of which Martin Buber speaks when he defines the "I-thou" relationship, love that is focused on the well-being of the "thou." I have decided to translate this concept as "loving well."

2. As to the origins of lesbianism, evidence comes from people's lives. Some women claim that they had erotic same-sex attractions from the time they were three; others claim to experience these feelings for the first time late in life. Both groups tell the truth. Women come to terms with lesbianism at different speeds and in different ways. For a fuller discussion about the issue of choice and biology, see Judith Plaskow, "Lesbian and Gay Rights: Asking the Right Question," *Tikkun* 9 (March–April 1994): 31–32.

3. This argument is based in Audre Lourde, "Uses of the Erotic," in *Sexuality and the Sacred: Sources for Theological Reflection*, ed. James B. Nelson and Sandra P. Longfellow (Louisville: Westminster/John Knox Press, 1994), 75–79.

4. *Mishnah Avot* 2:5.

5. The *New York Times* covered the story on four occasions in 1993: March 31, when CBST refused the organizers' suggestion that they could march, but without their banner (B2); April 21, when compromise was reached that CBST could march with the Reform movement's Zionist group (B12); May 5, when the *Times* profiled Sharon Kleinbaum, "Luckiest Rabbi in America Holds Faith amidst the Hate" (Alex Witchell, C1); and finally on May 8, when the synagogue was barred from marching and decided to hold a separate event (A16).

6. Barbara Rosenblum and Sandra Butler, *Cancer in Two Voices*, 2d ed. (Duluth, Minn.: Spinsters Ink, 1996).

7. This idea was first developed by Carol Gilligan, *In Different Voice* (Cambridge: Harvard University Press, 1992). It has been debated in feminist scholarship for many years.

8. Carter Heyward, *Our Passion for Justice* (New York: Pilgrim Press, 1984).

9. David Biale comments that "for a Jewish woman to adopt sexual identity, and even more to adopt lesbian identity, is to challenge the myths of the asexual Jewish woman." See David Biale, *Eros and the Jews* (New York: Basic Books, 1992), 225.

10. Iris Marion Young, *Justice and the Politics of Difference* (Princeton: Princeton University Press, 1990).

*Part 3*

# TAKING BACK
# THE CHRISTIAN SCRIPTURES

# 17

# Matthew and Mary of Magdala

## Good News for Sex Workers

### THOMAS HANKS

*Churches have selectively used the "good news" to exclude sexual minorities and sex workers. Tom Hanks questions the heterosexual presuppositions behind interpretation of Matthew. He raises an equally plausible hypothesis of Matthew as queer, countering the tradition of heterosexist interpretation. For Hanks, Matthew proclaims good news to sexual minorities and sex workers. Influenced by his years of living in Latin America and reading liberation theologians, Hanks is suspicious of the feminist rescue of Mary Magdalene from a tradition that has understood her as a prostitute. Hanks takes the traditional reading of her as a sex worker to proclaim good news for sexual minorities. Hanks founded Other Sheep to provide an outreach to sexual minorities in Latin and South America. It has established forty resource centers for sexual minorities in their struggles for liberation.*

Somehow the shockingly subversive Gospel of Matthew, the toll collector ("publican" in our older translations), often comes across in our Sunday schools and stained-glass windows like some doleful IRS representative about to summon you for a final audit against which you will have no defense. Yet it is Matthew alone of our Gospel writers who preserves Jesus' words to the religious leaders of his day:

> "Truly I tell you, the IRS bureaucrats and the sex workers are going into God's just new order ahead of you. For John [the Baptist] came to you in the way of liberating justice and you did not believe him, but the IRS bureaucrats and the sex workers believed in him, and even after you saw it, you did not change your lifestyle and believe in him."
> (21:31–32)

According to second-century church tradition, Matthew was written by the toll collector Matthew/Levi, whom Jesus called to be a disciple (9:9) and later commissioned as one of the twelve apostles (10:3). Current scholarship dates the Gospel around 85 C.E. and suggests that Matthew/Levi, the toll collector and apostle (eyewitness), may be more the ultimate authority behind the Gospel rather than the final editor/author of the edition we have. The author is commonly recognized as being a Jewish Christian, writing in and for the multicultural believing communities (synagogues and house churches) of Antioch in Syria (Matt. 4:24; Acts 11:19–20; 13:1–3). Matthew's Jewish background is evident everywhere: the opening genealogy, the fourteen citations of prophecies Jesus fulfilled, concern even for the minutiae of Moses' law (5:17–20; 23:1–3), and the initial limitation of Jesus' mission to the lost sheep of the house of Israel (10:5–6; 15:24). The emphatically Jewish viewpoint and emphasis on things Jewish have led scholars to see a miniature self-portrayal in Matthew's citation of Jesus' description of the faithful scribe:

> "Therefore every scribe who has been educated for leadership in God's just new order is like the master of a household who brings out of his treasure what is new and what is old." (13:52)

Matthew's Gospel culminates in the Great Commission (28:16–20) to make the community of Jesus' followers multicultural and share his good news with all "nations" (cultures, ethnic groups). Matthew's Gospel alone gives us Jesus' Magna Carta for the best-known sexual minorities of his day, the eunuchs, who were excluded from cultic participation by Moses' law (Deut. 23:1) but welcomed and celebrated by the prophet Isaiah (56:1–8) and later by the early church (Acts 8:26–40):

> For there are eunuchs who have been so from birth, and there are eunuchs who have been made eunuchs by others, and there are eunuchs who have made themselves eunuchs for the sake of the kingdom of heaven. (Matt. 19:12)

Eunuchs did not fulfill patriarchal expectations for the kind of penetrative sex with women that could result in procreation, but we should not assume that "eunuch" meant "sexless," since other alternatives were open to many of them. Matthew had no wife (like Jesus, Paul, and the other twelve apostles, Peter alone excepted), so he undoubtedly saw himself as a kind of "eunuch," portrayed in Paul's description of a variety of sexual minorities.

Such factors, long known to students of Matthew, leave us with an obvious question that no one seems to have posed: why would a nice Jewish boy, so devout and well educated, decide to become a despised "publican" (a notoriously dishonest profession in service of a hated empire and thus traitor to the Jewish people)?! The association of publicans with prostitutes, which Matthew makes explicit in his famous dinner party for Jesus (9:9–13), need not indicate that all publicans were incorrigible womanizers. Rather they shared with the prostitutes the shame and stigma of social exclusion.

Perhaps the most likely scenario is that Matthew did not decide to "run away" from home (like the prodigal son of Luke 15) but was kicked out for being an "abomination" (gay) and thus had to enter the only profession open to him! Some such traumatic rupture with his parents best explains the weird (queer?) combination in the Gospel of fervent Jewish piety along with the lifestyle of a hated publican whose only friends are other traitors and prostitutes. The rejection by his family might well have occurred in his early teens if he refused to enter into a marriage arranged by his father (Gen. 24).

Scholars who still maintain pretensions of "objectivity" will consider the gay reading of Matthew "novelistic," but they overlook how mythological is their own traditional heterosexist reading, rooted in childhood fairy tales of princes marrying Cinderella types and continually reinforced by homophobic censorship of alternative lifestyle images. The incapacity to plant and water alternative hypotheses is a sign, not of scholarly objectivity ("fairness" would be a more appropriately humble norm), but of ideological captivity to the dominant culture.

Obviously we cannot "prove" any gay hypothesis from the data at hand, but is there a shred of evidence to support the alternative hypothesis? Are we to believe that Matthew was just a "normal" heterosexual who first inexplicably betrayed family, faith, and nation to become a publican but then later decided that he could best serve God and find fulfillment by shelving God's command to "be fruitful and multiply" (Gen. 1:28) and join up with Jesus' band of itinerant bachelors (Luke 14:26; 18:29)? The more closely we scrutinize Matthew's Gospel, with the clash in its stringent dialectic between fervent Jewish piety and scandalous lifestyles, the less likely does the traditionally assumed "heterosexual" hypothesis appear. Logically one might also explore a "bisexual" hypothesis, but I fail to see how it might account for the strong conflictive dialectic apparent in the data from Matthew.

Matthew's gender-bending sexuality surfaces even in his opening genealogy (1:1–17), where he first subverts patriarchy by slipping four women into what was supposed to be a list of male descendants (according to the traditional Jewish literary genre; cf. Luke 3:23–38 with no women before Mary). But Matthew includes only women who were either (unclean) Gentiles or married to (unclean) Gentiles, all of whose irregular sexual unions would be viewed as undermining traditional patriarchal "family values": the harlots, Tamar and Rahab, the Moabitess Ruth (who boldly seduced Boaz), and Bathsheba (adulteress wife of the Gentile Uriah). One expects a certain expertise in simple math from an educated toll-collector-turned-scribe, but Matthew "queers" his math in his genealogy, pretending to find groups of fourteen, when careful counting by scholars reveals that (like militant gays who "can't even march straight") our publican either can't count straight or (like a thoroughbred queer) decides not to (1:14; see the commentaries for various befuddled "explanations").

Jewish writers delighted in the literary device known as "inclusion," by which the writer returns at the end of his piece to his starting point. So we should not be surprised to find Matthew playing up the role of women, particularly Mary of Magdala, at the conclusion of his Gospel (28:55–56, 61; 28:10). Mary of Magdala for centuries suffered from scholarly neglect on the part of white male advocacy scholarship. This tradition, ever posing as alone rational and objective (and never advocating anything), long affirmed that women could not be ordained as church leaders because the Great Commission (Matthew's conclusion, 28:16–20) was directed only to eleven male disciples.

A more coherent reading of Matthew's Gospel and conclusion would show that in the Great Commission Jesus is graciously inviting the cowardly "losers" (the "eleven") to join up with the courageous women, led by Mary of Magdala, who had already begun to proclaim the good news of his triumph over death. From the early centuries of Christianity, the church fathers have confused her as the penitent prostitute (confusing the forgiven harlot of Luke 7:36–50 with the noble Mary of Magdala in Luke 8:1–3, whose only failing was that she had to be exorcized of seven demons). The feminist scholarship in this area is excellent, makes fascinating reading, and certainly advances enormously our comprehension of Mary of Magdala, the Scriptures, the traditions concerning her, and the male distortions (posing as objective history) concerning her.[1]

However (perhaps because I have associated too long with Latin American theologians under the spell of the Masters of Suspicion) I cannot help but detect the aroma of another plot—alas this time a feminist one: in the feminist scholarly works dedicated to rescuing the Magdalene from her traditional disreputable reputation, we find a strong antisex bias. This bias makes it almost as difficult for many of them to write the word "prostitute" as it is for some of the older generation to get out the word "homosexual" (not to mention "queer"). In the male plot, centuries of scholars distorted the Magdalene's history in order to exclude women from ordination and church leadership. Now, when the ecclesiastical battle is over ordination of sexual minorities, we find feminist scholars using (or abusing) the Magdalene's history to present her as a paragon of sexual "virtue" (i.e., abstention) comparable only to the Virgin Mary.

I would suggest that closer attention on the part of all of us to Matthew's subversive perspective on sexual minorities might result in better understanding of Jesus' revolutionary teaching—and prove liberating not only for "virtuous" women but also for sexual minorities of all genders. Obviously from our limited historical data and our distant perspective, we can no more "prove" that Mary of Magadala was a prostitute than we can "prove" that Matthew was queer. However, before dismissing as ideological "advocacy" scholarship the hypothesis that Mary the sex worker could be a church leader on par or superior to Peter, we should look just as critically at the alternative hypotheses.

Just what was Mary of Magdala's profession? Feminist scholarship reminds us that Mary of Magdala, the first witness to the resurrection and "apostle to the apostles," did not deny Jesus three times as did Peter. Could not this Mary be a sex worker, repentant of her sin, but not of her sexuality (not even necessarily a sex worker become seamstress)? Why could she not be a church leader on par with Peter and Paul as a woman and as a sexual minority? (Feminist scholars properly remind us of the common white male distortion resulting from always posing questions as either/or instead of both/and.)

In addition to Matthew's emphasis on publicans and sexual minorities (prostitutes, eunuchs, women in irregular unions) and his apparent use of inclusion with Mary of Magdala reechoing the women, including prostitutes, in the opening genealogy, we have the fact that the other women associated with the Magdalene are identified by their "family values" ("mother of..." or "wife of..."), while Mary of Magdala is simply identified by her city or origin (a port town of ill repute, as feminist scholarship makes clear). Evidently Mary of Magdala had no husband and no children. Unlike Dorcas, the widow-become-seamstress, or Lydia, the seller of purple goods (Acts 9; 16), Mary of Magadala is never explicitly identified as having any respectable profession. No family ties are indicated, yet she is indicated to be a person of considerable economic resources, as sex workers or courtesans often were in her context (Matt. 27:55–56; Mark 15:40–41; Luke 8:1–3).

In a society where "nice" women stayed at home, Mary of Magdala and a few other gender-benders felt free to travel about with a band of itinerant single males and ministered to them from their wealth—a scandalous lifestyle in a conservative patriarchal Jewish environment. The ambitious "mother of the sons of Zebedee" (Matt. 20:20) is never identified as the "wife" of Zebedee since she evidently followed the example of James and John and abandoned her husband to join Jesus in his itinerant ministry (4:21–22; 27:55).[2] Matthew portrays women shattering patriarchal tradition and reclining at table with the men (9:10–13; 11:19; 14:21; cf. Luke 7:36–50). In a society where men were not even expected to talk to women in public (John 4), Mary of Magadala felt free to grasp Jesus' feet (Matt. 28:9), and she even had to be rebuked for clinging to him (the famous Noli me tangere of John 20:17). Evidently she was a woman who felt comfortable (not "sexually harassed") with socially disapproved physical contact with males (in fact, Jesus sounds more like the one who is being "sexually harassed"!).

In both Matthew and John, therefore, it is not the male Jesus who takes the initiative in physical contact but Mary of Magdala. This character trait will be viewed as negative only by patriarchal males (who think males should always initiate physical contact with women) or by women who are hypersensitive about physical contact with men (often lesbians or/and victims of male sexual abuse in childhood), who want their ample "space" secure and consider any uninvited physical contact with men as "harassment." Even if not a prostitute, Mary of Magdala might be a good role model for all concerned in cultures where physical touch has become so problematic and litigious.

Is Matthew's queer penchant for proclaiming good news to sexual minorities and sex workers (possibly including Mary of Magdala) contradicted by the data from the other Gospels that has been scrutinized by feminist scholarship? Was it only a patriarchal male plot that led to the medieval identification of Mary of Magadala (Luke 8:1–3) with the penitent prostitute of Luke 7:36–50? Certainly it is reading into Luke's narrative to insist that Mary of Magdala must be the prostitute of the preceding text in Luke 7, but that does not prove that Mary was not a prostitute. Why else would Luke take Mark's comments about Mary and the other women who ministered to Jesus, beginning in Galilee (Mark 15:40–41), and move them from the passion story to place them immediately after the episode of the prostitute who anointed Jesus' feet with her tears? Would this not be an ideal way of both preserving the prostitute's memorable act and suggesting something of Mary's background to those not prejudiced against prostitutes? Luke's forward placement would protect Mary's later reputation as apostle to the apostles and church leader for those who were not yet ready for such a radical as Jesus. Luke makes clear that Jesus accepted publicans and prostitutes as friends within his circle of disciples, but perhaps he only dared hint that they were also accepted as church leaders (see the Samaritan woman in John 4).

When the Gospel writers describe in explicit detail other exorcisms involving only one demon, why are Mary's "seven demons" left as such a vague blur (Luke 8:2)? Second Testament scholars point to Luke's tendency to eliminate or change passages in Mark unfavorable to those whose subsequent career makes them worthy of respect. Granted, tradition hates a vacuum, and originally anonymous figures often get tagged with just about any name that will rescue them from anonymity. There were, however, sometimes wise and loving reasons for not supplying names and occupations of all whose story appears in scripture (see the nameless woman taken in adultery, whose male partner somehow managed to escape; John 8:1–11).

Another factor worth weighing is the almost universal human tendency to use euphemistic language to describe sexual matters ("Adam knew Eve . . ."). The fact that scripture nowhere explicitly identifies Mary of Magdala as a prostitute does not justify the kind of flat denial of the possibility common in recent feminist scholarship. Perhaps Matthew's queer preoccupation with sex workers is only the first step in the growing male plot to defame Mary's character. But then again, given Jesus' penchant for friendship with publicans, prostitutes, and sexual minorities (shared by Matthew), why not follow the clues about Mary's profession and weigh the alternatives?

Whatever the uncertainties of biblical interpretation, medieval Christianity identified Mary of Magdala with the prostitute of Luke 7:36.[3] This identification generated indifference, prejudice, and further marginalization of sex workers. Some feminist scholars need to be reminded that sex workers, lesbians, and many other sexual minorities are women too. If sex workers are to be denied their traditional patron saint in the name of more accurate biblical scholarship, we should at least at the same time make clear that Jesus and his authentic followers welcomed sexual minorities without discrimination.

Another narrative in which Matthew ventures out of the closet is the healing of the centurion's slave (Matt. 8:5–13; Luke 7:1–10; John 4:46–54),[4] one of but two miracle stories depicting Jesus as healing from a distance. The "unclean" Gentile centurion's insistence that he is not worthy to have a famous Jewish rabbi enter his home might well remind us of common humorous efforts to "dedyke the house," classically portrayed in both the original French and later Hollywood versions of *La Cage aux Folles*. Finally, the importance of the story to early followers of Jesus is indicated by the fact that Luke places it immediately after his version of the Sermon on the Mount, perhaps a counterpoint to Moses' ten plagues leading to the Exodus and the Ten Commandments.

The first of Matthew's ten miracles stories (nine of which are healings) is the cleansing of a leper. The biblical terminology may signify a variety of skin diseases. In order to heal the unclean man, Jesus touches him (contrary to Lev. 13–14, where "lepers" contaminate all who touch them). Since male-male anal sex (without condoms) also renders participants "unclean" (in both Lev. 18; 20 as well as Rom. 1:24–27), Matthew's linking of the cleansing of a leper (8:1–4) with the healing of the unclean (Gentile) centurion's beloved slave (8:5–13) is further indication that Matthew recognized the sexual dimension of the centurion's love for his slave and presented Jesus as blessing the relationship with his powerful word of healing. Matthew's concluding emphasis on the greatness and adequacy of the centurion's faith (8:10–13) reminds readers that Jesus came, not to break up loving consensual same-sex relations (however some of his contemporaries may have misinterpreted Leviticus), but to heal and empower them. Sexual minorities, like everyone else, can experience authentic freedom through their faith in the Liberator God of the Exodus, incarnate in the poor carpenter from Nazareth.

If we are correct in our perception that Matthew was queer, we can appreciate how important the issue of details in the Mosaic law would be for him. In the Sermon on the Mount, Matthew presents Jesus as beginning a process of deconstruction of the apparent rigorous legalism of 5:17–20 (see 23:1):[5]

> "But I say to you that every one who is angry with his brother will be liable to judgment and whoever says to his brother 'sissy' will be answerable to the Sanhedrin, and whoever says 'you bugger' will be liable to fiery Gehenna." (5:22)

Then in the ten miracle stories (nine healings) in Matthew 8–9, we find Jesus subverting the law by touching an "unclean" leper, restoring an apparently gay relationship by healing the Roman centurion's beloved slave, touching an unclean corpse to resuscitate it, etc. Healings in place of the plagues of Exodus, blessing of homoerotic relationships, which everyone (wrongly) assumed to be an abomination according to Leviticus! Matthew's deconstruction is thorough and devastating but so subtly achieved that most readers get swept along into revising their views and abandoning their prejudices without realizing what is happening to them. After Jesus' assurance of his concern that not a jot of Moses' Torah is going to be jettisoned, the readers' defenses are down, and Matthew manages to slip Jesus into the place of supreme authority traditionally held by Moses: "Who cares whether that nice Roman centurion has a gay lover—after all, when kings and emperors are desecrating the Jewish Temple with their idols, that centurion will build us a synagogue with his own money! Maybe we should stop calling people like that 'faggots.' Perhaps Alexander the Great was right after all, and gays can be good soldiers! Whatever those two verses in Leviticus mean, the local synagogue reader must be misinterpreting them if he thinks such devout and generous people are an unclean abomination."

The rigorous dialectic evident in Matthew's struggle to be respectful to every detail of Torah, yet free from the law as a disciple of Jesus, and this stunning process of deconstruction carried out from the beginning to end of Matthew's Gospel are just what we might expect from someone wrestling with the queer bent in his own capacity to love God and neighbor. Contemporary scholars correctly detect many differences in the persons and theologies of Matthew, Paul, and John. However, each is best understood when we recognize their queerness and appreciate the enormous struggle this would have meant for pious Jewish males in their patriarchal society of the first century,

understand how Matthew, Paul, and John discovered in Jesus of Nazareth God's agent for integral human liberation, who loved them in their peculiarity (Gal. 2:20) and taught them to accept their queerness as a spiritual gift (Matt. 19:11–12; 1 Cor. 7:7),

and then see how their books represent a kind of "coming out" to themselves in the presence of God, leading to a radical and thorough deconstruction of their internalized homophobia (for which the misinterpretation of Torah common in their day had been a major cause).

Many gays like myself, impacted by evangelical teaching in our youth, can easily empathize with Matthew's long struggle with the jots and tittles of scripture and his dramatic encounter with a Christ who at times apparently affirms, yet more often transcends, them. Shortly after my own evangelical conversion I left home for Northwestern University and became an active student leader in InterVarsity Christian Fellowship, a student movement with a strong emphasis on inductive Bible study, evangelism, and world mission. After theological studies this led to two decades of submission to ex-gay quackery to "cure" my homosexuality, "marriage" (perhaps more accurately, a failed scientific experiment), and twenty-five years of service with an evangelical mission board in Latin America. Moving from Costa Rica, during our last three years with the mission board (1986–88), in Buenos Aires I began at last to partake of the sacrament of coming out. Like Matthew, I sensed a deep call to follow Jesus in ministry to those marginalized and despised by traditional religions. This led to our resignation from the board (which does not even permit separation, much less divorce). From 1989 until 1991 in my personal crisis (deprived of salary, health insurance, rejected by most friends), I was immensely helped as I worked closely with the Universal Fellowship of Metropolitan Churches (UFMCC) in Latin America. However, my denomination (Presbyterian) did not defrock me, and the UFMCC could not give priority to the trench warfare within the mainline churches. With a few old friends and several new ones who shared a similar vision, in 1992 we sensed God's leading to begin a Multicultural Ministry with Sexual Minorities, which soon took the name Other Sheep.

Our Antioch was St. Louis, but soon from Mexico, John Doner and José Hernández undertook a "Mission Jesus Style" (as a same-sex couple traveling light). Within six months they were able to visit virtually every country in Latin America by bus and established some forty resource centers with

Spanish materials for sexual minorities (PFLAG for parents and friends, contemporary scientific materials on homosexuality, Safer Sex, affirming theological and biblical materials). Traditional mainline and evangelical agencies have not even been able to acknowledge the presence of some forty million lesbigays in Latin America, much less work with them. We believe God has raised up Other Sheep as an ecumenical catalyst to respond to needs like this and obey the Great Commission to "teach all nations" (Matt. 28:16–20) to obey Jesus' teachings (often transcending Moses' laws).

In the worldwide struggle of sexual minorities for liberation, freedom, justice, and love, the significance of Matthew's good news to the poor and oppressed is enormous. The Great Commission that concludes the Gospel reminds us that much of primitive Christianity's dynamic growth was due to their capacity to "think globally" as they acted locally. Paul's paradigmatic pioneering efforts to develop a global network of Jesus' followers (envisioned in Matt. 28:16–20) might remind local individuals and groups (in the often isolationist U.S.A.) of their need to show solidarity with sexual minorities in other countries through international entities such as ILGA (International Lesbian and Gay Association) and Other Sheep (Multicultural Ministries with Sexual Minorities).

Matthew's sensitive dialectical deconstruction of cruel legalism shows us how to respect details in the Scriptures dear to the pious—and yet experience that freedom from the yoke of the law (Gal. 5:1; Acts 15:10), for which Jesus and Paul are outstanding paradigms. Above all, the breadth of Jesus' own solidarity with humans in their suffering and oppression (the economically poor, women, the sick and physically challenged, sexual minorities, persons of every culture and color) calls us out of our ghettos and narrow ideological myopia into the kind of global rainbow coalition that can alone challenge and transform the existing international power structures that oppress us. Any attempt to think globally and act locally for human liberation, of course, must begin with a radical personal commitment at first daunting but ultimately affirming of all that we most deeply desire and seek:

> "Come to me, all you that are weary and are carrying heavy burdens, and I will give you rest. Take my yoke upon you, and learn from me; for I am gentle and humble in heart, and you will find rest for your souls. For my yoke is easy and my burden is light." (Matt. 11:28–30)

## Notes

1. Carla Ricci, *Mary Magdalene and Many Others: Women Who Followed Jesus* (Minneapolis: Fortress Press, 1991/94); Jane Schaberg, "How Mary Magdalene Became a Whore," *Bible Review* 8, no. 5 (October 1992): 30–37; Susan Haskins, *Mary Magdalen: Myth and Metaphor* (New York: Harcourt, Brace, 1993); Mary R. Thompson, *Mary of Magdala: Apostle and Leader* (Mahwah, N.J.: Paulist Press, 1995); Esther de Boer, *Mary Magdalene: Beyond the Myth* (Harrisburg, Pa.: Trinity Press International, 1996/97).

2. Emily Cheney, "The Mother of the Sons of Zebedee (Matthew 27:56)," *Journal for the Study of the New Testament* 68 (1997): 13–21.

3. Haskins, *Mary Magdalen*, 317–65.

4. The probability that the centurion's relationship with his slave included a sexual dimension has been pointed out by various scholars: Gerd Theissen, *In the Shadow of the Galilean: The Quest of the Historical Jesus in Narrative Form* (London: SCM Press, 1986/87), 106; Michael Gray-Fow, "Pederasty, the Scantian Law, and the Roman Army," *Journal of Psychohistory* 13 (1986): 449–60; Donald Mader, "The *Entimos Pais* [Beloved Slave] of Matthew 8:5–13 and Luke 7:1–10," in *Homosexuality and Religion and Philosophy*, ed. Wayne R. Dynes and Stephen Donaldson (New York: Garland, 1992), 223–35; James E. Miller, "The Centurion and His Slave Boy" (unpublished seminar paper for the Society of Biblical Literature, 1997). This probability has been systematically ignored by heterosexist male advocacy scholarship. Virgilio C. Corbo, "Capernaum," in *The Anchor Bible Dictionary*, ed. David Noel Freedman (New York: Doubleday, 1992), 1:866–69.

5. Warren Johansson, "Whoever Shall Say to His Brother, Racha (Matthew 5:22)," in *Homosexuality and Religion and Philosophy*, ed. Wayne R. Dynes and Stephen Donaldson (New York: Garland, 1984/92), 212–14.

# 18

# Coming Out, Lazarus's and Ours

## Queer Reflections of a Psychospiritual, Political Journey

### BENJAMIN PERKINS

*In this essay, Benjamin Perkins uses the Lazarus narrative as a starting point for exploring the sacramental elements of coming out and the psychospiritual, political journey of the queer person. As an Unitarian Universalist Christian, Perkins takes Lazarus's story and draws parallels between it and the modern-day understanding of the coming-out process-event.[1] Consequently, coming out itself should be understood as a sacrament and should be celebrated liturgically as such. Finally, Perkins asserts that Lazarus's story is one of praxis: God's, the individual's, and the community's. All must do their part in a nexus of liberation.*

## Reimagining Lazarus's Story

The story of Lazarus's resurrection continually haunts and captures my imagination,[2] more than perhaps any other New Testament story. In the narrative, which is one of the longest in the New Testament, Jesus has been preaching in the villages beyond the Jordan River when he receives news of the illness of his beloved Lazarus. Although Jesus knows about Lazarus's illness, he does not leave immediately but instead waits two days before making the journey to Bethany, where Lazarus lives with his sisters Mary and Martha, all of whom were Jesus' close friends. By the time Jesus arrives, Lazarus has been dead for four days, and there is a stench. Jesus weeps for Lazarus, but he also scolds Martha for her disbelief that Lazarus would live again. And, upon praying to God, Jesus commands Lazarus to life and then commands those in Lazarus's midst to unbind him.

As I enter the text, I am struck by its unrelenting power to convey that life can come from a lifeless situation and existence, which has deep resonances for anyone who has lived a closeted existence. Lazarus's story, in my estimation, is a queer tale because the themes contained within it speak to the psychospiritual journey of queer persons. For instance, in my own personal experience of coming out, I remember distinctly telling my friends that I felt as if I had been given a new life, that the hopelessness and despair that shrouded me like a thick cloud had lifted. Thus for me, and many other queer individuals, it takes no stretch of the imagination to embody the narrative and, miraculously, bring it to new life! This is the wonderful, reimaginative possibility that lies within this biblical text. Some would argue that this is the reimaginative possibility that lies within all biblical texts.

Lazarus's story gives me permission, no, authority, to look at my own process of coming out as a sacramental journey. Therefore, I take seriously Jesus' command to "come out." I also take equally seriously Jesus command to those surrounding Lazarus to "unbind him, and let him go!" What follows is a result of my encounters with the Lazarus narrative and its life-giving hope. As such, this is not an exegetical essay, which has been done countless times; rather, I have decided to explore the implications of the narrative as a queer story that calls us to come out and to be unbound. My hope is that such an exploration will serve as one of many that explore the joy and beauty contained within a text that has oftentimes been read only to serve heterosexist interests. To this I exclaim, "No more!"

In this essay I will argue that Lazarus's story can be understood as a coming out and, as such, should be celebrated as a sacrament, which I define as an event that celebrates the renewal of life and the Unitarian Universalist principles of "the interdependent web of existence" and "the inherent worth and dignity of every person."[3] Additionally, the Lazarus narrative appears within the Johannine book of signs, which has a sacramental quality of pointing out how God is revealed within the human world. Sacraments call us to remember the sanctity of our existence and our relationship to the Divine. Here I am reclaiming the concept of a sacrament from more narrow definitions because I believe that it is a compelling way to underscore the Unitarian Universalist commitment to the idea that each human being is infinitely precious and that we as a faith community are dedicated to realizing these principles in our actions. Therefore, the sacrament I call us to celebrate is personal, spiritual, communal, and unapologetically political. Ours is a prophetic tradition, and it is in that spirit that I want to reclaim the sacrament and its provocative imagery. Additionally, I use the imagery of sacrament as a way of smashing the idols of theological heterosexism by celebrating the psychospiritual journey of the queer person, thereby challenging the parochial idea that heterosexuality is the only "valid" sexual expression.

By reframing and reimagining coming out as a sacrament, we bring a communal and, hopefully, liturgical recognition to a process-event that has traditionally been given a lukewarm reception by those in religious settings, even in a "liberal" denomination like Unitarian Universalism. In addition, bringing attention to the queer person's religious journey serves to educate those ignorant of how religious discourses have been used in the service of denying the humanity of queer persons; it does so by the mere fact that such a service is needed at all, suggesting a paucity of liturgical recognition of the gifts that queer people bring to the religious community.

My position in this essay is deeply informed by my multiple identities—that of a queer African American male, a Unitarian Universalist, and a progressively minded, marginal Christian theology student, who has also studied psychology extensively.[4] All of these locations influence my view and continuously inform the work that I do. Additionally, my view of sexuality is one that is neither wholly essentialistic nor constructivistic, but rather lies somewhere in between. Put more simply, I believe that identity, sexual and otherwise, is not fixed, nor is it free-floating. I use the term "queer" because it is useful, especially when speaking about a group of individuals who are marginalized because of their sexual identity and, most importantly, because identity does tell us something about who we are as profoundly relational beings.

Also, because I self-identify as a Christian, the faith tradition of my fore-mothers and fathers, this essay uses unabashedly Christian imagery, in which I am fairly conversant. I realize that this poses a uniquely Unitarian Universalist challenge to those in my reading audience, namely, those who may not have a Christian background. I will make every effort humanly possible to explain and illuminate Christocentric concepts whenever and wherever I deem it necessary to do so. And finally, most importantly I ask for a degree of latitude and charity as I embark on a task that, I believe, merits serious consideration and affirmation.

## Coming Out as Sacrament:
## Naming the Sacred Process-Event

Queer author Michael Nava writes that the coming-out process for queers is similar, if not identical, to being born again: "Being 'born again' and 'coming out' are transcendent experiences that produce a profound change in perception. You never look at yourself, your life, or your culture the same way again."[5] Additionally, queer theologian Chris Glaser has suggested, along with others, that coming out is a sacrament, not unlike baptism or any of the other sacraments observed by the church.

I view the coming-out phenomenon as a "process-event." Coming out, when understood as a sacrament, suggests powerfully that something is occurring that is moving us toward a deeper understanding of ourselves, our world, and our Source. In John 11, Jesus calls to Lazarus, shouting for him to come out of the tomb. Lazarus is called forth to life. For queer individuals the parallel is unmistakable: we are called out in a process that moves us toward a greater integrity in our relationship to self and others. As radical theologian-priest-educator Matthew Fox describes, "[the] sacrament of 'coming out' [is a] kind of letting go: a letting go of images of personhood, sexuality, and selfhood that society has put on in favor of trusting oneself enough to be oneself."[6] Coincidentally, what I am suggesting is that this move toward integrity and authenticity is best understood biblically. Here I am reminded most immediately of the words of Jesus found in saying 70 of the Gospel of Thomas, "If you bring forth that which is within you, that which is within you will save you; if you do not bring forth that which is within you, that which you do not bring forth will destroy you."

## Coming Out and the Hermeneutic of Reimagination

Another useful tool that helps us to frame the coming-out process-event in religious/spiritual terms is hermeneutics, the principles of interpretation, specifically of biblical texts.[7] Many, if not all, of the contemporary liberation, feminist, and gay theologies start with the principle of the hermeneutic of suspicion, the idea that the reader must be wary of traditional interpretations of any biblical text because they have been interpreted with heretofore unacknowledged biases, be they sexist, racist, and/or homophobic.[8] The hermeneutic of suspicion has been remarkably useful for the kind of genealogical analyses that have helped destabilize many of the deeply entrenched problematic aspects of biblical interpretation. Queer French philosopher and social critic Michel Foucault's work is indispensable here because it underscores what truly is at stake when one engages in such genealogical analyses:

> Criticism is a matter of flushing out that thought and trying to change it: to show that things are not self-evident as one believed, to see that what is accepted as self-evident will no longer be accepted as such. Practicing criticism is a matter of making facile gestures difficult. In these circumstances, criticism (and radical criticism) is absolutely indispensable for any transformation.[9]

For Foucault and others who use genealogical analysis, this method can be likened to pointing out that the emperor's new clothes are not new, nor are they clothes! More frankly stated, oftentimes the genealogical method has the primary result of exposing the hypocrisy of the so-called self-evident aspects of culture, particularly religion and its unchallenged assumptions and dogma.

But while the hermeneutic of suspicion and the attendant genealogical analyses have done a great deal, they alone are insufficient because they do not engage the interpreter in an equally important task of revitalizing and reimagining what the biblical texts might be saying to a contemporary audience. Feminist biblical scholars like Elisabeth Schüssler Fiorenza, for instance, have been particularly cognizant of this criticism and have taken up the cause by utilizing a "hermeneutic of reimagination."[10] In the hermeneutic of reimagination the interpreter enters a text to look for the silences, possibilities, and dangerous memories "lost beneath nearly two millennia of patriarchal and ecclesial formulations."[11] This interpretive principle allows queers and other marginalized groups to take the biblical texts and ask the revolutionary question, "What if?" Most importantly for the queer reading of the Lazarus narrative, it allows us to "imaginatively release the elements of struggle and resistance within the text into [our] lives."[12]

The story of Lazarus's resurrection is ripe for a hermeneutic of reimagination, for it is a coming-out story. Lazarus is dead, and he has been called to new life by the power of God—a God who acts but also commands that Lazarus and the community do their parts. It is crucial that we remember that it is Lazarus who must answer the call to come out and the community who must unbind him.[13] Such a reimagination reminds us that coming out is far from an individual event; it must take place in community.

## Lazarus's and Our Coming Out: Making Connections in a Sacramental Journey

Queer Christian liberation theologian Robert Goss states, "To sacramentalize is to pay attention. It is what a community does when it names and claims ordinary human experience as holy, connecting them with history and propelling them into the future."[14] If we take Goss's definition seriously, coupled with Tillich's contribution and the hermeneutic of reimagination, then the coming out of Lazarus from the tomb and our coming out have an unmistakably sacramental quality: "Coming out as sacrament means recognizing God's word acting in our life, delivering us from the closet, guiding and sustaining us, and promising us a new and more meaningful life."[15]

Therefore, with our political, philosophical, and theological framework for understanding the coming-out process, we need to look now at how the sacramental nature of the coming-out process-event in the Lazarus story unfolds and how it parallels the modern-day coming out for queer persons.

In drawing such parallels, we will find deep psychospiritual resonances that lead even more credence to the thesis that coming out is a sacrament. With this in mind, I have chosen to organize the Lazarus story into five themes/movements that reflect the sacramental journey: fear, commitment, doubt, resurrection, and commission.

## Fear

Fear is one of the first themes we encounter in the Lazarus story. Mary and Martha are both afraid because they fear that Lazarus will die if Jesus does not come to heal him. In coming out, many of us fear that we will die untimely deaths at the hands of a heterosexist, homophobic society. The recent brutal murder of Matthew Shephard, for example, simply underscores this frightening reality for queers.

In addition to the fear that Mary and Martha have, it is also apparent that the wider society is fearful, fearful of Jesus' power to perform signs and wonders. The disciples are afraid that Jesus will be stoned if he returns to Judea. And the Pharisees are afraid of what Jesus' power truly signifies: God's coming out! They will do whatever it takes to quash the inbreaking good news and reign of God.

The Lazarus story, however, implicitly calls us to move beyond fear. Jesus intuits that it is only through loving that fear can be extinguished. He loves Lazarus and moves through the fear of persecution and death to get to him. We, like Jesus, also have to move through fear to arrive at love—love of ourselves and love for a world that oftentimes seeks to destroy us. It means that we learn to love in spite of fear in the hope that something far more glorious lies just beyond the horizon of our awareness: true freedom.

## Commitment

Jesus' love for Lazarus serves as an exemplar for all who struggle to love and be in the face of fear, ignorance, and hatred. Thus Lazarus's story is also one of commitment. Jesus' passionate love for Lazarus, as evidenced by the tears that he sheds, transcends even death. Such a fierce and unapologetic display of emotion continues to be a great source of comfort to me, reminding me of Paul's assertion that "neither death, nor life, nor angels, nor rulers, nor things present, nor things to come, nor powers, nor height, nor depth, nor anything else in all creation, will be able to separate us from the love of God in Christ Jesus our Lord" (Rom. 8:38–39).

In the Lazarus story Jesus knows that nothing can separate him from God's love or his love for Lazarus; therefore, Jesus commits himself to Lazarus even though he knows the fear and hatred that such a commitment incites. Jesus will not be deterred. It is no coincidence that we queers also find ourselves in a similar situation. We know that our coming out signals a commitment that is oftentimes met with fear, derision, and even violence. Our commitment to be ourselves means that we too will clash with the holier-than-thou, modern-day Pharisees (also known as the religious right, in its many guises). However, we must cling to the promise that we are loved by God in unfathomable depths and that nothing can change that beautifully irrevocable fact.

## Doubt

It is difficult to maintain our commitments. While there are moments of unwavering and unflagging devotion, there are often equally as many moments of intense doubt and recrimination, and we begin to grow fainthearted and waver in our commitment to be queer. In the Lazarus story a similar thing happens: both Mary and Martha, who loved Jesus and were committed to his ministry, did not grasp fully the immediacy and power of God's love; they doubted its ability to transcend space, temporality, and death, as evidenced by the fact that they both utter the same words: "Lord, if you had been here, my brother would not have died" (John 11:21, 32).

Like Mary and Martha, I have also doubted God's power to transform the death-dealing effects of homophobia, heterosexism, and racism into a life-affirming existence where all are celebrated for the many unique gifts they bring to creation. During my darkest moments in "Christian" reparative therapy, I thought that it would have been far better for me if I were heterosexual, if God had simply "been there" before my queerness developed. Today I realize that my queerness, in Jesus' words, "is for God's glory" (John 11:46).

## Resurrection

Fortunately, in the depths of our despair, doubt, and anguish, the miraculous happens—life bursts forth from death and hopelessness. Lazarus is called forth from the tomb. And like Lazarus's coming out of his tomb, we too are called out of our closets/tombs. We are called to leave a mode of existence that encourages dishonesty and deception for a life that celebrates authenticity and vulnerability. In answering this call to come out, we are also resurrected.

Curiously, throughout Lazarus's story we suspect that the miraculous will happen and that he will be resurrected. Martha herself believes that Lazarus will be resurrected, not immediately, but rather on "the last day" (John 11:24b). She does not grasp the immediacy of God's power to transform the present hopelessness she feels. Put another way, Martha grasps the "not yet" aspect of resurrection but not the "already."

In coming out, we queers also grapple with the urgency of our call to leave the entombed closet and the future hope that someday we will reflect fully the glory of our Creator. I yearn for that day. But the Lazarus story challenges us and does not let us off the hook: we, like Lazarus, are called to leave our closets/tombs and inhabit the world as resurrected beings; we are not called to wallow in an eschatological daydream! For many, myself included, it means finding environments that welcome and celebrate our courage to be, and it means that we must actively challenge attitudes and policies that directly perpetuate the existence of closets.

## Commission

The final theme in the Lazarus story starts with Jesus calling Lazarus to come out and ends with Jesus' command to those in the resurrected Lazarus's midst to "unbind him, and let him go!" Lazarus has, in fact, done his part by answering the call to come out; however, for the story to end there would make the resurrection event a marginally interpersonal one that leaves the wider community out entirely. I suspect this is why Jesus commands those around Lazarus to do the unbinding.

Clearly because Jesus calls forth the community to do its part in Lazarus's coming out and unbinding, he also avoids a problem that often befalls coming-out rhetoric: hyperindividualism. Such rhetoric misses the pivotal fact that any coming-out journey requires a community of witnesses who can aid and celebrate the individual in his/her life journey of being and be-coming fully made in God's wonderfully polymorphous image. Simply stated, coming out is both an individual and communal event.

Jesus' words to Lazarus's community are, in my opinion, a commission, much like the Great Commission found in Matthew 28:19–20. And because of this, coming out, like the baptismal commission, is a sacrament, for it calls us to remember and commemorate the power that calls us forth from the entombed closet. When I recall the coming-out sacrament that Jesus insti-tutes at Lazarus's resurrection, I remember the joy of being liberated from heterosexist and homophobic expectations not my own, the joy of being liberated from deception and its hurtful consequences, and the joy of being liberated from a way of being that is life extinguishing. Finally, in recalling the sacrament of coming out, I remember the joy of being liberated to laugh and love fully and unrepentantly, the joy of actively challenging injustice and making strides toward a more humane world, and, most importantly, the joy of God's remarkable gift and responsibility of being queer.

## Conclusion: The Unbinding Must Continue

Coming out as a sacrament is a deliberately provocative image. To sacra-mentalize it is to bring much needed attention to a process-event that, as I have shown via Lazarus's story, requires a great deal of fortitude to initiate and continue. Unitarian Universalism is perhaps in one of the best positions, theologically and politically, to affirm and celebrate coming out, for it has been on the leading edge of sexual justice matters in the religious communities for many decades. Unfortunately, such a progressive position also invites complacency. It invites us to believe that by simply accepting queer people into our midst, we have done the work of justice making.

Coming out is not only sacramental; it is also prophetic. Coming out calls everyone to account for his or her deeds and misdeeds—it is a double-edged sword, allowing us to celebrate our victories, while at the same time piercing hypocrisy and complacency. If we have truly done our work, then we as a religious community will be deeply unsettled by what we find: homophobia and heterosexism that are entrenched in almost every aspect of our religious lives, even the religious lives of we religious liberals. As a result, it serves and will continue to serve as a witness to us that much work needs to be done. We are a pilgrim church, which means that we can never rest on our laurels, especially when the inherent worth and dignity of all individuals are still not fully recognized. So, then, the obvious question is, what next?

Fortunately, the Unitarian Universalist Association's Office of Gay, Lesbian, Bisexual, and Transgender Concerns (OGBLT) has created the "Welcoming and Affirming Congregation Program," which is designed specifically for congregations that seek to do the prophetic work of sexual justice making.[16] In many ways, I envision a coming-out liturgy as the beginning of such a journey to new life, reconciliation, and communion.

When I started writing this paper, I found myself reflecting on what coming out has meant to me and how the communities I have been a part of impacted that process, for better or worse. The image of Lazarus, as I recounted earlier, kept recurring for me, particularly the image of Jesus commanding those in Lazarus's community to unbind this resurrected man. For me, it underscores beautifully the nexus of God, humanity, and community—each has a part to play in this drama. Thus my experience has, like Lazarus's, reflected this nexus: God has called me out of the lifeless existence of the closet, I have answered this call, and I have continued the journey, thanks to the communities that have unbound me. I am profoundly grateful to those who have assisted me and given me the courage to be queer, and thus my challenge to Unitarian Universalism (and other faith traditions) is to continue "unbinding us and letting us go"!

# Notes

1. Calling coming out a process-event reflects the belief that it is both discrete and continuous.

2. John 14:1–44.

3. Unitarian Universalist Association, *Unitarian Universalist Association Principles and Purposes* (Boston: UUA, 1997).

4. I use the term "marginal" here not as a value judgment but as a location. I see myself as "doing" Christianity on the margins because of my social location. This, I believe, gives me a perspective on Christianity that is oftentimes not the dominant view, especially around issues of race, class, and sexual orientation. I see it both as a challenge and an opportunity.

5. In Brian Bouldrey, ed., *Wrestling with the Angel: Faith and Religion in the Lives of Gay Men* (New York: Riverhead Books, 1995), 178.

6. Matthew Fox, *Wrestling with the Prophets: Essays on Creation Spirituality and Everyday Life* (San Francisco: HarperSanFrancisco, 1995), 257.

7. While there is no canon in Unitarian Universalism, many still regard the Bible as instructive and, to varying degrees, even normative. This is especially true for Unitarian Universalist Christians, like myself.

8. Elisabeth Schüssler Fiorenza, *Bread Not Stone* (Boston: Beacon Press, 1995), 15–18.

9. Michel Foucault, *Michel Foucault: Politics, Philosophy, Culture* (New York: Routledge, 1988), 155.

10. Elisabeth Schüssler Fiorenza, *Sharing Her Word: Feminist Biblical Interpretation in Context* (Boston: Beacon Press, 1998), 77.

11. Robert E. Goss, *Jesus ACTED UP: A Gay and Lesbian Manifesto* (San Francisco: HarperSanFrancisco, 1993), 62.

12. Ibid., 110.

13. John 11:43–44.

14. Goss, *Jesus ACTED UP*, 126–27.

15. Chris Glaser, *Coming Out as Sacrament* (Louisville: Westminster John Knox Press, 1999), 82.

16. Information about the Welcoming and Affirming Congregation Program can be obtained through the Unitarian Universalist's Office of Gay, Lesbian, Bisexual, and Transgender Concerns, located at 25 Beacon Street, Boston, MA 02115.

## 19

# The Beloved Disciple

## A Queer Bereavement Narrative in a Time of AIDS

### R O B E R T   E .   G O S S

*Robert Goss narrates a bereavement story of personal loss of a spouse. It is a story that has been rehearsed hundreds of thousands times in the last decades of the twentieth century. The relationship between Jesus and the beloved disciple has long been intuited by gay men as possessing an erotic configuration. Goss builds upon the erotic relationship between Jesus and the beloved disciple to speak of the loss of his lover of sixteen years and the ensuing grief. He narrates how his continued bonds with his deceased spouse help transform grieving into solace. Personal grief looks for linking objects for sustaining continued bonds with the deceased. Bereaved survivors of HIV loss found the need to localize the presence of the deceased in the Names Project through memorial quilts. Goss finds his own story within the larger narrative configuration of the beloved disciple's loss of Jesus and the transformation of his grief to resurrection solace.*

The women at the tomb were observing the customs of mourning. They were weeping for Jesus. Their eyes were full of tears when the realization hit them that Jesus was not in the grave. For the poor, for widows, for a colonized nation, the eyes are the organs that register pain. The Marys were using their eyes in the graveyard, but not like the Greeks. They "saw" Jesus through tears.... The community was grief-stricken, the women were wailing. It was awful; and if you haven't lost someone you love, then you can't even begin to understand what it was like. Sixty years afterward, the churches had four sanitized little stories about a trip to a garden and a lovely surprise. But it wasn't like that when it happened. Grief may also be the precondition for resurrection, and tears for permitting their eyes to see.[1]

The women companions of Jesus saw him through grieving eyes. They watched his agonizing death on the cross and tearfully discovered the empty tomb. Grieving women had a special role in ancient Jewish burial customs; they were primarily anointers (Mark 14:3–9) and mourners. Often they functioned as interpreters, using the religious and cultural resources to find meaning in tragic death. Jewish women often made imaginative use of such resources in order to find the meaning. Their interpretative practices surrounding death were an accepted part of their role as mourners. Perhaps they reflected over the words in Zechariah 12:10: "I will pour out on the house of David and the inhabitants of Jerusalem a spirit of compassion and supplication, so that, when they look on him whom they have pierced, they shall mourn for him, as one mourns for an only child, and weep bitterly over him, as one weeps over a first-born" (RSV). If they remembered this text, the women may have discovered faint echoes of solace that Jesus would be wrapped in divine care. The women might have anticipated that Jesus' teaching would survive his death, and they looked to the day of reunion and vindication, the resurrection of the dead. Meanwhile, they wept over his death and wept over the thought of his decaying body. Their grief was a prelude to their faith where the empty tomb signified the resurrected Jesus. He was alive not only in appearances but also in his words and actions remembered in faith. Jesus' bodily presentations became recognized in the bodies of the poor, the ill, other classes and ethnicities, the breaking of the bread, and deliberate actions for justice.

According to the Gospel of John, the beloved disciple was at the foot of the cross with the grieving women. The beloved disciple, I will argue, spent his time in a household dominated by women. As the women disciples mourned, I imagine that the beloved disciple participated in their mourning rituals and their attempts to make sense of Jesus' tragic death. As a gay man, I identify with the beloved disciple's connections to women, his passionate love of Jesus, his grief and bereavement struggle for resurrection faith. As a survivor of the loss of a spouse to HIV illness, I will read the texts about the beloved disciple as a bereavement narrative searching for solace in the midst of sorrow. Just as the beloved disciple found solace in a continuing bond with the crucified and resurrected Jesus, so the hope also remains to those men and women who have experienced loss through HIV, breast cancer, and a myriad of other human tragedies.

## The Beloved Disciple

Heterosexual scholars often read the texts between Jesus and the beloved disciple as a spiritual or symbolic relationship in which the beloved disciple portrays the Johannine community or represents the ideal disciple. Only recently have there appeared several monographs that attempt to identify the beloved disciple as a historical figure.[2] Biblical scholar Sjef Van Tilborg provides a provocative treatment of the relation of Jesus and the beloved disciple as the pederastic relationship of the older male as lover (*erastes*) to the beloved younger male (*eromenos*), similar to what is found in Plato's *Symposium*. This pederastic model of older male to younger male provides an educational model in the Greco-Roman world of the first century C.E. Van Tilborg notes the reluctance of scholars to entertain the classical pederastic model for the beloved disciple:

> The reason that scientific exegesis did not connect the relation of the teacher Jesus to his beloved disciple with this typical educational background is, probably, that sexuality is present in the majority of the concerned texts, either explicitly mentioned or at least not far off. The love for the *pais* in the context of education and training has sexual connotations in Greek and Hellenistic thought and action that cannot be brought in line with the asexual text of the Johannine Gospel.[3]

Van Tilborg understands that the author uses a nonsexual pederastic model to portray the intimate teacher/disciple relationship of Jesus and the beloved disciple.

I intend to "queer" the texts about the beloved disciple, to disrupt its traditional heterosexist readings as purely symbolic or as asexual. There are homoerotic echoes that a queer reading surfaces. The late John Boswell writes, "Certainly, the most controversial same-sex couple in the Christian tradition comprised Jesus and... the beloved disciple. The relationship between them was often depicted in subsequent art and literature as intimate, if not erotic."[4] For centuries, the beloved disciple has remained a powerful metaphor for homoerotic friendship and love, and even today gay men intuit an identifiable love relationship between Jesus and the beloved disciple.[5]

The beloved disciple is never identified by name. Tradition has recognized the beloved disciple as John. For me, however, Lazarus has been the most likely candidate for the beloved disciple, who makes his debut in the Gospel as the unnamed disciple (John 1:35). Biblical commentators have frequently posed the question whether the anonymous disciple with Andrew is identifiable as the beloved disciple. From the perspective of a reader familiar with the Fourth Gospel, the anonymous disciple could easily be understood as the beloved disciple. I argue for Lazarus from two particular vantage points: (1) the intertextual evidence of John's Gospel and (2) the identification in the Secret Gospel of Mark of the youth that Jesus raised from the dead and who undergoes a sexual initiation.[6] Lazarus lives in the household of Martha and Mary, his older sisters. He always seemed a lot "softer" than dominating males in first-century C.E. Judea or even the male-identified Martha, who ran the household. Lazarus's sisters sent Jesus a message, "Lord, he whom you love is ill" (John 11:3). He is introduced into the narrative as the one Jesus loved. All the subsequent passages that mention the beloved disciple follow the Lazarus narrative, and in fact, the same language used of Lazarus is also used of the anonymous "beloved disciple." Finally the Jewish observers at the tomb comment on Jesus' weeping for Lazarus: "See how he loved him" (John 11:35). There are clearly emotional and intimate bonds of affection between Jesus and Lazarus. In the extracanonical fragments from the Secret Gospel of Mark, the youth raised from the dead is clearly Lazarus and is referred to as "the youth whom Jesus loved." Both intertextual and outside tradition points to Lazarus as the most plausible candidate for the beloved disciple, and I choose to read Lazarus as such.

The beloved disciple certainly shared the grief of the women at the foot of the cross and at the tomb. As a gay male, I identify with the beloved disciple. Was he "soft" (*malakos*) or just youthful (*paidikos*)? It is inconceivable for me to imagine the beloved disciple in a household of women neither grieving nor sharing their attempts to find meaning within the tragic death of Jesus. It is in the grieving process, I will suggest, that the grieving women and the beloved disciple discover the presence of the crucified Jesus. I lost my spouse of sixteen years and my brother on the same day through HIV. This essay will trace the course of my inner representation of Frank's journey with HIV, his death, the resolution of my grief through continuing bonds with his spirit, and my reengagement with life. The bereavement process often includes a movement from tragic loss to strengthening the continuing bonds with the deceased and the creation of new narratives of hope.

In *Reviving the Tribe*, Eric Rofes has detailed how loss through HIV illness has traumatized gay men as a community.[7] Bereavement has been a critical issue for the survivors of multiple loss of HIV for nearly two decades. Though Rofes outlines a plan for the revival of the gay male community, he leaves undeveloped the spiritual aspects of grief as part of such a revival. Spiritual phenomena are an important aspect of the experience of bereavement and grief for many gay men during the AIDS pandemic.[8] In their grief, gay men, including myself, often report a persistent bond with their deceased partners. They experience a heightened sense of the past with memories of their lovers and their friends. Although deep loss intrudes on their lives at every turn, they do not dissolve their intimate and familial bonds at death. These bonds provide a creative dimension to their lives as they work to resolve their grief and reengage a world beyond multiple loss.[9] Often grief is not abandoned but transformed through continued bonds with the deceased into solace, particular memorials, compassionate care, a quilt panel, and empowered action.

## John 11:17–44

What if we read the traditional account of the raising of Lazarus from the dead from the literature of otherworldly and ecstatic journeys in late antiquity? Otherworldly journeys were connected by ancient Near Eastern and Mediterranean cultures to the human problem of death, and they have some corresponding features to our contemporary near-death experience. We can easily contextualize the Johannine texts regarding the raising of Lazarus with the literature of near-death experience in the ancient Jewish narratives of apocalypses and chariot mysticism.[10] Like near death-experience, otherworldly and ecstatic journeys have always tried to glimpse what lies behind the veil of earthly life, and they were perfectly normal and natural phenomena both in the Jewish and the Greco-Roman world. Divine authoritization is evident in the call narratives of the Hebrew prophets such as Isaiah and Ezekiel. Visionary travel to the otherworld is a core symbol in the proto-chariot (*merkabah*) mysticism of the first century C.E.

Imagine Lazarus fading away in death, and his spirit leaves his body. His spiritual body lingers for a while as he watches Mary and Martha prepare his body according to Jewish burial custom. His sisters find themselves lamenting the loss of their brother, peppering the laments with ritual prayer of the kaddish. Lazarus is wrapped in clothes and spices and buried that day. His Pharisee study group, or *haburah*, believed in resurrection from the dead. On many table occasions, Jesus also spoke about God's resurrection of the dead. He wonders at his own spiritual body, "Was this a resurrected body?" He notices that it gives no shadow. Bewildered, Lazarus tries to speak to his sisters and companions surrounding his body, but they are unable to hear him. With his spiritual body, he enters a chariot and travels upwards towards a place of light. He wonders if this is the chariot that also transported Ezekiel and Enoch to the heavens. His *haburah* had often read from the scroll about Enoch, who had been saved and transported to the heavens. Enoch's scroll was always one of his favorite books, and he remembers it as he climbs into the chariot to the heavens.

Within the heavenly light, there is a presence who is loving and welcoming him. Surely this must be Abraham. He remembers Jesus' tale about a rich man and a man named after him. Lazarus died and found himself in the bosom of Abraham. Was he now in the bosom of Abraham? Lazarus feels a strong sense of love, surrounded by light and love. He reviews his life, his practice of the precepts (*mitzvot*), the oral Torah, and the visionary message of Jesus. The gentle presence asks him, "Is there anything else that you need to accomplish?" He now hears the voice of Jesus, "Lazarus come forth." Lazarus finds himself, tugged between heaven and earth, between the loving presence and the voice of the man he loved. I imagine him in a wrestling match between the radiant beauty of the light and his erotic bonds to Jesus. Lazarus answers his heavenly messenger's inquiry with a firm, "I must go back and love Jesus." He returns from his otherworldly journey to his love. Death provided him with an occasion for a dramatic unmasking of his heartfelt bonds and love for Jesus. The words of Jesus ring in his ears: "I am the resurrection and the life" (John 11:25). Death not only galvanized the imagination of Lazarus, but Lazarus's death and resurrection also galvanize my own imaginative faith with the narrative text.

It was January 10, 1990. The week before we were tested for HIV, but the Red Cross would not allow us to come together for our test results. I was scheduled for the earlier appointment. I went and received my test results of remaining HIV negative; I was back home within fifteen minutes. Frank left and did not arrive back promptly. My anxiety increased geometrically with each five minutes, and after a half hour, my anxiety turned to panic and tears. I knew in my heart the truth of the situation and sobbed. When Frank arrived, his face washed of color and filled with tears confirmed what I dreaded. We wept together like Jesus at the tomb of Lazarus. We wept for ourselves and for the dreams of our lives together. We never dreamed that one of us would be positive while the other remained negative. Mixed antibody status was a near-death experience for us, and we both began a grieving process at the separation that was destined by those test results.

Our test results were an experience of loss. Frank faced his own mortality while I worked through tremendous guilt over my negative antibody status. I wanted to be positive as well and share Frank's fate. As a mode of judgment, near-death life review allows for self-examination and self-judgment. We examined our life together and made significant judgments and life decisions in the next two months. Frank left our business to head the Sharing Center, an activity program for HIV-positive folks, while I went back to Harvard University to finish my educational requirements and dissertation for my doctorate. Death trivializes the insignificant actions of our lives and highlights what is truly significant. Lazarus, I imagined, realized what was significant and insignificant after his postmortem experience. He courageously followed Jesus into Jerusalem and lived through the traumatic events that Passover.

## John 13:23–25

Here we have the actual physical intimacy of the beloved disciple with Jesus at the final farewell meal. The Gospel narrates how the beloved disciple's act of reclining in the *kolpos* (literally "pocket") or undergarment of Jesus. *Kolpos* is used to describe the garment extended from the breast to over the genital area. At dinner, the beloved disciple is depicted in the singular place of honor, resting on Jesus' chest (*stethos*). The beloved disciple who rests in the *kolpos* is physically intimate with Jesus. The phrase *en to kolpo* used in the Septuagint translation of the Hebrew Scriptures has a number of meanings, including an explicit sexual relationship.[11] The text is ambiguous enough for a nonsexual as well as a sexual reading, but I choose to read the beloved disciple's reclining in the *kolpos* of Jesus contrary to erotophobic (or perhaps homophobic) biblical readings. There is a recognized sexual intimacy between Jesus and the beloved disciple at this final meal. Raised as a Catholic Christian, sexual intimacy and final farewell meals have always made sense to me. There is embodied and intimate presence within both acts. Those who hold to the hypothesis that Jesus was celibate may debate whether Jesus was sexually intimate with the beloved. I choose to understand Jesus as sexually intimate with Lazarus.

Sexual intimacy and the eucharist have always been an intimate part of Frank's and my own spirituality.[12] Each Sunday morning we made sexual love, followed by eucharist at the dining room table. Both sexual love and eucharist were intimate and embodied, sacred moments of lovemaking. In our lovemaking, we choreographed our fused bodies in an ecstasy of pleasure and prayer. My head would often recline on Frank's *kolpos* covering his hairy chest. In sexual ecstasy, we celebrated deep love and deep spirituality. When body and mind are joined meditatively together in lovemaking, the sexual/spiritual potential moves beyond the ordinary orgasmic threshold of both partners into a new dimension of reality. There was a sense of oneness with each other and a deep sense of Christ's presence in a dynamic energy flow embracing our bodies. There was a letting go and a surrender to rapture that transported us into a meditative realm of consciousness where boundaries dissolved and where the body of Christ was experienced in intimate touch, taste, smell, and play. There were times that I saw Christ's face within Frank's face as we made love.

We made love and extended that sexual love into our weekly celebrated eucharists. Both were intense experiences of lovemaking with God. Our passionate letting go was carried into our prayer around the table as we broke bread and shared the cup of Christ' love. We experienced communion intimacy in the bedroom and at the altar. Eating the consecrated bread and wine was as intense communion as our intimate lovemaking. As a gay lover, how often I rehearsed this passage.

## John 19:25b–27

Often I imagined how painful it was for the beloved disciple to watch the man he loved be crucified. I watched a crucifixion for more than two years as Frank struggled with HIV, was hospitalized several times, wasted away, and experienced AIDS-related dementia. Many people dying from complications of HIV have experienced a gruesome, rapid bodily deterioration. I have likened their dying to crucifixion, where gravity weighs down the body on the cross and suffocates the crucified as they are physically weakened. I understood how helpless the beloved disciple felt while watching the death of the man he loved. The beloved disciple was the only male follower at the cross, for the other male disciples were afraid of the ruling authorities (John 20:19). He could have opposed the Romans and joined Jesus on an adjacent cross. Sometimes I felt that way, wanting to become HIV-positive and be with Frank.

In John 19:26–27, Jesus places his mother in the care of the beloved disciple and the beloved disciple in the care of his mother: "Woman, behold your son! . . . Behold, your mother" (RSV). Jesus appointed the beloved disciple as his own successor, legal heir to assume the familial responsibility for his mother and accept the responsibility for continuing his own ministry. The beloved disciple created a family of choice with the mother of Jesus. I have often witnessed the repetition of this adoption event at the death beds of gay men dying of AIDS with their lovers and their families. It is the powerful entrusting of unfinished business in the face of death and personal tragedy. Gay lovers and mothers of deceased gay men have reenacted this narrative too many times, forming a human quilt to share their grief and a community seeking solace in the midst of tragedy.

I experienced a version of this adoption event for myself as Frank was placed on a respirator in the last days of his life. I stood grieving at the bedside of my own spouse while his arms were bound, cruciformed to the hospital bed railings to prevent him from pulling out the respirator. Each day I was on one side of the bed, and his mother on the other side, his two major concerns as he died. Weeks before his death, Frank spoke to his mother, asking her to take care of me when he died. He spoke to me of his concerns for his mother's welfare after his death. I can no longer hear this text without hearing Frank's voice and seeing his body racked in pain on the respirator.

I gently massaged with body lotion his heels bruised and bloodied, wounds incurred from his fighting against the respirator. It was an anointing of his body to ease his pain and prepare him for his passage. I stood awake, keeping vigil to the pounding rhythm of the respirator and watching his agony. But who could sleep with the respirator's pounding sounds that tormented the man I loved? Though his living will and his durable power of attorney were entered into his medical chart, he was placed on a respirator against his own wishes. I threatened the hospital with legal action. The night that the hospital staff took him off the respirator, Frank awoke and asked me what was happening. I told him, "You're dying, and I will always love you." He weakly spoke, "I love you." Those were the last words that he uttered.

Many partners give their partners permission to die. When timed correctly, it eases the passage of the spirit from the body. The night before Frank died, I prepared a last Passover eucharist. I placed a morphine patch on myself to be in communion with Frank; I administered the eucharist elements to him. Our two dogs lay in vigil near Frank's hospice bed; occasionally, one of them would tenderly lick his hand. Like the *haggadah* recital of the Passover meal, I rehearsed our life together from our days as Jesuits to owning an executive search specializing in agricultural biotechnology. I included the humorous and fun times, our joys and our struggles, and the shortness of our time spent together. I spoke how God brought us together, how God continued to be with us in our life together, and how God would continue to keep us together.

Beginning a litany of letting-go exercises for Frank, I gave him permission to die. Ten days earlier he had given me permission to live and love again. I tried the Tibetan meditation practice of *pho-wa*, attempting to transfer Frank's consciousness from the body. I envisioned myself as midwife, assisting his transition and birth into another life. Next day at 11:16 in the morning, he died in a fetal position, passing beyond physical existence. I washed his face and anointed him with the sign of the cross. The scripture verse became very real: "When Jesus had received the wine, he said, It is finished" (John 19:30). Frank died while I stood vigil like the beloved disciple at the foot of the cross.

## Resurrection as the Continuing Bonds with the Crucified Jesus

I went to the grave each day the first week. I was numb. I prayed; I ached. The death of Frank threatened my constructed meaning of life and robbed me of energy for living. I imagine that the same emotional devastation, hopelessness, despair, and sadness arrested the beloved disciple as he grieved. On the third day, something happened to the crucified Jesus that changed the beloved disciple and transformed his grief into solace and empowered action. I too went on pilgrimage to the cemetery each day with the hope of the beloved disciple who ran to the tomb of Jesus when he heard the amazing tale of Mary Magdalene. On the day of resurrection, the beloved disciple peeked into the tomb, noticing the face cloth that had been on Jesus' head, not with the linen wrappings on the floor, but rolled up in a place by itself. He entered and saw the grave clothes and the face cloth, and he believed. The beloved disciple needed no one to explain the meaning of the empty grave, the clothes thrown on the stone floor, and the neatly rolled up face cloth. His deep and intimate relationship with Jesus produced a sensitivity to Jesus' resurrection. The beloved disciple hoped, remembering that Jesus frequently spoke about something greater than themselves in the reality of God's love, their love, and their love of God. In his grief, he came to believe in the resurrected presence of Jesus, and the love relationship was restored albeit a spiritual, yet intimate, presence.

According to John 21:24, the beloved disciple is the author of the words and the deeds of Jesus. His activity culminates in the writing of a book, a narrative that has a long complex history of development and narrative that has been long treasured by men who loved men. Resurrection was not enough; there was a need for linking objects of remembering, to invoke the memory of Jesus in faith. I suspect that he remembered a verse from Exodus that my old sacramental theology professor, Ed Kilmartin, frequently quoted to talk about God's memorial presence: "In every place where I cause my named to be remembered I will come to you and bless you" (Exod. 20:24). The beloved disciple maintained a continuing bond with the crucified and risen Jesus through his writings, eucharist, community, and justice. As the years passed on, the beloved disciple relived the memories of his experiences of the words and deeds of Jesus. The Gospel, eucharist, community, and actions for justice became his linking objects to the presence of the risen Jesus. They became signposts of presence or continuing bonds in the midst of the physical absence of Jesus and a reengagement with life beyond crucifixion. The beloved disciple continues a belief that the relationship with Jesus persists, transcending death, and that the love between them actively continues.

The irony of spiritual presence in the midst of physical absence never became so poignant until after the death of Frank. I attended the grave in order to experience again the sense of pain. My pain was initially a primal means of remembering him and maintaining an ongoing relationship. I half expected to find some sign of his presence, looking for my own particular sign similar to the neatly rolled up face cloth. I wanted something to happen to overcome my numbness at Frank's absence and to believe like the beloved disciple. The tomb was filled with the body empty of life, and my personal emptiness engaged desperately the empty tomb. I sought Frank's presence in the absence of life at his grave site.

Bereaved gay men often experience a presence of the spirit of the lost person in direct communication in the form of an exchange of thoughts, a vision, symbolic communications, dreams, and vivid recollections of the deceased. Presence in the midst of physical absence is never a substitute for physical presence of a loved one, but sometimes there is nothing else! Part of gay grief work involves recalling the events leading up to the death of lover and friends, trying to make sense of what tragically has happened. During the process, telling the story and retelling even humorous events are of utmost importance to the bereaved. Some mourners make a quilt to commemorate the loss, to make sense of death, and to search for presence in physical absence. We build that presence on our memories. In grieving over physical absence, we often discover presence—identifying it with the energy and love, traditionally designated as the spirit that was in the deceased. We continue a familial and loving bond with the deceased.

During the week of pilgrimage to the grave site, I heard the Bette Midler rendition of "The Wind beneath My Wings" from the movie *Beaches*. It was Frank's favorite song, and it was sung at his funeral. As I listened, the song transformed me. It was a linking memory that evoked a vivid sense of Frank's presence. Even still today when I hear that song, Frank's presence becomes vividly alive to me. Pictures, shared objects, clothing that still carried his scent, eucharist, music, dreams, memories, and favorite spots were my numerous doorways. Linking objects became my numinous door to Frank's presence. When linking objects are invoked in memory, they evoke the spiritual presence, and eventually I found blessings with them and the ability to celebrate the giftedness of our love. Every time I went to a worship service with the breaking of the bread and sharing of the cup, I found vivid recollections of our eucharistic lovemaking. The words "This is my body given for you" evoked the passionate giving of our bodies in lovemaking. For erotophobic Christians, this seems blasphemous, but for embodied Christians, it is at the heart of the mystery of God's incarnation. These memorials brought a numinous sense of presence: "Do this in remembrance of me." Every time I prayed, the presence of Christ evoked also Frank's presence. There was certainly a merging of presences, as we often did in the prayer of lovemaking. I found solace in the memory of our life together and comfort in Frank's spiritual presence.

The persistence of Frank's presence in the midst of his physical absence empowered me to redefine our relationship and give it new shape. In our life together, we were committed to justice doing. It grew out of our lovemaking and the realization that Christ was intimately involved in our sexual union. Our lovemaking involved us in opening our household to marginalized folks, creating Food Outreach, a major AIDS service organization in St. Louis, fighting the homophobia and racism of the Cracker Barrel Restaurant chain, joining ACT UP and Queer Nation, struggling against Christian extremism and hatred, working for environmental justice, and much more. Frank's presence continues to beckon me to work for justice and to care for the disenfranchised, the marginalized, and the outcast. These deliberate actions for justice remain as linking objects of my lovemaking with Frank and Christ. Doing justice is a legacy of finding his presence and continuing our inclusive love.[13] The resurrection of Jesus encourages Christian mourners to maintain contact with the deceased and to work for the living. The story of the beloved disciple and his love relationship with Jesus helps queer Christians to refigure lives to take into account loss, absence, and presence.

## "My Heart Goes On"

There is no loss of love in physical separation; in fact, there may be an increase of love as the continuing relationship moves from grief into solace.

Achieving solace does not mean forgetting loss or the pain, but moving on with life means taking a part of our love and our loss with us. Solace becomes learning to live with absence and presence simultaneously, being able to cry and smile at the same time.

Celine Dione's popular song "My Heart Goes On" speaks of bereavement, absence, and presence and captures a melancholy of transient love suffering loss, grieving absence, and finding solace—a theme easily applied to the tragedies of HIV-related deaths for the last two decades and queer bereavement. The song speaks of absence and presence simultaneously. It imagines a continuing bond with the loss of a lover, the transforming power of love, and expresses a hope of survival in remembered actions of love. I look forward to the day when death will die, when there will be no need for justice, and when all beloved disciples, lovers, and Christ are reunited in an erotic dance of joy and communion.

## Notes

1. Marianne Sawicki, *Seeing the Lord: Resurrection and Early Christian Practice* (Minneapolis: Fortress Press, 1994), 92–93.

2. Vernon Eller has identified Lazarus of all possible candidates for the beloved disciple, while James Charlesworth has more recently argued for Thomas the Twin. Vernon Eller, *The Beloved Disciple: His Name, His Story, His Thought* (Grand Rapids: Wm. B. Eerdmans, 1987); James H. Charlesworth, *The Beloved Disciple: Whose Witness Validates the Gospel of John* (Valley Forge, Pa.: Trinity Press International, 1995).

3. Sjef Van Tilborg, *Imaginative Love in John* (Leiden: E. J. Brill, 1993), 79.

4. John Boswell, *Same-Sex Unions in Premodern Europe* (New York: Villard Books, 1994), 138.

5. For St. Aelred, see John Boswell, *Christianity, Social Tolerance, and Homosexuality* (Chicago: University of Chicago Press, 1980), 224–26. See also Jeremy Bentham's views: Louis Crompton, *Byron and Greek Love: Homophobia in the Nineteenth Century* (Berkeley: University of California Press, 1985), 225–83. For more contemporary views, see Hugh Montefiore, "Jesus: The Revelation of God," in *Christ for Us Today*, ed. W. Norman Pittenger (London: SCM Press, 1968), 101–17; Malcolm Boyd, "The Sexuality of Jesus," *The Witness* 74 (July–August 1991): 14–16; Robert Williams, *Just As I Am* (New York: Crown Publishers, 1992), 116–22.

6. Morton Smith, *Clement of Alexandria and a Secret Gospel of Mark* (Cambridge: Harvard University Press, 1973). Many scholars feel that the fragment may be from the second-century C.E. Carprocratian sect who thought Jesus engaged in homoerotic sex.

7. Eric Rofes, *Reviving the Tribe: Regenerating Gay Men's Sexuality and Culture in the Ongoing Epidemic* (New York: Haworth Press, 1995).

8. T. Anne Richards and Susan Folkman, "Spiritual Aspects of Loss at the Time of a Partner's Death from AIDS," *Death Studies* 21 (1997): 527–52. See also Richard P. Hardy, *Loving Men: Gay Partners, Spirituality, and AIDS* (New York: Continuum, 1998). I was one of the partners inverviewed for Hardy's book.

9. I am indebted to Dennis Klass and his work on the continuing bonds of mourners for the deceased. See Dennis Klass, "Solace and Immortality: Bereaved Parents' Continuing

Bond with Their Children," *Death Studies* 17 (1993): 343–68; "The Deceased Child in the Psychic and Social Worlds of Bereaved Parents during the Resolution of Grief," *Death Studies* 21 (1997): 147–75; *The Spiritual Lives of Bereaved Parents* (Philadelphia: Taylor & Francis, Brunner/Mazel, 1999), 297–304.

10. See Carol Zaleski, *Otherworldly Journeys* (New York: Oxford University Press, 1987); John J. Collins, "A Throne in the Heavens: Apotheosis in Pre-Christian Judaism," in *Death, Ecstasy, and Other Worldly Journeys*, ed. John J. Collins and Michael Fishbane (Albany: SUNY Press, 1995), 41–56; Alan F. Segal, "Paul and the Beginning of Jewish Mysticism," in ibid., 95–122.

11. See, for instance, some of the sexual instances: Genesis 16:5; Deuteronomy 12:7; 28:54; 1 Kings 12:8; Sirach 9:1. Rudolf Meyer, "kolpos," in *Theological Dictionary of the New Testament*, ed. Gerhard Kittel (Grand Rapids: Wm. B. Eerdmans, 1965), 3:824–25; L. Robert Arthur, *The Sex Texts: Sexuality, Gender, and Relationships in the Bible* (Omaha, Neb.: MCC, 1994), 22.

12. Robert E. Goss, "Passionate for Christ: Out of the Closet into the Streets," in *Male Lust: Pleasure, Power, and Transformation*, ed. Kerwin Kay with Jill Nagle and Baruch Gould (New York: Haworth Press, 1999), 297–304.

13. See Robert E. Goss, *Jesus ACTED UP: A Gay and Lesbian Manifesto* (San Francisco: HarperSanFrancisco, 1993), 161–76. The book was dedicated to his memory. It expressed our legacy to love and justice.

## 20

# "And Then He Kissed Me"

## An Easter Love Story

### JAMES MARTIN

*This is a queer retelling of the resurrection loosely based upon the Emmaus road account from Luke's Gospel. While this work is fictional in nature, it is shaped by the author's values, personal experiences, and aspirations as a gay man. This story challenges our boundaries of beliefs regarding the types of relationships Jesus the person would have chosen to pursue. Set within the author's context of an encounter with Jesus, it encourages its readers to contemplate what their own encounter with Jesus on a human level might be. This story is the author's contribution to the witness of the connection between spirituality and sexuality. While some may not wish to encounter Jesus as lover, the story brings clarity to and enriches the diverse experience of a personal relationship with Jesus the Christ and our God.*

Throughout Christian history there has been an underground of Christian men sexually attracted to men, and they intuited that Jesus was one of them. Traditional Christian doctrine has maintained that since Jesus was without sin, he did not engage in sex. It is difficult for the church to envision a sinless Jesus who is also sexual. It has been difficult for the church to envision healthy sexuality between its members. I want to imaginatively read and retell the story about Jesus at Emmaus (Luke 24:28–35) from a gay man's perspective. It is a story about resurrection and the naked vulnerability of Jesus in sexual giving and receiving, and it is an empowering narrative of self-discovery and self-acceptance of the giftedness of my sexual feelings towards men.

The idea for this story was based upon a pastor-colleague's search for new ways that we, as pastors and preachers, could help people fall in love with Jesus. With that thought in mind, I began to imagine what it would be like for me, as a gay man, to fall in love and have that kind of relationship with the Jesus whom we know as fully human. The result of that imagining is this story.

## A Gay Reading of the Emmaus Story

My name is Joseph. I live in Emmaus, a village about seven miles from Jerusalem. It was just a little more than a week ago that he came into my life. We spent just a weekend together, but my life will never be the same.

He was traveling through my village with some of his friends. We met in the market just before sundown at the beginning of the Sabbath. I still can't believe that it happened. It was one of those typical cruising things gay men do, a lot of eye contact and smiles.

I'm usually not very good at that sort of thing because I'm a little too shy. However, that afternoon I was bold. My attraction to him gave me all the courage I needed. To say that he was my type would be a gross understatement. He was perfect in every way. Big dark eyes, classically handsome, medium frame, just a little taller than me, smooth olive complexion, everything that defines my type. I couldn't believe what I was seeing. It was as if my thoughts had been the blueprint for his creation. Now, here he was ... right here in my village.

There was more to this than physical attraction though. There was something more about him, something so deep, that drew me to him. I began following him around the market. I was trying so hard to let him know that I was cruising him. When he moved to a different seller, I would move to a different one too. I remained just close enough that when he would look up, he could see me smiling at him.

He made me fall in love with him that afternoon. He was so sweet as he looked up at me to find me looking at him. He would smile back with that smile of his, and he would gaze into my eyes. It was as if he came to know me so completely ... with just a look. We continued our dance until he finished his buying.

I had drifted to within just a couple of yards from him. I was so close that I could almost reach out and touch him. Just as I was about to take the first of those few steps toward him to invite him home for the Sabbath meal, he started toward me.

"Would you like to spend some time with me?" he asked in a tone that assured me he was as exhilarated and as nervous as I.

Perhaps I was too impetuous that afternoon, but I just couldn't help answering, "Yes ... a lifetime." You should have seen his eyes brighten and the happy smile that signaled his approval when I responded.

"Let's go for a walk," he suggested, "show me your village."

Thus we began our tour of Emmaus.

"My name is Joseph," I said.

"Joseph," he repeated with such a look of fondness, "was my father's name. I love that name."

My heart was soaring.

"Show me where you live. I want to meet your mother," he insisted after we had walked for a while.

As encouraging as that may have been in that moment, I felt a sense of dread. My mother isn't so very proud of me. She has bought into what the rabbis have said. She's sure that I am an abomination. When we buried my father, she refused to allow my life partner to stand with us as family as we said the kaddish. That was a hurt from which Benjamin never recovered, and I'm sure that it had a lot to do with the ending of our relationship.

I've been so lonely since then. I just want to share my life with someone. I can't change the truth that I want that someone to be another man. I'm not even sure that I would want to change, if I could. Now I was finally meeting someone in whom I recognized that this just may be possible. I was afraid of what may happen once my mother entered the picture.

I tried to talk him out of it. I explained everything, but he was so persuasive. He told me that everything would be fine. He convinced me as he took my hand in his.

We walked along, and he pulled me close to him. He looked deeply into my eyes, as though he were looking into my soul, and he whispered to me again that everything would be fine. I couldn't believe that this was happening. If you only knew how often I had walked down this road dreaming of exactly what I was realizing in these moments. . . .

When we came to my home, he held onto my hand all the way to the door, but the opening was too small for us to enter together. My happy outlook became even brighter when my mother received him with a hospitality that I've never seen her offer to anyone else before. Just before we left to continue our walk, my mother whispered to me, "I like him." Her usual advice would have been, "Find a nice girl, settle down, have sons." This change in her should have overwhelmed me, but I could focus only upon him . . . and what may lie just ahead for us. My mother seemed to kiss me good-bye in a way that communicated she knew I wouldn't be coming home that night.

I fought the urge the whole time we visited with my mother to go to his side, just to take his hand again. I think he knew that and felt the same himself because he stepped to go through the small door first and then reached back with his hand to take mine again.

We began to walk, but not with any sense of destination or direction. Thoughts of what might be raced through my mind. I was delirious with awareness that my dream may be coming true. I paid no attention to where we were going, yet I knew our path. We headed into the countryside, hand in hand through a wheat field until we reached the woods. We walked into the trees, and then he stopped and drew me to him in an embrace that felt so secure and yet so gentle.

He looked into my eyes with such knowing. His eyes were so tender and so loving. He spoke my name softly... and then he kissed me. His kiss was like nothing I had ever known before. It wasn't a stranger's kiss. It was a kiss filled with a depth of love that only long-term lovers know. We spoke no words in those following moments, but we communicated much with our eyes. Then he took my hand, and we started to walk again. I knew where we were going, and yet at the same time I had no idea of where he might be leading me. My only thought was that I hoped he would kiss me again... and where that might lead.

I was totally oblivious to the fact that we were walking together along my favorite path—the one I have walked along alone so many times, each time wishing I had a partner to walk with me. After a while he stopped. Finally looking away from him, I realized that he had led me to my secret place. To this place my favorite path always brings me. To this place I come to escape and think and solve my problems. To this place I come to hope that someday again someone will love me and will want to share his life with me. I always leave here feeling better about myself and my life. Sometimes too, though, I fantasize about making love to my special someone here at this place. He looked at me as if he knew that.

We sat down together and embraced... and then he kissed me again. His kiss made me feel so confident, so wanted. This was so unlike my other experiences of this kind—no awkwardness, no shyness—this was not a stranger's touch. How I longed to make love to him.

"Tell me more about yourself," he whispered to me.

I'm not sure how he did it, but he so distracted me that after a while I realized I had been telling him my life story. His eyes pulled every bit of it out of me: what it was like growing up with my religious parents, coming to terms with my sexuality and coming out, my failed relationships, my search for love and a life with a partner. Dusk passed into night, and we continued to talk.

He did some talking too. He had some very definite ideas about religion and the realm of God, about our people truly being free, about new ways of knowing and experiencing God. I guess he should have; he said he was a rabbi. You would have never expected it though by the friends with whom he was traveling. There was a tax collector and a few peasants, but the one who puzzled me the most was the harlot. He had such compassion for people. I loved that about him. I loved his big heart.

After a while, he cradled my head in his lap. I remembered again how much I wanted him, and I began to focus again on my longing for him. He began stroking my hair with his gentle hands and then looked into my eyes with what I knew was his longing too. I closed my eyes for just a moment as I savored the softness of his hands. The next thing I knew it was morning, as I awoke to find myself in his embrace. It was a sleep that I hadn't known for some time.

"Maybe this morning it will happen," I repeated over and over in my head, as if I were praying. He began to awake in a few moments, and he beamed a loving smile at me as he opened his eyes. I pressed close against him as my passion began to lead me. He pressed his body back against mine but then reminded me that temple service would soon be starting. All too soon after that we began making our way back to the village, hand in hand, again. He took me home and promised that he would see me at the Temple; he needed to find his friends first.

I was giddy to think that I would be able to sit with him at temple service. I hoped for a large crowd at the Temple. That meant we could sit almost as close together as we had embraced that morning. My senses couldn't take in enough of him. I ached to feel his flesh against mine. He filled my every thought.

At the service, however, he took a leading role, teaching us from the Torah and the Prophets. He made it all seem so easy to understand. His ideas were so simple. His message was that God cares most about what is within our hearts. I had never experienced God's love and acceptance at temple service as I did that morning. Temple service ended. I stood and watched from the far side of the room as he spoke briefly to one of his friends and then began making his way to me. I cringed thinking he would be ruining his credibility by his association with me. Everyone now would be sure to think the same of him as they do of me. That thought seemed to be the farthest one from his mind as he took me by the hand leading me out of the Temple.

"Are you ready for another day together?" he asked me.

So we were off. We wandered about the village, walked from hillside to hillside, and then almost at dusk we reached what now had become our secret place. I was sure we would finally make love.

This night turned into a duplicate of the night before, except this night he had me talking of my hopes and of my dreams. I drifted off to sleep again with my head cradled in his lap.

When we awoke, his troubled spirit was quite apparent. "I must go to Jerusalem," he said, "but I will be back."

Despite my disappointment, I quickly accepted his word. I thought that he was going to celebrate Passover, and I trusted him when he said that he would return to me. He took me home again, and then he kissed me, just outside my mother's door. I didn't say anything, but I watched him, feeling so helpless, until he was out of sight. I spent the rest of that week regretting that I hadn't gone with him.

The next Sabbath came and then ended. I looked for him all that first day of the following week, watching for him from the roof until it was time for bed. I waited all the next morning for him and then at midday decided I would go to Jerusalem to find him. I was sure all I had to do was look at the Temple. After all, he called it his father's house.

It was evening before I reached the Holy City. I couldn't help sensing a strange mood as I made my way through the streets. There had been a public execution four days before. As I searched about the Temple, I overheard people discussing it. It seemed a miracle had occurred. One of the three crucified had been resurrected. I had to sit down when I overheard someone say he was one of the three executed.

I don't know how long I sat there in the Temple courts or when I began to wander aimlessly through the streets of Jerusalem. When I came upon his woman friend, the harlot, I begged her to tell me what had happened.

"It's true," she informed me, "he was killed . . . horribly."

She caught me as I began to collapse in grief. She forced me to confront her eyes as she tried to console and comfort me with her words. "When I, along with his mother and his aunt, went to the tomb yesterday to anoint his broken body, we found nothing," she began. "An angel said to us, 'He has risen . . . we would find him in Galilee,'" she continued her argument. "Come with me to the others; they will tell you," she implored me.

She was so insistent as she tugged on my arm. I could find no words to speak to her or the rest of his friends. I turned from her and began my journey back to Emmaus.

"I had expected to walk this road with him, hand in hand as his life partner," I contemplated with every step. Despite her story I knew he would never be coming back to me.

When I reached the village, I couldn't face being alone, so I made my way to the home of some friends. My association with Cleopas, and his partner Antonitus, was just another part of my life that brought me the scorn of my neighbors. They were good friends, trusted friends. Zionist bigotry, disguised as religion, could never keep me from loving them. I hadn't seen my friends for some time though. They had gotten all caught up in some religious movement. They had been following some new prophet.

"Oh, we're just returning from Jerusalem too," Antonitus explained to me.

It was then that I began to sob. Cleopas and Antonitus were so loving to me in those moments. They put their arms around me and held me as I wept. When I regained my composure, they listened as I told them my story but said nothing, looking at one another in amazement.

After a long silence Cleopas looked at me and said, "He was here just last night, Joseph. He broke bread with us...we saw him!"

Then for the next few minutes I listened to their story. I wanted so badly to believe them, but I just couldn't. I had come so close to happiness.

I politely said my good-byes to these friends. As I trudged back to my home, I felt concern about what this new religion was doing to them. I fought for sleep that night. My only rest came during the dream about my life with him. It was a wonderful dream that ended much too soon.

I went through the motions of my life the next day. In late afternoon I felt drawn to our secret place. I sat there missing him, missing what I imagined would have been our life together...feeling hopeless and helpless, worthless and alone. As I began to weep, I felt a familiar hand upon my head. I couldn't believe this was happening. I rose and turned...and it was he. He was more beautiful to me than even before, but I sensed something very different about him now.

"I promised you that I would come back," he said to me, as he reached to take me into his arms.

"I was told you were killed," I began to whimper as I fell into his embrace.

"What Mary and Cleopas and Antonitus told you was true," he said, "everything they told you."

We talked of that for some time as he held me.

Then he said, "I must leave you again."

"No...please...don't go," I pleaded as I interrupted him. "Don't leave me; stay with me."

"I'll always be with you," he whispered to me. "Seek me among my friends, and you will find me."

There was a long silence between us as I gazed into his eyes—into the eyes that enfolded me with security and caring and happiness. He bent his head down toward me as if to say something, but he was unable to form the words. And then he kissed me, one last time.

"Know this, Joseph," he whispered, "I will always love you."

And with those words he vanished from sight.

I stood there astonished for a few moments, and then I felt a sense of peace that I had never known. As I made my way home that evening, it all left me: all my fear, all my failures, all my self-doubt, all my embarrassment, all my pain, all the emptiness, all the loneliness, all of it was gone. His resurrection was my resurrection, you see. All because he loves me.

## Postscript

There is more of me written into the character of Joseph than I would really care to admit. My own hopes and dreams as a gay man informed the outcome of the story, in that Jesus fell in love with me as completely as I fell in love with him. It is the completeness of that love that, I believe, led him to Jerusalem and his cross. I suspect that there are many gay Christians who share similar feelings about Jesus.

To be loved as much as we love is an inherently human characteristic. While we understand that within the human family there are many ways to love and to be loved, those of us from the queer nation deserve to have a sense of dignity restored to our own diverse hopes and dreams and experiences of love. Jesus is the one who can restore that dignity, for ultimately it is Jesus who is the lover of all our souls.

# 21

# "To Cut or Not to Cut"

## Is Compulsory Heterosexuality a Prerequisite for Christianity?

### THOMAS BOHACHE

*Many denominations remain welcoming but not affirming of queer Christians. The price for inclusion is celibacy. That queers live and practice Christianity shocks homophobic churches. Thomas Bohache reads Paul's letter to the Galatians as a contemporary manifesto of sexual inclusion. The early Jesus movement was shaken to its foundation over the inclusion of the Gentiles into their assemblies, for it did not conceive of including Gentiles within its communities without compelling them to undergo circumcision and observe the Jewish precepts. Much to the shock of the Jerusalem community of Peter and James, God poured the Spirit upon Gentiles as Gentiles, not as converted observing Jewish members (Acts 10:45–46; Gal. 3:1–5). Bohache reads Galatians as a proclamation of the good news that "we're queer, we're Christians, and we're church."*

At first glance, the letter of Paul to the Galatians might seem an odd choice for an essay in an anthology of queer biblical interpretation.[1] However, if we look at this letter anew through questioning, queer eyes and if we are able to put aside our preconceived notions of what this text has always meant and how it has always been interpreted, I believe that we will be pleasantly surprised. There are several reasons for looking anew at Galatians.

First, I believe that the Pauline corpus needs to be redeemed for queer Christians. For too long the mention of the name "Paul" has caused a knee-jerk reaction in the homosexual community because so many of his works have been used as texts of terror by fundamentalist Christians in their campaign of gay bashing and sex negativity.[2] This reaction is one of fear, anger, and/or outright dismissal. However, there is much in Paul's letters that can speak to the sexually disenfranchised if we are willing to read the silence and to apply a feminist critical hermeneutic of suspicion,[3] knowing and acknowledging that we are not necessarily getting the full story because of millennia of heterosexist and patriarchal interpretation. Second, I believe that it is *fun* to "play" with the Scriptures to see what they might hold for us if we are willing to use our imaginations. Every Sunday preachers of various denominations, faith traditions, and theologies feel free to bring whimsy and wonderment into their sermons on scriptural texts. Why should we not do so in the field of biblical interpretation as well? If the normal everyday person were shown that readers and hearers do not have to approach the Bible only with seriousness and morbidity, I believe the result would be that more and more people would regard the Bible as a living, breathing book with questions and answers for today's world.[4] Third, and most important, Paul's letter to the Galatian churches has a particular message of liberation for queers who are seeking to reconcile their sexuality and their spirituality, just as it did for those original readers who were wondering what they had to do as Gentile outsiders to embrace the new Christian faith.

Now, let us look at Galatians, first examining the situation leading up to Paul's letter, then what Paul has to say to his readers, and, finally, what Paul might say to us in a queer context.

## Background

Much has been written about the letter to the Galatians, probably because it is believed to be one of Paul's earliest extant letters and because it lays out a rudimentary version of Paul's theology supporting his ministry to the Gentiles.[5] However, as E. P. Sanders cautions in his work on Pauline thought, if one seeks a systematic theology or "theoretical thought" in Paul, one will look in vain.[6] The two letters of Paul that discuss in detail the Gentile mission and how Christianity relates to Judaism are Galatians and Romans. As Sanders points out, the occasion of these two letters is different. In Romans, the later work, Paul is giving an overview of his beliefs to a church he has not previously visited, whereas in Galatians Paul is addressing in a polemical fashion a specific situation being faced by churches with whom he had a long-standing relationship.

What was that situation? No one knows for certain because there is no independent witness to describe the situation that moved Paul to write this letter.[7] A satisfactory reconstruction might go like this:[8] Christianity began as a small sect within Judaism. Eventually Christians were expelled from the synagogues and began to be regarded as heretics by the Jewish officials because the Christians believed that their founder Jesus, called Christ, was God, which was seen as contradicting the Torah's command of monotheism. After this break with Judaism, Christianity began to spread outward from Palestine all over the Mediterranean world. Many "Gentiles" (a Latinization of the Septuagint Greek *ta ethne*, "the nations," referring to all non-Jews) were converted to the new Christian faith, leaving behind their pagan cultic practices. This introduction of Gentiles into Christianity caused some initial confusion because heretofore all Christians had been Jews and therefore subject to the Law, or Torah; now the question began to be asked whether Gentiles should convert to Judaism prior to converting to Christianity.

Around this same time Paul was converted to the Christian faith by a direct experience of the risen Christ.[9] Paul began ministering to the Gentiles, founding churches all over the Mediterranean. His view of the "Gentile question" was that Gentiles need not become Jews in order to be Christians. He apparently founded churches in the region of Galatia and considered himself in a parental position vis-à-vis these congregations. Sometime after he left the area, however, a group referred to as "Judaizers" began preaching to the Galatian churches. These Judaizers were Jewish Christians who had remained faithful to the Torah and its various laws, including dietary restrictions and the necessity of circumcision. Their message to the Galatians was that if they wanted to remain Christians, they must begin adhering to the Torah and be circumcised. Obviously this contradicted the "gospel" that Paul had preached to the Galatians.[10]

To rebut the position of the Jewish Christian missionaries, Paul writes his letter to the Galatians. In this letter he must both defend his own status as an apostle and explain, biblically, his reasons for not requiring Gentile converts to be circumcised and accept the Law.

## The Letter to the Galatians

Paul begins by clearly stating that he was made an apostle by direct apprehension of a message from Jesus Christ.[11] Thus he preaches not by human authority but from divine mandate. The preaching the Galatians have been receiving from the Judaizers is contrary to the very gospel that they received from Paul, which he himself had received from Christ. For Paul, Christ is everything, and to Christ is due all human loyalty.

Paul tells the Galatian Christians that if they have accepted God through faith in Jesus Christ, then they need not take upon themselves any other regulations. He explains that the Law (the Hebrew Torah) had been given to the Jews as a caretaker or guardian (*paidogogos*) until the sending of the Messiah (Greek *Christos*, Christ). With the coming of Christ, the Law was abrogated. Therefore, to become Jews in order to become Christians made nonsense of the Christian message, for to do so would be to take on an unnecessary burden. When one is "in" Christ, one does not need the Law.[12] Thus, to undergo circumcision is redundant, Paul states. One need not change the way one is born in order to come to God through Jesus Christ.[13]

Paul encourages the Galatians to embrace the freedom that they possess in Christ, rather than the bondage being forced upon them by the Judaizers, even going so far as to say that if the Law is still valid, then Jesus died for nothing. Paul utilizes proof-texts from the Hebrew Bible (particularly from Gen. 12–21) to show that Christians inherit the promise given directly to Abraham and Sarah from God, generations before the giving of the Torah at Mount Sinai. Abraham (uncircumcised himself) was judged righteous by God because of his faith, not through any rules he followed. Christ, as a descendant of Abraham through Sarah, is a child of the promise and fulfills for Christians the Abrahamic covenant. On the other hand, the Jews, according to Paul, in continuing to keep the Law and in not accepting Christ, are heirs, not of the promise, but of Hagar the slave woman, who was cast out.[14]

Paul urges them not to be slaves to other gods, cautioning them that to undergo circumcision is to turn away from their faith in Jesus Christ. Paul uses the practice of circumcision to represent everything that has been superseded in the Law by Christ's coming. Indeed, so angry is he at those who would confuse the Galatian Christians by demanding circumcision that he says he wishes they would go one step further and castrate themselves!

Paul concludes his advice to the Galatians by reminding them that in Christ's own words true fulfillment of the Law is to love one's neighbor as oneself. He reminds them that Christianity carries with it the duty to practice ethical behavior but reiterates that what is called for is not bodily observance but rather spiritual observance. All that matters is that the Christian has been created anew; to be pleasing to God, one need do nothing else than accept God's grace through faith in Jesus Christ.

## An Interpretation

In biblical times, circumcision was foundational to Jewish identity, while noncircumcision was a sign that one was not in covenant with the Hebrew God.[15] For the first (Jewish) Christians, the mark of circumcision was proof that they were good, observant Jews and that Christianity was a continuation and fulfillment of Judaism. But other peoples, non-Jewish, also practiced the custom. As Christianity became a religion of its own, separate and apart from Judaism, circumcision began to lose its importance as a religious sign. As it has today, the issue of circumcision became more and more a medical debate rather than a religious one.[16]

At the time that Paul wrote his letter to the struggling Christians in Galatia, however, there were differing opinions among the various groupings of Christians as to whether circumcision was mandatory for Gentiles who were embracing the Christian faith. Galatians and Acts both describe, in different ways, the institutional procedures that resulted in Gentiles not being required to be circumcised as a requirement for entry into Christianity. Paul, when he left Galatia, had believed that the whole matter was settled, but then, as now, churches were "magnets" for those who wished to cause problems and to rehash issues in less-than-healthy ways![17] Outsiders began to criticize Paul and preach another gospel—a gospel of circumcision for those who would seek to know Christ.

This is where the letter to the Galatians has incredible impact for queer Christians. Today the debate rages as to whether gays and lesbians should be welcomed "just as we are" in the churches of Christianity.[18] Some have taken the attitude of "love the sinner, hate the sin";[19] they require, not that one give up one's homosexual orientation, but rather that the homosexual practice celibacy.[20] Others insist that homosexuality is unnatural and sinful; a minority of these individuals even believe that it is the result of demon possession.[21] The requirement of these "good Christian believers" is that gay and lesbian people pray and take other steps (including exorcism!) toward changing our sexuality. We even read about and see and hear stories of "conversion" from homosexual to heterosexual orientation; the so-called ex-gay movement continues to influence adherents.[22]

For queer Christians facing this debate and seeking to know God in the midst of it, I contend that Galatians is directly relevant; it is, as it were, "manna from heaven" sent by our loving God, who would not have us perish in the desert of denial, confrontation, and rejection, for the issues seem remarkably the same. Must one "cut away" a basic part of oneself in order to approach God?[23] It is my thesis that noncircumcision, as a symbol for nonacceptance of the entire Hebrew Law, is directly comparable to homosexuality because both challenge long-accepted standards of religious entry requirements. Paul's opponents believed that circumcision, regarded as foundational to Jewish and therefore Christian identity, must be required for salvation through Christ. In like manner, those who would seek to exclude "unrepentant" homosexuals from churches today are demanding compulsory heterosexuality as a requirement for a relationship with God in Christ.

So how would one read Galatians from a queer perspective? Most importantly, we need to remember that for generations the letter to the Galatians has been regarded as Paul's great declaration of freedom in Christ Jesus.[24] Hebrew Bible and Talmudic scholar Daniel Boyarin states:

> [I]t is productive to read Paul as a Jewish cultural critic. My suggestion
> is that there is a great deal in his letters that suggests [his] primary
> motivation...was a passionate desire that humanity be One under

the sign of the One God—a universalism, I have claimed, born of the union of Hebraic monotheism and Greek desire for univocity.[25]

Thus, for Paul, the Christian message, indeed the very integrity of the gospel, depended upon universality and inclusivity—the welcoming into God's realm of all people through Jesus Christ. To him "the Christian Event [was] the vehicle of this transformation of humanity" itself,[26] the reversal of prior religious systems of insiders and outsiders.[27]

In his role as a cultural critic trying to grapple with the issues disturbing the peace of the Galatian churches, Paul comes to the conclusion that uniquely Jewish customs are not going to save Gentiles.[28] Circumcision as an entry requirement is now replaced by faith and baptism (Gal. 2:15–21). Righteousness (*dikaiosune*, literally "being adjudicated blameless") comes through God's grace alone, not through anything human beings might do or refrain from doing. Therefore, Paul's logic suggests, if people have faith in God's grace, it does not matter whether they are heterosexual or homosexual, whether they practice their sexuality or not. What may have been regarded as an entry requirement is no more, for we are free in Christ. No one is made righteous (or "justified," a translation of the Greek verb *dikaioo*, from the same root as *dikaiosune*, above) by the works of the Law.[29]

Moreover, Paul tells queer readers that one does not have to change what is intrinsically a part of the self in order to come to God. Is this not a corollary to what Paul says in Romans 1:26–28, a standard "text of terror" for queers? His entire point in talking about people acting contrary to nature (*para phusin*) is that men and women are not doing sexually what they were created to do. That is, men are betraying their nature as penetrators, becoming passive like women, while women were abandoning their passiveness to become active penetrators.[30] As children of God's promise, we need not fall back on what human beings tell us we must do or not do to inherit the realm of God: "If I were still pleasing others, I would not be Christ's follower" (Gal. 1:10). We, like the Galatians, should concentrate instead on living a moral, ethical life, loving our neighbors as ourselves, and displaying the fruits of the Spirit: love, joy, peace, patience, kindness, generosity, faithfulness, gentleness, and self-control (Gal. 5:22–23). I wonder what the world would be like if homophobic Christians concentrated on this Pauline list rather than the one contained in 1 Corinthians 6:9–10!

Beyond the specific topic of circumcision, there is another aspect of freedom that is addressed in Galatians and that is essential to a queer reading of the letter. This is the elimination of distinctions in Christ, which has been an important area of research in feminist reconstruction of early Christian history.[31] In Galatians 3:26–28, Paul quotes what most scholars believe to be a primitive Christian baptismal formula:[32]

All of you are children of God through faith in Christ Jesus. For as many of you as were baptized into Christ have put on the mantle of Christ. There is no longer Jew or Greek, no longer slave or free, no more male and female; for you are all one in Christ Jesus.

The importance of these three verses cannot be underestimated, for Paul's repetition of the formula has "momentous implications,"[33] not only for gender roles and status but also for sexuality in general, including sexual orientation. Scholars of both genders have emphasized that in the communal experience of the earliest Christians—at baptismal services—these words were spoken to "act out" tangibly the earliest Christian belief that in being baptized the new Christian entered into a new creation in which social distinctions of gender, race, and class had no meaning.[34] When baptized persons went under the water, they left behind in that water the former person, and in emerging from the water and putting on a fresh garment, they were literally "putting on" Christ, which meant embracing radical freedom (cf. Col. 3:10; Eph. 4:24.).[35] One must also bear in mind that the first Christian baptisms were mostly likely performed nude,[36] which points toward an elimination of the sexual shame and alienation elicited by the fall of humanity.

Much has been made of the wording of the third phrase in verse 28. Instead of paralleling the previous two phrases ("Jew or Greek... slave or free"), the third phrase uses the construction "male and female," instead of what one might have expected—"man and woman." Using "male" and "female" emphasizes sexuality. Though one can think of "men" and "women" as "desexed" creatures, it is the maleness and femaleness of the human creature that is the wellspring of our sexuality. It has been suggested that the use of these particular words is to recall the words of Genesis 1:27, "male and female [God] created them," in which sexuality is created and the human creature is now differentiated by gender and sexuality.[37]

A feminist interpretation would point out that in this baptismal formula one sees expressed a return to the divine plan of mutuality.[38] A queer interpretation, however, can go further and say that not only are we able to see a return to the divine plan of mutuality and reciprocity between creatures, but moreover we are also able to see the blending and merging of the sex roles into one harmonious vision of "male and female" together. No longer must we have the macho male and the fragile female relegated to different spheres or even different genders: We can have all of it right here and right now by virtue of our freedom from God! This, in my view, is tantamount to a dissolving of sexual orientation in favor of neither homosexual nor heterosexual beings but just sexual beings, however that sexuality might manifest itself.

As previously stated, Paul begs the Galatians not to give up their freedom by returning to the ways of the Law, including the physical cutting of circumcision. To illustrate this point, he introduces the famous and puzzling allegory of Sarah and Hagar in Galatians 4:21–31. Paul makes the descendants of Abraham through his chief wife Sarah (including Jesus) stand for those who participate in freedom (i.e., the Gentile Christians), while the descendants of Abraham through the slave woman Hagar represent those who remain under the burden of slavery (i.e., the Jews who follow the Law). Paul reminds his readers that Sarah, originally childless, was blessed by God through the fulfilled promise of free children. The proof-text he employs is a fitting one with which to end our queer reading of Galatians, for it is from the book of the prophet Isaiah:

> "Rejoice, you childless one, you who bear no children,
>     burst into song and shout, you who endure no birth pangs;
>   for the children of the desolate woman are more numerous..."
>                          (Gal. 4:27, quoting Isa. 54:1)[39]

The reason that this proof-text can speak as powerfully to queer Christians today as it did to the Gentile Christians of Paul's day is as follows. This portion of Isaiah is sandwiched between two famous passages that involve eunuchs, the sexually disenfranchised of the biblical world.[40] Just a few verses previously, Isaiah has described one who "was oppressed, and...afflicted, yet...did not open his mouth.... By a perversion of justice [this one] was taken away.... [and] cut off from the land of the living" (Isa. 53:7–8). This is the passage of scripture that the first Gentile convert to Christianity—the Ethiopian eunuch—was reading when he had his salvation experience (Acts 8:26–40). And just two chapters after the verses quoted by Paul comes the important declaration of God's providential loving care for the sexually disenfranchised:

> Do not let the foreigner joined to [God] say,
>     "[God] will surely separate me from the people";
>   and do not let the eunuch say,
>     "I am just a dry tree."
>   For thus says [God]:
>   To the eunuchs...
>   I will give, in my house and within my walls,
>       a monument and a name
>       better than sons and daughters;
>     I will give them an everlasting name
>       that shall not be cut off. (Isa. 56:3–5)[41]

May we not see this as a clue for the queer community encoded in the pages of scripture? Now certainly I am not suggesting that Paul himself meant to give such a clue. However, if we are going to play with the Scripture, as I proposed at the outset of this essay, then why should we not consider these "coincidences" as fodder for such play in the setting of a queer biblical interpretation? Other marginalized groups have certainly seen words meant for them within the pages of scripture,[42] so why not the faith community that reads from the social location of sexual orientation?

## Conclusion

To cut or not to cut? The conclusion that I reach is the conclusion that Paul reached almost two thousand years ago. No! To be pleasing to God, one need do *nothing* except believe. For Christians, that belief is manifested through our confession that Jesus of Nazareth became Christ and offers salvation to all through the good news of his life, the tragedy of his death, and the power and mystery of his resurrection.

What this means for queer Christians is this: We do not have to circumcise the foreskins of our sexual orientation in order to be acceptable to Almighty God. Our status as children of God is not dependent upon outside forces or rules or lists of sins created by human beings. Like the Galatians, we need not submit to a yoke of slavery, for we are free heirs of the promise. Over and over again, Paul urges the Galatians to accept their freedom (Gal. 5:1, 13). Should we not do so as well? I believe that God urges us to turn our backs on modern-day "Judaizers" who, as a requirement for entry into the reign of God, would have us submit to a standard—heterosexuality—which was not meant for us.

As he nears the end of his letter, Paul offers some pastoral advice: "Live by the Spirit, I say" (Gal. 5:16); and that bit of advice is ours today. Elsewhere in the New Testament, the words of Jesus remind us that the restless Spirit "blows where it chooses" (John 3:8). That Spirit—the part of the Divine that each of us breathes in and breathes out—has chosen to blow through and reside in gay, lesbian, bisexual, and transgendered people, whether others approve of it or not. In Paul's words, human distinctions are cast aside: "A new creation is everything!" (Gal. 6:15). May we as queer interpreters of God's Word recognize that new creation in our midst and share it with the rest of our world.

We are assured in Genesis 1:26–27 that each one of us is created in "the image and likeness" of God. That means that wherever we see humanness, we encounter God. When we see lesbian mothers and gay fathers, we are seeing God! When we see leathermen and leatherwomen, we are seeing God! When we see the transgendered coming home to their bodies, we are seeing God! When we see young "gender-bending" queers who don't label themselves either gay or lesbian, we are seeing God! We must never destroy that divine image by ignoring or stifling that piece of our human "god-ness"—sexuality—with which we have been gifted by a loving God of amazing diversity.

I believe that queer people of faith have been given a tremendous responsibility. Through our struggles, we are empowered to heal the rupture that traditional religion has created between sexuality and spirituality. Perhaps we are better equipped to do this than others because society is so preoccupied with our sexual expression that we have often been relegated to society's periphery as sexual and spiritual outlaws.[43] Now is the time to claim our power—the validity that comes from being daughters and sons of God. Sexual theologian James Nelson tells us that incarnation, a foundational tenet of Christianity, is all about embodying God and welcoming the Divine into our humanity. Many Christians are unable to do that, however, because they have been alienated from their sexuality. "But," James Nelson asserts, "if we do not know the gospel in our bodies, we do not know the gospel. We either experience God's presence in our bodies or not at all."[44] Queer folks are fortunate in that we are deeply in touch with our sexual natures. In order to claim our rightful inheritance as children of God, we must own our experiences as sexual and spiritual beings. Only we know the ways in which God speaks to us in our divine humanness. Outsiders cannot tell us, as they couldn't tell the Galatians, what we are to do with our bodies and how we are to experience the incarnation of Christ. Our very ability to make love is our power to "be Christ-ed," and our right to experience sexual diversity without interference is our very capacity to embrace the many faces of the Divine, whose image we bear in our bodies and in our sexualities.

## Notes

1. I use the term "queer" to include gay men, lesbians, bisexuals, the transgendered, seeking and questioning folk, people who are nonsexual or differently sexual, as well as those accepting and supportive heterosexuals, who, like my own father, are "queer" in a homophobic society. I am indebted to Robert Goss for introducing me (in a series of conversations in July 1995) to the concept of "queer" as a verb, standing for the proposition of shaking up the status quo. See his seminal work *Jesus ACTED UP: A Gay and Lesbian Manifesto* (San Francisco: HarperSanFrancisco, 1993).

2. The term "texts of terror" was originally used by feminist biblical scholar Phyllis Trible in her book of that title (Philadelphia: Fortress Press, 1984) as a way of describing biblical texts that have been used to silence and oppress women. The term was adopted for a queer milieu by Robert Goss in *Jesus ACTED UP*, 88–89.

The traditional texts of terror for queers from the Pauline corpus are Romans 1:26–28 and 1 Corinthians 6:9, as well as 1 Timothy 1:18 in the Deutero-Pauline corpus.

3. The terms "reading the silence" and "hermeneutic of suspicion" are tools of feminist biblical interpretation used and explained most notably by Elisabeth Schüssler Fiorenza in *Bread Not Stone: The Challenge of Feminist Biblical Interpretation* (Boston: Beacon Press, 1984).

4. For an example of such "bringing to life" of scripture, see Peter J. Gomes, *The Good Book: Reading the Bible with Mind and Heart* (New York: William Morrow, 1996).

5. The following commentaries were consulted in preparation of this essay: Hans Dieter Betz, *Galatians: A Commentary on Paul's Letter to the Churches in Galatia*, Hermeneia (Philadelphia: Fortress Press, 1979); J. Louis Martyn, *Galatians: A New Translation with Introduction and Commentary*, Anchor Bible 33A (New York: Doubleday, 1997); Frank J. Matera, *Galatians*, Sacra Pagina 9 (Collegeville, Minn.: Liturgical Press/Michael Glazier, 1992); and John J. Pilch, *Galatians and Romans*, Collegeville Bible Commentary 6 NT (Collegeville, Minn.: Liturgical Press, 1983).

6. E. P. Sanders, *Paul, the Law, and the Jewish People* (Minneapolis: Fortress Press, 1983), passim but esp. 3–15; *Paul and Palestinian Judaism: A Comparison of Patterns of Religion* (Minneapolis: Fortress Press, 1977), 433–31.

7. The book of Acts cannot be considered an independent authority with which to compare Galatians for accuracy. See Betz, *Galatians*, 10–11; Sanders, *Paul and Palestinian Judaism*, 432.

8. See the explanation of Christian origins contained in W. H. C. Frend, *The Rise of Christianity* (Philadelphia: Fortress Press, 1984), chaps. 3–4; and Everett Ferguson, *Backgrounds of Early Christianity*, 2d ed. (Grand Rapids: Wm. B. Eerdmans, 1993), chap. 6. On the expulsion of the Christians from the synagogues, see J. Louis Martyn, *History and Theology in the Fourth Gospel* (Nashville: Abingdon Press, 1968; 2d ed., 1979).

9. Galatians 1:11–16; for a different version, see Acts 9.

10. There has been much discussion as to the identity of these "Judaizers." Traditionally they have been referred to as "opponents" (Betz, *Galatians*, 90ff.); more recently, however, it has been suggested that the term "agitators" (Matera, *Galatians*, 7ff.) or "teachers" (Martyn, *Galatians*, 117ff.) be used to indicate that they had some solidarity with the Christian movement.

11. I have used my own translation for the discussion contained in this essay.

12. I choose not to discuss in this essay the issue of whether this attitude of Paul's is anti-Semitic (which in itself is an anachronistic term when applied to Paul). As stated previously, Paul's thought on this entire subject is far from systematic. See Krister Stendahl, *Paul among Jews and Gentiles and Other Essays* (Philadelphia: Fortress Press, 1976); and W. D. Davies, "Paul and the People of Israel," *New Testament Studies* 24 (1977): 4–39, reprinted in idem, *Jewish and Pauline Studies* (Philadelphia: Fortress Press, 1983).

13. Peter was taught this same lesson in his vision of clean and unclean foods in Acts 10.

14. In his allegory of Sarah and Hagar in Galatians 4, Paul appears to be saying that the Jews were never intended to be inheritors of God's promise, which is at odds with what he says elsewhere in this same letter and in the letter to the Romans.

15. Unfortunately, when one speaks of circumcision, the discussion takes a decidedly androcentric slant because of Judaism's origin as a patriarchal religion. While women were of course Jews, they did not carry on their bodies the sign of the covenant as men did; their ties to Judaism were through their fathers and their husbands. For a feminist discussion of women's inclusion in the covenant, see Judith Plaskow, *Standing Again at Sinai: Judaism from*

*a Feminist Perspective* (New York: HarperCollins, 1991). For an excellent recent discussion of circumcision in Judaism, see Daniel Boyarin, *A Radical Jew: Paul and the Politics of Identity* (Berkeley: University of California Press, 1994), 26–38.

16. See Billy Ray Boyd, *Circumcision Exposed—Rethinking a Medical and Cultural Tradition* (Freedom, Calif.: Crossing Press, 1998), as well as frequent debates in the letters to the editor of *Machismo* magazine (New York: Princeton Publishing). Women and feminist-identified men have also begun to discuss (and condemn) the practice of so-called female circumcision in African and Islamic countries. See Alice Walker and Pratibha Parmar, *Warrior Marks: Female Genital Mutilation and the Sexual Blinding of Women* (London: Jonathan Cape/Random House, 1993); and Mary Daly, *Gyn/Ecology: The Metaethics of Radical Feminism* (Boston: Beacon Press, 1978), chap. 5.

17. For a modern discussion of this problem, see Kenneth C. Haugk, *Antagonists in the Church: How to Identify and Deal with Destructive Conflict* (Minneapolis: Augsburg, 1988).

18. In 1998 the Anglican communion rejected the validity of homosexuality as a recognized and acceptable lifestyle at the historic "Lambeth Conference." See, e.g., *The Washington Post* throughout July and August 1998; and most recently, a response by Bishop John Shelby Spong, "Christianity Caught in a Timewarp," in *The Voice* (September 1998): 2.

19. This pithy slogan goes all the way back to Anita Bryant's crusade to "save the children" in Dade County in the 1970s and is still alive and well in statements by various Christian denominations.

20. John J. McNeill, *Freedom, Glorious Freedom: The Spiritual Journey to the Fulness of Life for Gays, Lesbians, and Everybody Else* (Boston: Beacon Press, 1995).

21. As recently as August 1998, I myself while on America Online received an "instant message" from a woman who had seen in my profile that I was a gay clergyman. One of her first and most persistent questions was, "But don't you believe that homosexuality is caused by a demon?"

22. Advertisements have been placed in major American newspapers (e.g., *The New York Times*, *The Los Angeles Times*, and *The Washington Post*, July–August 1998) declaring that homosexuality can and must be cured. Alleged "ex-gays" are frequent visitors to daytime television talk shows.

23. See Chandler Burr, *A Separate Creation: The Search for the Biological Origins of Sexual Orientation* (New York: Hyperion Books, 1996); Simon LeVay, *The Sexual Brain* (New York: MIT Press, 1993); and idem, *Queer Science: The Use and Abuse of Research on Homosexuality* (New York: MIT Press, 1996).

24. "It is the Magna Carta of Christian freedom and the charter of evangelical faith." Edward P. Blair, *The Abingdon Bible Handbook* (Nashville: Abingdon Press, 1975), 277, paraphrasing Martin Luther.

25. Boyarin, *A Radical Jew*, 106.

26. Ibid.

27. See Alan F. Segal, *Paul the Convert: The Apostolate and Apostasy of Saul the Pharisee* (New Haven: Yale University Press, 1990).

28. Boyarin, *A Radical Jew*, 117.

29. One might even go so far as to say that the "texts of terror" for queers in Leviticus no longer have force and effect, for they have been abrogated in Christ!

30. See Bernadette J. Brooten, *Love between Women: Early Christian Responses to Female Homoeroticism* (Chicago: University of Chicago Press, 1996). Brooten's thesis is that *para phusin* is used by Paul to refer to human beings performing acts contrary to that for which

their bodies, in a heterosexist, patriarchal culture, were thought to have been created (i.e., men being penetrated and women penetrating).

31. Elisabeth Schüssler Fiorenza, *In Memory of Her: A Feminist Theological Reconstruction of Christian Origins* (New York: Crossroad, 1983), esp. chap. 6.

32. Betz, *Galatians*, 181–85.

33. Sheila Briggs, "Galatians," in *Searching the Scriptures*, vol. 2, *A Feminist Commentary*, ed. Elisabeth Schüssler Fiorenza (New York: Crossroad, 1994), 219.

34. Betz, *Galatians*, 189–200; Schüssler Fiorenza, *In Memory of Her*, 218; Briggs, "Galatians," 218–19; and, especially, Wayne A. Meeks, "The Image of the Androgyne: Some Uses of a Symbol in Earliest Christianity," *History of Religions* 13 (1974): 165–208.

35. Schüssler Fiorenza has pointed out that it was in response to such freedom that the subsequent Deutero-Pauline letters included the "household codes" (*haustafeln*) ordering wives to be subservient to their husbands (Col. 3:18; Eph. 5:22; 1 Pet. 3:1) and slaves to obey their masters (Eph. 6:5; 1 Pet. 2:18), as part of what she calls the "patriarchalization" of the church. *In Memory of Her*, chap. 7.

36. Lawrence Hull Stookey, *Baptism: Christ's Act in the Church* (Nashville: Abingdon Press, 1982), 103.

37. Betz, *Galatians*, 195, Phyllis Trible, *God and the Rhetoric of Sexuality* (Philadelphia: Fortress Press, 1978), chap. 1.

38. E.g., Riane Eisler, *The Chalice and the Blade: Our History, Our Future* (New York: Harper and Row, 1987), chap. 9. Meeks has pointed out that many cultures have a myth of the "original androgyne" who existed before sexual differentiation. "The Imagine of the Androgyne," 197. See also Robin Scroggs, "Paul and the Eschatological Woman," *Journal of the American Academy of Religion* 40 (1972): 283–303.

39. This is the NRSV translation of Galatians 4:27. The quotations from Isaiah that follow are also from the NRSV, inclusified.

40. For the connection between eunuchs and gays and lesbians, see Nancy L. Wilson, *Our Tribe: Queer Folks, God, Jesus, and the Bible* (New York: HarperSanFrancisco, 1995). Left unexplored is the obvious connection between eunuchs and transgendered folk.

41. It is significant to a queer reading that the word translated "cut off" would have appeared in the Greek Septuagint version of both Isaiah 52 and 56 as a form of the Greek *tome* (verb *temno*), which is the root of the word for circumcision *peritome*, employed by Paul.

42. For example, African Americans since slavery times have seen in the Exodus story a clue for them of what God had in store for them as a people. This reality is reflected in the recent essays regarding reading the Bible from various social locations (but not sexual orientation!) contained in *The New Interpreter's Bible*, vol. 1 (Nashville: Abingdon Press, 1995).

43. See Christian de la Huerta, *Coming Out Spiritually: The Next Step* (New York: Jeremy P. Tarcher/Putnam, 1999), esp. chap. 1.

44. James B. Nelson, *Between Two Gardens: Reflections on Sexuality and Religious Experience* (New York: Pilgrim Press, 1983), 17–18.